THE UNITED STATES SUPREME COURT

Volume 6

The
Conservative Court
1910-1930

Norman Bindler

GROLIER EDUCATIONAL CORPORATION
Danbury, CT

Grolier Educational Corp.

The United States Supreme Court

George J. Lankevich, Editor

George J. Lankevich, *The Federal Court, 1787-1801*.
Adrienne Siegel, *The Marshall Court, 1801-1835*.
Martin Siegel, *The Taney Court, 1836-1864*.
Robert Fridlington, *The Reconstruction Court, 1864-1888*.
Howard Furer, *The Fuller Court, 1888-1910*.
Norman Bindler, *The Conservative Court, 1910-1930*.
Robert Mayer, *The Court and the American Crises, 1930-1953*.
Arnold S. Rice, *The Warren Court, 1954-1969*.
Arthur L. Galub, *The Burger Court, 1969-1986*.
Arthur L. Galub and George J. Lankevich, *The Rehnquist Court, 1986-1994*.

Photographs of the Supreme Court justices provided by the Supreme Court Historical Society, Washington, D.C.

Copyright © 1995, 1986, The History of New York City Project, Inc. Edited and updated by Grolier Educational Corporation 1995. Portions of this material were originally published under the title *The Supreme Court in American Life*.

ISBN 0-7172-7439-X

Manufactured in the United States of America

Gary Hermalyn, Project Director

For Paula

Contents

Part III

Introductory Note

The Supreme Court of the United States is an effective and very human institution, but it also stands as a symbolic, almost sacred, icon of the American nation. Almost every school child knows that the Constitution established the judiciary as an independent third branch of government, yet few mature citizens can confidently assert that they understand how the Supreme Court became the respected final arbiter of American life that it is today. And rationally, how is it possible that an institution composed of unelected men serving for life and deliberating in secrecy, is accorded the authority to bend the other branches to its will? By what alchemy have independent Americans become submissive to Court decisions which are as final as the ukase of a tsar? To study the human and institutional development of the Supreme Court in terms free of legal jargon, and to relate the history of the Court to the wider concerns of American life, is the purpose of these volumes.

The Founding Fathers who wrote America's Constitution were wise and prudent men. It took them eight times as long to define the powers of Congress (Article I), and three times the space to create the Presidency (Article II), than to organize the judicial branch (Article III). The Fathers were concerned with potential abuse of power, and devoted most of their efforts to devising intricate mechanisms to limit the exercise of government authority. Showing more faith in the judiciary, they did not set qualifications for Supreme Court Justices, mandate a Chief Justice or establish a court system. Once the Court's jurisdiction was defined at Philadelphia, the only limitations placed upon the Justices were the Senate's right to reject candidates (a right since exercised twenty-six times), Congress' power to impeach, the people's right to amend the Constitution and the Justices' own sense of self-restraint and wisdom. Yet from such meager origins developed a Supreme Court which has, on over one hundred occasions, invalidated acts of Congress and set aside well over a thousand statutes passed by state legislatures. The Court has thus displayed awesome power throughout our history, perhaps far more than the Fathers ever suspected it would enjoy. The successive volumes of this series will trace the development of the Court's judicial power, introduce the men who interpreted the Constitution, and study the society that inspired and surrounded the decisions of the Justices.

The Court has become central to our national life because it is the arena in which two basic American attitudes contend. Americans revere and respect the law, yet they also believe in the determining nature of the will of the people. Congress legislates in the name of the people, but the Court has the responsibility of testing statutes against American ideals and the words of the Constitution. That such a task has political ramifications is hardly surprising. As often as the Court has seized the opportunity to decide major cases, it has as frequently avoided controversial issues. Powerful as it can be, the Court is often important for what it chooses not to decide. If the Court sometimes appears to "follow the election returns," does that not imply judicial sensitivity to public opinion? A central theme of these volumes is the unending tension between the desires of the people, the dictates of the Constitution, and the decisions of the Justices. "We are under a Constitution," wrote Justice Hughes, "but the Constitution is what the judges say it is." One of the enduring marvels of American society is that the people have been so willing to admit the Justices' right to determine the meaning of our fundamental law and permit them to say "no" to the initiatives of the elected representatives of the people.

These volumes emphasize biography because the decisions of the Court are produced by the experience, prejudices and convictions of its changing membership. America's Supreme Court asserts that it does not make the law, it only decides what the law is; yet the attitudes of the men and one woman who have had the final word in our political process are critical to that discovery. As a kind of reward for their even-handed efforts, Justices seem far more likely to be labeled "great" than are Presidents or members of Congress. This accolade appears to be more freely given precisely because the nation believes its Justices act on a more rigorous and unforgiving standard. The law, more so than the practice of politics, seems to make greater demands of men. During our history as a nation, the Justices of the Supreme Court have invalidated acts of Congress, accepted slavery, dissolved trusts, ordered reapportionment and given their approval to abortion; such actions invariably shook the nation. Yet our Justices have no monopoly on wisdom or competence. The Constitution awards authority to the Court, but not omniscience. Understanding the Court demands that we know its membership, as well as the law they are sworn to uphold.

American history has given to our Supreme Court enduring prestige, but the willingness of society to accept Court decisions testifies as well to the national faith in law and the Constitution. The people, the law and the Court mutually support each other. Although the members of each Court temporarily enjoy the right to decide questions of law, they are keenly aware that they must protect broadly-held moral principles, legal precedent, and unspoken tradition as well. The interaction between the Justices and the society that called them to serve remains one of the enduring dramas of American history. If that relationship becomes clearer for readers, the authors of these volumes will have created the useful tool and reference work they intended.

Editor's Foreword

The Supreme Court of the period 1910 to 1930, reflected America's prevailing political and economic philosophy; *laissez-faire* ideas and concepts were held sacrosanct by presidents, congressmen, and a majority of the Court, a social theory that was generally viewed as liberal and progressive, yet today such beliefs are considered conservative or even reactionary. While there were exceptions, this meant that in most of the cases brought before the high bench the Justices sought to protect a free economy, limit government intervention into the lives of its citizens and void legislation designed to effect social reform. Most leading Americans during the early twentieth century strongly believed that the best society was one where there was almost complete economic freedom; in short, in their estimation the marketplace reigned supreme. While the free market engendered the growth and development of the world's greatest economy, it exploited labor, destroyed the environment and blocked the way for social reform. The Supreme Court generally supported this unenlightened view of society even during the years prior to the First World War when liberal Republicans and their Democratic sympathizers were vigorously promoting a program of political and social change. If American society was to advance into the twentieth century, it had to overcome retrogressive forces represented by such institutions as the Supreme Court.

Unrestricted competition was considered critical to the success of capitalism. Yet shortly after the Court dissolved the Standard Oil Company for violating the Sherman Anti-Trust Act (1890) in *United States v. American Tobacco Co.* (1911), the Justices reversed themselves and refused to break up this monopoly on the ground that the tobacco trust was not altogether an "unreasonable" one. The Court had adopted an old principle, "rule of reason" promoted by Chief Justice Edward Douglas White, which permitted the Court to determine whether or not the behavior of a large company was in the public interest. Although this approach apparently was in conflict with laissez-faire doctrine, it found support in most sectors of the economic community, especially big business. Moreover, important conservative policymakers were also expounding the position that although monopolies might destroy small enterprises and cause higher prices, they did not necessarily endanger the national well-being. There were critics, of course, like Justice Oliver Wendell Holmes who argued that the "Constitution is not intended to embody a particular economic theory, whether of paternalism...or *laissez-faire,*" but their complaints were out of the mainstream of thought. In *United States v. United States Steel Corp.* (1920) the Court exonerated the great trust, a decision which for all intents and purposes ended discussion of the corporate issue until the New Deal.

If big business received strong support from the Courts, labor organizations suffered from discrimination by the judiciary. The Clayton Anti-Trust Act (1914) specifically exempted unions from prosecutions as trusts and forbade federal courts to issue injunctions in labor disputes. Yet in *Duplex Printing Co. v. Deering* (1921) the Supreme Court decided that certain labor union practices such as secondary boycotts constituted illegal interference with interstate commerce and were therefore enjoinable. This, of course, weakened the Clayton Act considerably, and during the 1920s, all manner of labor injunctions were issued by unsympathetic, probusiness judges. Another example of antilabor bias came when the Supreme Court, in *Truax v. Corrigan* (1921), declared unconstitutional an Arizona statute forbidding state courts the right to grant injunctions against picketing. And in *Bedford Stone Co. v. Journeymen Stone Cutters' Association* (1927) the Justices upheld the use of an injunction against a union which had instructed its members not to work on stone that had been cut by nonunion labor. In virtually all cases pitting property against labor, the Courts favored the owners of property; the Justices had emasculated the Sherman and Clayton acts, and labor was severely hampered in its efforts to protect itself, especially against unyielding employers.

After 1910, the Supreme court upheld as constitutional a series of statutes that protected the health, morals, and welfare of the people. In *Hippolite Egg Co. v. United States* (1911), for example, the Court sustained the Pure Food and Drug Act (1906) and in *Hoke v. United States* (1913) the Justices ruled that the Mann (White Slave) Act (1910) was constitutional. Yet in a disturbing turnabout in *Hammer v. Dagenhart* (1918), the Keating-Owen Child Labor Law (1916) was invalidated in a 5-4 decision. In his dissent Justice Holmes implied that his fellow Justices had been more influenced by conservative social philosophy than by constitutional precedent. While the Court upheld legislation which outlawed narcotics, impure food, spoiled meat, and prostitution, the Justices found that they were unable to destroy the great evil of child labor because the "statute was not a regulation of commerce by an outright prohibition." As always, in a contest between property and labor, property rights took precedence. *Hammer* was seen as a key test of the Court's willingness to allow important social legislation to stand. Justice William Rufus Day, speaking for the majority, ignored the plight of small children who labored under terrible conditions by arguing that the products of child labor "were in themselves harmless, and their movement in commerce was also harmless."

When the United States joined the Allies in the world war on April 6, 1917, Congress, with President Woodrow Wilson's approval, imposed limits upon the freedoms of speech and press. The Espionage Act (June 1917) and the

Sedition Act (May 1918) made it a felony to attempt to cause insubordination in the armed forces, to obstruct the enlistment process, to convey false statements with the intent to interfere with military operations, or to send seditious material through the mails. By upholding these acts the Supreme Court severely curtailed the First Amendment in wartime; the Justices essentially agreed that the national government could punish any act which it regarded as interfering with the war effort. Even Justice Holmes, a longtime advocate of free speech, jointed his colleagues in upholding the Espionage Act (1917). He did, however, in *Schenck v. United States* (1919), argue that the statute did not supercede the First Amendmment, and offered a doctrine—"clear and present danger"—which could be used to test whether certain statements endangered the national security. Yet in *Pierce v. United States* (1920) Justice Mahlon Pitney discarded Holmes's test and declared that literature which had a *tendency* to cause insubordination and disloyalty in the military services should be banned. The "bad tendency" doctrine of the court was a major setback for civil liberties in general and freedom of speech in particular; for all intents and purposes democracy ceased to function in wartime. The Supreme Court proclaimed to Americans that open discussion of the merits and methods of a war would not be permissible.

During the 1920s, the Justices again imposed restrictions on personal liberty and freedom with affirmative decisions in *Gitlow v. New York* (1925) and *Whitney v. California* (1927). In the former case they validated a state anarchy law and in the latter decision they upheld California's right to outlaw syndicalism. This meant that the states as well as the federal government could limit the protections enumerated in the First Amendment.

The Supreme Court from 1910 to 1930, succeeded in establishing the principle that the sphere of economic enterprise must be free from serious federal and state interference. Conservative laissez-faire policies supported by big business became the accepted norm, and weak sectors of American society such as labor, small business, and defenseless children were forced to take a backseat and hope for a better day. Furthermore, not since the early years of the Republic were the civil liberties of citizens so narrowly limited. While the Court in theory defended the First Amendment, it permitted government authorities to curb dissent. Only when the Great Depression resulted in the administration of Franklin D. Roosevelt, did the Court reevaluate its prevailing conservatism; with reluctance, government support of an ailing economy was promoted, and an attempt was made to place labor on an equal footing with business. Serious work to repair the damage done to the personal freedoms of Americans would not begin until the postwar period. To understand and elucidate the actions and the attitudes of this most conservative of all Supreme Courts is the purpose of the following pages. From the perspective of our day, the Court of 1910-1930 seems outrageously anachronistic, yet it reflected accurately the spirit and the expectations of a growing nation.

PART I

The United States Supreme Court

■ ■ ■ ■ ■

Chronology
1910-1930

Chronology

1910

July 4	Melville Weston Fuller, Chief Justice of the Supreme Courts since 1888, dies in Sorrento, Maine, at the age of seventy-seven.
August 31	Theodore Roosevelt proclaims the "New Nationalism" in a speech at Osawatomie, Kansas.
October 10	Justice Charles Evans Hughes succeeds David Josiah Brewer on the Supreme Court. Hughes had been nominated to the bench by President William Howard Taft on April 25, 1910, and was easily confirmed.
November 8	In the national elections Progressive Republicans and Democrats hand Old Guard Republicans a set of major defeats. The Democrats win control of the House of Representatives for the first time since 1894, and a Democratic-Liberal Republican coalition often dominates the Senate.
	Oregon adopts the presidential preferential primary by popular vote.
	The state of Washington adopts women's suffrage by constitutional amendment.
November 20	Justice William Moody resigns from the Supreme Court due to illness.
December 5	The United States Immigration Commission presents a forty-one-volume report recommending restrictions, especially on unskilled labor.
December 12	Frederick W. Lehmann assumes the office as solicitor general.

December 19   Justice Edward Douglas White is elevated to the Chief's chair by President Taft.

1911

January 3   Justice Willis Van Devanter is sworn in as White's replacement as Associate Justice. Justice Joseph Rucker Lamar succeeds William Henry Moody.

Bailey v. Alabama, 219 U.S. 219, invalidates as violating the Thirteenth Amendment a state peonage law which required individuals to pay their debts by working on the land of creditors.

Muskrat v. United States, 219 U.S. 346, reiterates that the Court will not give an advisory opinion in a case not involving a "case or controversy" within the meaning of the Constitution.

February 3   The electric self-starter for automobiles, invented by Charles F. Kettering, is demonstrated.

March 3   Due to Judicial Code revision the federal courts undergo modernization. For example, the old Circuit Courts are abolished and the District Courts become the trial courts of general jurisdiction, a number of obsolete procedural laws are discarded, and the appellate jurisdiction of the Circuit Courts of Appeals is enlarged.

March 13   *Hipolite Egg Co. v. United States,* 220 U.S. 45, sustains the provisions of the Pure Food and Drug Act (1906) which prohibits the sale of adulterated foods and drugs in interstate commerce. This case is one of several in which the Supreme Court supports Congress's right to pass legislation regarding health, morals, and welfare of the community. Congress holds this critical power through its constitutional right to regulate commerce between the states.

Flint v. Stone Tracy Co., 220 U.S. 107, sustains a federal tax on the income of corporations. Shortly, the Sixteenth Amendment will endow Congress with the constitutional "power to lay and collect taxes on incomes. . . " *Flint* helps to create the right climate for the adoption of the amendment.

March 25   Fire destroys the Triangle Shirtwaist factory in New York City. About 145 persons (mostly women) are trapped and killed.

May 3   *Standard Oil Co. v. United States,* 221 U.S. 1, finds Standard Oil Company in violation of the Sherman Anti-Trust Act (1890) and the Court orders that the oil trust be dissolved. In coming to this decision the Justices use the principle of "rule of reason" which means that the dissolution of the Standard Oil Company is a reasonable, plausible, and intelligent act, and in the public interest.

United States v. Grimaud, 220 U.S. 506, agrees that administrative rulings have the force of law and violation of them might entail punishment as infractions of a criminal statute. In short, the Court accepts delegation of a large element of administrative discretion to the executive branch of government as constitutional.

Oklahoma v. Kansas Natural Gas Co., 221 U.S. 229, clarifies the differences between a state's power to prohibit the taking of its natural resources and the right to deny their transportation in interstate commerce.

Gompers v. Bucks Stove and Range Co., 221 U.S. 418, finds that an antitrust order enjoining a secondary boycott in the form of published charges of unfair trade is not a violation of the First Amendment. (One version of a secondary boycott is the attempt to restrain trade by compelling third parties, persons not directly involved in a labor dispute, to refrain from engaging in business activities with a struck company.)

May 29   *United States v. American Tobacco Co.,* 221 U.S. 106, unlike the Standard Oil case, does not dissolve American Tobacco. This trust is not an unreasonable one since not all combinations or monopolies in restraint of trade are illegal; only those which are unreasonable or against the public interest.

June 9

Carry Amelia Nation, temperance activist, dies in Leavenworth, Kansas, at the age of sixty-four.

October 16

Progressive Republicans meet in Chicago and nominate Robert M. LaFollette as their candidate for the presidency.

October 20

Southern Railway Co. v. United States, 222 U.S. 20, upholds a federal statute on railway safety devices as constitutional, even when such devices are not used in interstate commerce. Such cases demonstrate the Court's willingness on occasion to enlarge the powers of the federal government at the expense of those of the states.

December 18

The United States abrogates an 1832 treaty with Russia because of that country's refusal to honor passports of Jewish-Americans and of certain clergymen.

1912

January 6

New Mexico becomes the forty-seventh state.

January 12

Textile workers, many of them members of the Industrial Workers of the World (IWW), go on strike in Lawrence, Massachusetts, over the issue of reduced wages.

January 15

Second Employers' Liability Case, 223 U.S. 1, finds the first liability act unconstitutional because it included intrastate as well as interstate activities. The law is amended in 1908, and the Court now upholds its constitutionality.

February 14

Arizona becomes the forty-eighth state.

February 19

Pacific States Telephone Co. v. Oregon, 223 U.S. 118, agrees that the proposition that the Constitution guarantees the states a republican form of government is not a question for the Court to decide.

March 12

The Girl Scouts are founded by Juliette Low.

March 18	Justice Mahlon Pitney succeeds John Marshall Harlan to the Supreme Court.
April 9	In the White Phosphorous Matches Act a tax is placed on hazardous matches in an effort to eliminate them from the marketplace.
April 14-15	The British liner, *Titanic,* on her maiden voyage, sinks in the North Atlantic.
May 12	The Socialist Party of America nominates Eugene V. Debs (Ind.) for president and Emil Seidel (Wis.) for vice president.
June 5	U.S. Marine land in Cuba to protect American interests.
June 7	*Savage v. Jones,* 225 U.S. 501, upholds a statute which prohibits the importation of substandard dog food for public health reasons, arguing that this measure does not place an unreasonable burden on the constitutional principles of interstate commerce.
June 22	William Howard Taft and James S. Sherman are renominated by the Republican party.
July 2	Woodrow Wilson (N.J.) is nominated on the forty-sixth ballot by the Democratic party. Thomas R. Marshall (Ind.) is chosen as candidate for the vice presidency.
August 5	The Progressive "Bull Moose" party is organized in Chicago. Teddy Roosevelt accepts the nomination for the presidency on August 6. The candidate for vice president is Hiram W. Johnson (Calif.).
August 24	A parcel post system is created and authorized to go into service on January 1, 1913.
October 15	William M. Bullitt becomes the solicitor general.
November 5	In the national elections the Democratic party candidate, Wilson, defeats both the Republican Taft and the Progressive Roosevelt. Wilson receives 435 electoral

votes to Roosevelt's 88 and Taft's 8. The Socialist candidate, Debs, polls about 6 percent of the vote (900,000).

December 2   *United States v. Union Pacific Railroad Co.,* 226 U.S. 61, orders the Union Pacific and Southern Pacific railroad merger dissolved as a violation of the Sherman Anti-Trust Act (1890).

December 10   Elihu Root, statesman and lawyer, receives the Nobel Peace Prize.

1913

February 14   President Taft vetoes a bill calling for a literacy test for immigrants.

February 17   The Armory Art Exhibition opens in New York City and is the first showing in America of European modern art.

February 24   *Home Telephone and Telegraph Co. v. Los Angeles,* 227 U.S. 278, holds that injunctions of the Fourteenth Amendment apply to all persons.

Hoke v. United States, 227 U.S. 308, sustains the Mann (White Slave) Act of 1910. Justice Joseph McKenna argues for the Court that the commerce power of the Constitution could be used to promote the general welfare. This case is one of many that helps to enlarge federal police power during the Progressive Era.

February 25   The Sixteenth Amendment is adopted. "The Congress shall have power to lay and collect taxes on incomes, from whatever source derived, without apportionment among the several States, and without regard to any census or enumeration."

Silk workers led by William "Big Bill" Haywood of the Industrial Workers of the World (IWW) go on strike in Paterson, New Jersey.

March 1   The Webb-Kenyon Interstate Liquor Act prohibits the shipment of liquor into states where its sale is forbidden. Prohibitionists consider this a victory for their movement.

The Physical Valuation Act empowers the Interstate Commerce Commission to make thorough investigations of property held or used by railroads under its jurisdiction with the view to establishing cost and physical valuation as a basis for rate making and the fixing of a reasonable profit.

March 4   Wilson is inaugurated as president. His program, "The New Freedom," calls for reforms in banking, tariffs, and business.

The Department of Commerce and Labor is divided into two departments.

March 5   James C. McReynolds assumes the office of attorney general.

March 12-   A hundred fifty thousand garment workers go on strike
April 21   in New York City protesting long hours, low wages, and the refusal of union recognition. They win on all points.

April 7   *McDermott v. Wisconsin,* 228 U.S. 115, again sustains the Pure Food and Drug Act (1906) and rules that the law applies to indivudal purchases and consumers.

April 8   President Wilson, reviving a practice abandoned by Jefferson, personally addresses both houses of Congress.

May 2   Official recognition of the new Chinese Republic is extended by President Wilson.

May 10   Congress designates the second Sunday in May as Mother's Day.

May 19   A California law is enacted which in effect excludes Japanese-Americans from the ownership of land.

May 31   The Seventeen Amendment is ratified. "The Senate of the United States shall be composed of two Senators from each State, elected by the people therof, for six years; and each Senator shall have one vote. . . . " Progressives consider this a victory for the democratic process since a number of legislatively appointed senators had been identified with big business.

June 9

Minnesota Rate Cases, 230 U.S. 352, upholds railroad rate-fixing by a state commission. The exclusive authority of Congress over interstate commerce does not inhibit state action in nonconflicting areas.

June 10

Lewis Publishing Co. v. Morgan, 229 U.S. 288, upholds statutes which require statements of ownership of periodicals as a condition for use of the mails since these laws do not endanger the freedom of the press guaranteed by the First Amendment.

July 15

The Newlands Act authorizes the creation of a Board of Mediation and Conciliation to adjust disputes between interstate railroads and their employees.

August 30

John W. Davis assumes the office of solicitor general.

October 3

Under the provisions of the Underwood-Simmons Tariff Act Congress significantly reduces duties on such items as food, wool, iron and steel, shoes, and agricultural machinery. One object of this law is to stimulate trade with other nations. Since tariffs generally provide the federal government with considerable revenues, the act compensates for the loss of revenue by including a graduated tax on personal income. (The Sixteenth Amendment, ratified earlier, authorizes the imposition of income taxes.)

December 23

The Federal Reserve Act along with revisions and adjustments, creates a stable monetary and credit system; something which did not exist since the Civil War. The basic law provides for the division of the nation into twelve banking districts, each under the supervision of a Federal Reserve Bank. These Reserve banks exchange paper money for the commerical and agricultural paper that member banks take in as security from borrowers. The money supply is no longer at the mercy of precious metals. The Federal Reserve Board in Washington, D.C., which could appoint directors of the Federal Reserve banks and has some influence in determining interest rates, supervises the whole system.

1914

January 5	Henry Ford announces the adoption of a minimum wage of five dollars a day.
February 24	*Weeks v. United States,* 232 U.S. 383, holds for the first time that in federal court cases the Fourth Amendment bars the use of evidence secured through illegal search and seizure.
April 14	President Wilson orders the American fleet to Tampico Bay, Mexico, as a result of an incident involving the arrest of U.S. troops on April 9.
April 21	American forces land at Veracruz, Mexico, and capture the city.
April 25	The "ABC" countries (Argenting, Brazil, and Chile) offer to arbitrate the United States-Mexican dispute.
May 8	The Smith-Lever Act provides federal money on a matching basis for agricultural extension work.
June 8	In *Houston and Texas Railway Co. v. United States,* 234 U.S. 342, a majority of the Justices agree that the Interstate Commerce Act and the commmerce clause of the Constitution gives the United States government supreme power in rate making. Federal rate-fixing authority could override and amend a rate fixed by a state.
June 22	*The Pipeline Cases,* 234 U.S. 548, uphold the authority of the Interstate Commerce Commission to regulate pipelines. The commission is authorized to fix pipeline rates in interstate transportation under the Hepburn Act (1906).

June 28	Gavrilo Princip, a Serbian, assassinates Archduke Francis Ferdinand, heir to the imperial throne of the Austria-Hungarian Empire, in the provincial capital of Sarajevo, Bosnia. By early August the Central powers (Germany and Austro-Hungary) and the Allied powers (Great Britain, France, and Russia) are at war.
August 4	President Wilson issues an offical proclamation of neutrality for the duration of the world war.
August 5	The Bryan-Chamorro Treaty gives the United States the right-of-way for an interoceanic canal through Nicaragua.
August 6	Mrs. Woodrow Wilson (Ellen Axson Wilson) dies.
August 15	The Panama Canal is opened to the commerce of the world. The first ship actually passes through the Canal on January 7, 1914.
September 3	Thomas W. Gregory becomes attorney general.
September 26	The Federal Trade Commission Act authorizes the investigation of all interstate corporations, except carriers and banks, and the issuance of cease and desist orders in cases where unfair business practices exist. Unfortunately, the law does not define the term *unfair,* and the commission's ruling could be taken on appeal to the federal courts where during the 1920s and 1930s, conservative judges usually find for business.
October 12	Justice James C. McReynolds succeeds Horace H. Lurton.
October 15	In the Clayton Anti-Trust Act specific business practices such as price discrimination that tends to foster monopoly, "tying" agreements (which forbid retailers from handling the products of a firm's competitors), and the creation of interlocking directorates as a means of controlling competing companies are made illegal. This act also exempts labor unions and agricultural organizations from antitrust laws and curtails the use of injunctions in labor disputes. Unionists sometimes refer to the Clayton Act as the Magna Carta of labor.

November 3   In the national elections, the Democratic majority in the House of Representatives is reduced from seventy-three to twenty-five. The Republicans also make impressive gains in the key states of New York, Pennsylvania, Ohio, Illinois, Wisconsin, and Kansas.

November 23   U.S. forces depart from Veracruz, Mexico.

December 17   In the Harrison Anti-Narcotics Act all persons manufacturing or selling drugs have to register with the collector of internal revenue and pay a tax of one dollar. This law attempts to rid society of a social evil through the use of the commerce clause and taxing power of the Constitution.

1915

January 25   In *Coppage v. Kansas,* 236 U.S. 1, the majority argues that a state law outlawing "yellow-dog" antiunion contracts is unconstitutional since such a statute interfers with freedom of contract, a conservative position since it upholds the precepts of laissez-faire. Justice Oliver Wendell Holmes vigorously dissents and argues that the Court should not substitute its judgment for that of the legislature in matters of public policy.

January 26   Rocky Mountain National Park is established by Congress.

January 28   President Wilson vetoes a bill calling for a literacy test for immigrants. A new bill is passed over Wilson's veto in 1917.

                      The U.S. Coast Guard is created by Congress.

February 4   The German government declares the water surrounding the British Isles a war zone and states that they would sink all ships in the area.

February 8   *The Birth of a Nation,* a film depicting the Ku Klux Klan in a sympathetic fashion, is produced by D.W. Griffith, and has its first showing in Los Angeles.

March 4   The Seamen's Act initiated by Andrew Furuseth, president of the International Seamen's Union, mandates rigorous safety requirements on all vessels in the American maritime trade and declares that American and foreign sailors on vessels arriving at American ports are freed from their bondage to labor contracts.

April 12   *Chicago, Burlington, and Quincy Railroad Co. v. Wisconsin Railroad Commission,* 237 U.S. 220, holds that the Interstate Commerce Commission has the power to examine state regulations to determine their potential effect on interstate commerce.

April 22   The Imperial Germany Embassy publishes advertisements in Washington, D.C. newspapers warning travelers that vessels flying the flag of Great Britain or her Allies sailing in waters adjacent to the British Isles are liable to destruction.

April 30   President Wilson creates by executive order Naval Petroleum Reserve No. 3, the Teapot Dome, in Wyoming.

May 7   A German submarine sinks the British liner *Lusitania* off the Irish coast and almost 1,200 persons, including 128 Americans, lose their lives. President Wilson demands that Germany indemnify the victims and desist from attacking passenger ships. The German government eventually apologizes and agrees to pay an indemnity.

May 13   President Wilson appeals to the German goverment to halt sinking of unarmed merchantmen by submarines.

September 1   The German government pledges (Arabic Pledge) that unresisting liners would not be sunk without warning and without provision being made for the safety of passengers and crew.

September 16   The president of Haiti signs a treaty making his country a protectorate of the United States.

September 19   The first transcontinental wireless telephone call is made.

October 19   The United States government recognizes General Venustiano Carranza as president of Mexico.

November 1   *Truax v. Raich,* 239 U.S. 33, invalidates a state law which limits the number of foreign nationals who could be employed by local employers.

November 4   President Wilson presents a program to expand the army and navy; the campaign for "preparedness" has begun.

November 14   Booker T. Washington, black educator and advocate of economic independence of black Americans, dies in Tuskegee, Alabama.

November 25   The Ku Klux Klan of Reconstruction days is revived by Colonel William J. Simmons of Atlanta, Georgia.

December 4   Henry Ford's "peace ship" departs for Europe in an ill-fated attempt to end the war by a negotiated peace.

December 7   President Wilson urges Congress to increase military and naval expenditures.

December 12   *Hadacheck v. Los Angeles,* 239 U.S. 394, sustains a city ordinance requiring brickyards to be operated outside the city limits on the basis that it protects the public health.

December 18   President Wilson marries Mrs. Edith Bolling Galt, in Washington.

1916

January 24   In *Brushaber v. Union Pacific Railroad Co.,* 240 U.S. 1, the majority agrees that the Sixteenth Amendment (the income tax) invalidates *Pollack v. Farmers' Loan and Trust Co.* (1895) which had rejected certain federal income taxes on government bonds and lands.

February 10   The German government announces that its submarines would sink all armed merchant ships without warning beginning on February 29.

February 18	The Senate ratifies a treaty which makes Nicaragua a virtual protectorate.
February 21	*Tyree Realty Co. v. Andrews,* 240 U.S. 115, follows the rule set in *Brushaber* and upholds the income tax provisions of the Underwood-Simmons Tariff Act (1913).
February 28	Henry James, author, dies in London, England.
March 9	Francisco "Pancho" Villa raids Columbus, New Mexico, burns the town, and kills nineteen inhabitants.
March 15	American troops under General John J. Pershing are sent into Mexico to pursue and capture the Mexican revolutionary Pancho Villa.
March 24	The French steamer *Sussex* is torpedoed by the German navy. An American protest, known as the Sussex Pledge, persuades the Germans to promise not to sink merchantmen without warning.
May 15	American marine and naval forces seize Santo Domingo, Dominican Republic, and take control of the government.
June 3	The National Defense Act is the result of President Wilson's preparedness campaign. The regular army and National Guard are enlarged; a Reserve Officers Training Corps is established at colleges and universities; and a Citizens' Military Corps at military camps is created. The act also mandates a procedure for an inventory of industry.
June 5	Justice Louis Dembitz Brandeis succeeds Joseph Rucker Lamar.
June 7	The Republican party nominates Charles Evans Hughes (N.Y.) for the presidency and Charles W. Fairbanks (Ind.) for the vice presidency.
June 15	Wilson and Thomas R. Marshall are renominated by the Democratic party at its convention in St. Louis.

July 11
The Federal Highway Act, also known as the Bankhead Good Roads Act, provides funds on a matching basis for interstate highways.

July 18
In the Federal Farm Loan Act, Congress provides economic support for agriculture; the Federal Reserve Act had provided similar support for banking. A regional system with a national board is created to arrange long-term loans for farmers at rates below those of commercial banks.

July 22
A bomb is thrown during a Preparedness Day parade in San Francisco, killing ten persons.

August 11
The United States Warehouse Act; another act beneficial to farmers, authorizes bonded warehouses to issue receipts which are negotiable in themselves and acceptable as collateral for loans.

August 25
The National Park Service is established as part of the Department of the Interior.

August 29
A Council of National Defense is established by Congress and is charged with the responsibility of coordinating industry and resources for the national security and welfare.

In the Jones Act an elective Senate of the Philippine legislature is mandated, as well as lower suffrage requirements and senatorial consent to appointments made by the governor-general of heads of executive departments. Ultimate sovereignty, however, still remains in the hands of the United States.

September 1
The Keating-Owen Child Labor Act bars manufactured goods from interstate commerce when produced by underage children. The use of the commerce clause by the Congress in this statute will be ruled unconstitutional by the Court in 1918.

September 3
The Adamson (Railway Labor) Act is essentially a maximum-hour law which establishes an eight-hour day for railroad workers. It averts a national rail strike.

September 7   The Kern-McGillicudy Compensation Act establishes
                       a system of workmen's compensation for federal
                       employees.

                       In the Shipping Act Congress authorizes the creation of
                       the U.S. Shipping Board which is empowered to build,
                       purchase, lease, or requisition vessels through the
                       Emergency Fleet Corporation.

September 8   The Revenue Act is passed; among its provisions is the
                       creation of a tariff commission which looks into such
                       questions as unfair competition and "dumping" by
                       other nations.

October 9   Justice John Hessin Clarke succeeds Hughes.

October 16   The first birth-control clinic is opened in Brooklyn,
                       New York, by Margaret Sanger.

November 7   In the national elections, President Wilson defeats
                       Hughes, former Supreme Court Justice, by the narrow
                       margin of 277 to 254 in the Electoral College. The
                       popular vote is 9.1 million to 8.5 million. The Demo-
                       crats receive strong support from progressives and
                       those who want peace. So far, Wilson, who supports
                       preparedness, had kept America out of the war.

November 29   American military occupation of the Dominican
                       Republic is proclaimed.

December 18   President Wilson sends a communication to the war-
                       ring powers suggesting that they come to an under-
                       standing of each other's demands. He feels that neutral
                       America could bring about peace through negotiation
                       with the belligerents.

1917

January 8   *Clark Distilling Co. v. Western Maryland Railway Co.,*
                       242 U.S. 311, upholds the Webb-Kenyon Interstate
                       Liquor Act and also sustains West Virginia's prohibi-
                       tion law.

January 15	*Caminetti v. United States,* 242 U.S. 470, broadens the meaning of the White Slavery Act by holding that it applies to noncommercial as well as commerical traffic in women.
January 22	President Wilson gives his "Peace Without Victory" speech in the U.S. Senate.
January 27	The withdrawal of Major General John J. Pershing's troops from Mexico begins.
January 31	The German government announces that after February 1, her submarines would sink without warning all ships, belligerent and neutral, in a zone around Great Britain, France, and Italy, and in the eastern Mediterranean.
February 3	The United States breaks diplomatic relations with Germany.
February 5	An immigration act excluding all Asians from the United States is passed by Congress over Wilson's veto.
February 23	In the Smith-Hughes Act federal grants, matched by the states, for vocational training are provided and a Federal Board for Vocational Education is also created.
February 25	The American ambassador to Great Britain, Walter Page, transmits to Washington a message (Zimmerman Telegram) from the German foreign secretary, Arthur Zimmerman, to the German minister in Mexico City which instructs the minister to prepare an alliance with the Mexicans in the event that Germany goes to war against the United States.
March 2	In the Jones Act a large measure of self-goverment as well as American citizenship is granted to the residents of Puerto Rico.
March 4	Woodrow Wilson begins his second term as president.
March 13	After three years of vicious civil war, the United States government recognizes the Mexican regime once again

led by Venustiano Carranza.

March 14
The Czarist regime is overthrown in St. Petersburg and revolution breaks out in Russia. Within a year the Russians will be out of the world war.

March 18
German submarines sink three American merchant vessels without warning.

March 19
Wilson v. New, 243 U.S. 332, accepts the constitutionality of the Adamson Act which provides for an eighthour workday on interstate railroads, arguing once again that congressional authority over interstate commerce is a power granted by the Constitution through the commerce clause.

A food control program under Herbert Hoover, former director of the Belgium Relief Commission, begins.

March 31
The General Munitions Board is created by the Council of National Defense to procure raw materials and to manufacture armaments for the War and Navy departments.

The Virgin Islands are transferred from Danish ownership to American sovereignty, and are governed by the Navy Department until 1931.

April 2
Representative Jeanette Rankin (R. Mont.), becomes the first woman-member in the House of Representatives, just in time to vote against American entry into World War I.

April 6
Congress declares war against the Central Powers. The vote in the Senate is 82 to 6 and in the House 373 to 50.

April 9
In *Bunting v. Oregon,* 243 U.S. 426, the majority rules that an Oregon maximum-hour statute is a reasonable exercise of the state's police power. The law also affects minimum wages of women and children and the Court upholds these parts of the statute as well.

April 14
A Committee of Public Information under the journalist George Creel is created by President Wilson in order

to persuade Americans to support the war effort. A massive propaganda machine consisting of writers and speakers is mobilized to present a picture of a good and democratic America opposed to a bestial Germany.

April 16   The Emergency Fleet Corporation, a subsidiary of the United States Shipping Board, is chartered for the purpose of building ships for the war effort.

April 23   The War Loan Act authorizes the Treasury to issue $2 billion in short-term notes and $5 billion in bonds, $3 billion of which would be lent to the Allies.

April 24   In the Liberty Loan Act Congress authorizes the sale of bonds to the public. Most of the cost of the war is met by borrowing and Liberty and Victory bond campaigns produce billions of dollars. Other sources of revenue include income and excess-profits taxes.

May 18   The Selective Service Act allows the federal government to register and classify for military service all American men from 21 to 30 years of age. Later, it was amended in the Man Power Act (August 31, 1918) and men from 18 to 45 years of age are registered.

May 21   *New York Central Railroad Co. v. Winfield*, 244 U.S. 147, declares that the federal government preempts state authority in the area of workingmen's compensation even when the federal law does not provide a remedy. This case highlights the Court's attack upon reform legislation at this time.

Erie Railroad Co. v. Winfield, 244 U.S. 170, denies relief under state laws as in the *New York Central* ruling, on the ground that an injured worker is engaged in interstate commerce and thereby falls under federal law, although the federal statute affords no remedy.

In *Southern Pacific Railroad Co. v. Jensen*, 244 U.S. 205, the third suit for compensation heard by the Court, the majority argues that relief under state law is denied because federal law governs the subject of injury in maritime work on vessels owned by railroads.

June 11   *Paine Lumber Co. v. Neal,* 244 U.S. 459, holds, in this prolabor decision, that a private party could not petition for an injunction against a labor union under the Sherman Act unless he could show special injury to himself. Later, the Taft Court would overturn this concept of limiting the labor injunction.

Adams v. Tanner, 244 U.S. 590, invalidates a Washington state law forbidding employment agencies to collect fees from job hunters as a deprivation of a property right without due process of law. This represents a weakening of state power by the Court.

June 14   Major General Pershing arrives in Paris to establish the headquarters of the American Expeditionary Force.

June 15   In the Espionage Act Congress asserts that the federal government under the war powers of the Constitution could impose fines up to $10,000 and imprisonment up to 20 years for aiding the enemy or obstructing recruiting and training of troops. The postmaster general is also authorized to ban from the mails any material which he considers treasonable or seditious.

June 19   A special adjustment commission is established by the War Department to set wages and hours for workers engaged in constructing army camps.

July 2   A major race riot breaks out in East St. Louis, Illinois, and thirty-seven persons are killed.

July 4   The first units of the American Expeditionary Force reach Paris.

July 20   A Board of Control for Labor Standards is set up to regulate clothing manufacturers who supply army uniforms.

July 28   The War Industries Board is created to oversee all aspects of industrial production and distribution. The board has the authority to allocate scarce materials, standardize production, fix prices, and coordinate American and Allied purchasing.

August 10

The Lever Food and Drug Control Act authorizes federal controls over the production, distribution, and pricing of foods and fuels declared essential to the war effort. The statute also institutes wartime prohibition. Hoover, appointed food administrator by President Wilson, is empowered to fix wheat prices, establish a government corporation to purchase sugar and organize a national campaign to conserve food.

August 23

President Wilson establishes the Fuel Administration under Harry A. Garfield, president of Wiliams College; the agency's aim is to increase the output of coal.

October 3

In the War Revenue Act Congress authorizes a graduated excess profits tax ranging from twenty to sixty percent, reduces income tax exemptions, increases the income tax for individuals and corporations, increases the maximum surtax, and sets higher limits on excise and estate taxes.

October 6

The Trading with the Enemy Act attempts to prevent commerce between American producers and the enemy, establishes an Office of Censorship to control communication abroad, and creates an Office of Alien Property Custodian to take possession of property of belligerents and their nationals when found in the United States.

November 2

In the Lansing-Ishii Agreement, the United States recognizes that the Japanese have special interests in China, especially Manchuria and Shantung provinces. In return, Japan reaffirms her support of the Open Door and the independence of China.

November 11

New York State amends its constitution to grant women the vote.

December 7

War is declared against the Austria-Hungarian Empire by the United States.

December 10

Hitchman Coal and Coke Co. v. Mitchell, 245 U.S. 229, upholds the right of employers to seek an injunction against union organizers advocating a strike for union recognition.

December 28	All railroad transportation is put under the control of the United States Railroad Administration headed by William G. McAdoo, former secretary of the treasury.

1918

January 7	*Selective Draft Law Cases,* 245 U.S. 366, unanimously uphold the federal government's power to raise and support armies as provided in Article I of the Constitution. This decision effectively upholds the constitutionality of the Selective Service Act (May 18, 1917).
Janaury 8	In the Fourteen Points, a speech delivered before Congress, President Wilson enunciates a plan which calls for a peace treaty openly negotiated, freedom of the seas, the elimination of trade barriers, the reduction of armaments, greater concern for colonial peoples, European boundaries which would reflect the rights of minorities, and the estalishment of a League of Nations. Wilson hopes that these fourteen points will be the basis for the peace treaty to be negotiated after the war.
January 10	The House of Representatives adopts a resolution to submit a constitutional amendment for ratification by the states providing for federal women's suffrage.
January 14	*Goldman v. United States,* 245 U.S. 474, sustains the federal government's right to draft individuals for military service on the grounds that such power is not an unreasonable infringement upon individual liberty.
March 3	In the Treaty of Brest-Litovsk the Russian Bolsheviks negotiate a separate peace treaty with Germany.
March 4	Bernard M. Baruch, Wall Street broker, is made chairman of the War Industries Board. The board's powers are expanded to conserve resources, advise purchasing agencies as to prices, make purchases for the Allies, and determine priorities of production and distribution in industry.
March 19	Congress creates daylight savings time.

March 21	In the Railroad Control Act Congress fixes compensation for railroads under government management during the wartime emergency.
April 5	The War Finances Corporation is created to finance war industries.
April 8	The National War Labor Board, headed by former President William Howard Taft and a lawyer, Frank P. Walsh, is established by President Wilson in order to settle labor disputes occurring during the war. Numerous cases are heard and many strikes are averted.
April 10	The Webb-Pomerene (Export Trade) Act exempts American trade associations from the operation of antitrust laws so that American business could compete with English and French cartels during the war.
April 20	Under the Sabotage Act the willful sabotage of war materials, utilities, and transportation facilities is made a federal crime. This law is primarily aimed at the antiwar activities of the Industrial Workers of the World (IWW).
May 15	The first airmail service between New York City and Washington, D.C. is inaugurated.
May 16	The Sedition Act, essentially an amendment to the Espionage Act (1917), mandates severe penalties for persons convicted of willfully making statements interferring with the war effort and using disloyal, profane, or abusive language with reference to the American flag, the Constitution, or the form of government of the United States. As a result of this statute and the Espionage Act numerous periodicals lose their mailing privileges and therefore their readership; and literally thousands of pacifists, socialists, and antiwar advocates go to prison.
May 20	*Peck v. Lowe,* 247 U.S. 165, sustains a provision of the income tax law passed under the Sixteenth Amendment which allows the levying of a tax on the net income of a corporation derived from the sale of exported goods.

The Overman Act authorizes the president to coordinate or consolidate executive bureaus, agencies, and offices in the interest of economy and the more efficient concentration of governmental operations in matters relating to the war effort.

June 3   *Hammer v. Dagenhart,* 247 U.S. 251, by a 5-4 decision invalidates the first Child Labor Law. Justice William R. Day, writing for the majority, argues that the statute is not a regulation of commerce but an outright prohibition and as such is void. Justices Oliver Wendell Holmes and Louis D. Brandeis counter by stating that the majority is promoting their own social philosophy—conservative laissez-faire economics.

United States Glue Co. v. Oak Creek, 247 U.S. 321, sustains a local income tax on corporations even when this tax falls in part upon income derived from interstate commerce.

June 6-25   The Battle of Belleau Wood, the first sizable American action of World War I, breaks out.

June 8   The War Labor Policies Board, under Felix Frankfurter of the Harvard Law School, is empowered to set wages-and-hours standards for each major war industry.

June 10   In *Toledo Newspaper Co. v. United States,* 247 U.S. 402, the majority sustains the principle that holding a newspaper in contempt of court is not an infringement of the First Amendment.

September 14   Eugene V. Debs, Socialist party leader, is sentenced to ten years in prison for advocating pacifism in violation of the Espionage and Sedition acts.

September 19   In the District of Columbia Minimum Wage Law Congress fixes wages and hours for women-employees in the District of Columbia.

November 5   In the national elections, the Democrats lose twenty-six seats in the House of Representatives and six in the Senate, giving the Republicans control of both Houses.

November 11	An armistice goes into effect at 11:00 A.M. and the world war comes to an end.
November 21	Alexander King assumes the office of solicitor general.
December 4	President Wilson sails for France to attend the peace conference.
December 23	*International News Service v. Associated Press,* 248 U.S. 215, holds that a news service is entitled to protection from the pirating of its news by another news service, even though the news itself is part of the public domain.

1919

January 1	The War Industries Board is terminated; the first of the wartime agencies to end.
January 6	Theodore Roosevelt dies at Oyster Bay, New York.
January 18- May 7	The Paris peace conference is convened.
January 29	The Eighteenth Amendment is ratified. "The manufacturing, sale, or transportation of intoxicating liquors . . . is hereby prohibited."
February 20	Victor L. Berger, Socialist editor and leader, is indicted for conspiracy to violate the Espionage Act, and sentenced to twenty years imprisonment. The sentence is later set aside.
February 24	In the War Revenue Act Congress levies taxes on incomes, excess profits, estates, and the products manufactured by children.
	In the Child Labor Tax Act Congress attempts to prohibit child labor in interstate commerce by placing a heavy tax on goods produced by underage children. In using its ability to tax, Congress is attempting to accomplish the same ends as in the invalidated Keating-Owen Child Labor Act (1916).

February 25	One hundred million dollars is voted by Congress for the establishment of a European relief fund.
February 26	Grand Canyon National Park is established by Congress.
March 2	President Wilson appoints Herbert Hoover director general of the American Relief Administration
March 3	*Schenck v. United States,* 249 U.S. 47, unanimously upholds the Espionage Act as not violating the First Amendment. Justice Oliver Wendell Holmes applies the "clear and present danger" test and finds that Schenck's writings encourage real resistance to the draft. Moreover, the point is made that free speech is always under restraint, especially in time of war.
	United States v. Doremus, 249 U.S. 86, sustains a federal antinarcotic drug law (Harrison Act) as a reasonable use of the tax power; this is a police measure to outlaw a practice believed contrary to the general welfare.
March 5	A. Mitchell Palmer assumes the office of attorney general.
March 10	*Frohwerk v. United States,* 249 U.S. 204, applies the "clear and present danger" test to the Espionage Act and finds it to be constitutional.
	Debs v. United States, 249 U.S. 211, agrees that the First Amendment does not protect someone intentionally obstructing the military operations of the government. Debs therefore went to prison.
March 15-17	The American Legion is organized in Paris.
June 5	The Women's Suffrage Amendment is adopted by Congress and sent to the states for ratification.
June 9	*American Manufacturing Co. v. St. Louis,* 250 U.S. 459, sustains a state tax on local business rather than on interstate commerce.

June 28	Germany signs the Treaty of Versailles.
July 1	Daily airmail service is inaugurated between New York and Chicago.
July 4	Jack Dempsey wins the world heavyweight boxing championship by knocking out Jess Willard in the third round in Toledo, Ohio.
July 10	President Wilson presents the peace treaty to the Senate for ratification.
July 19	Race riots break out in Washington, D.C.; black soldiers are among those attacked by mobs.
July 27	Race riots erupt in Chicago and twenty-three blacks are killed.
August 11	Andrew Carnegie, industrialist, dies in Lennox, Massachusetts, at the age of eighty-three.
August 31	The Communist party is organized in Chicago.
September 3	President Wilson begins a nationwide speaking tour in support of the League of Nations.
September 9-14	Calvin Coolidge, governor of Massachusetts, uses the National Guard to break a strike by the Boston police.
Septebmer 10	The U.S. First Division and General John J. Pershing, back from Europe, march up Fifth Avenue in New York City.
September 22	Steelworkers strike U.S. Steel and other companies; demanding union recognition and the end of the twelve-hour day and seven-day week.
October 2	President Wilson suffers a stroke which incapacitates him for almost two months.
October 28	The National Prohibition Enforcement (Volstead) Act is passed over the veto of President Wilson and implements the Prohibition amendment.

November 1   A major soft coal strike breaks out under the leadership of union leader John L. Lewis.

November   U.S. Attorney General Palmer commences the "Red Scare" raids and arrests. Most of those arrested are later released for lack of evidence, but some aliens are deported.

November 10   Berger is reelected to Congress by his Wisconsin district.

In *Abrams v. United States,* 250 U.S. 616, the majority upholds the 1918 Sedition Act on the grounds that invoking disaffection during wartime is not protected by the First Amendment. In dissent, Holmes strongly defends freedom of speech.

November 19   The Senate blocks ratification of the Versailles Treaty as well as American membership in the League of Nations.

December 22   About 250 "anarchist, communist, labor agitator" aliens are deported and sailed to Russia.

December 24   The railroads are returned to private control by presidential proclamation (effective day March 1, 1920).

1920

January 2   The Red Scare continues as federal agents stage nationwide raids and arrests.

January 5   *Ruppert v. Caffey,* 251 U.S. 264, upholds the Volstead Act against the charge that it deprives breweries of property without due process of law.

January 16   The Prohibition amendment to the Constitution goes into effect.

January 26   *Silverthorne Lumber Co. v. United States,* 251 U.S. 385, holds that the Fourth Amendment protects corporations from unreasonable seach and seizure in criminal proceedings.

February 13 President Wilson forces Secretary of State Robert Lansing out of office, accusing him of holding unauthorized Cabinet meetings during his illness.

February 28 The Esch-Cummins (Transportation) Act returns the railroads to private control after wartime govermental operation, creates a labor arbitration board, and encourages railroad consolidation under the Interstate Commerce Commission.

March 1 *United States v. U.S. Steel Co.,* 251 U.S. 417, dismisses an antitrust case against U.S. Steel and brings to an end the trust-busting era.

Schaefer v. United States, 251 U.S. 466, takes a narrow view of what constitutes a "clear and present danger" under the Espionage Act, in finding against Schaefer.

March 8 *Eisner v. Macomber,* 252 U.S. 189, proclaims that stock dividends are not to be subject to income taxes.

March 19 The Treaty of Versailles agains comes to a vote in the Senate and fails to obtain the necessary two-thirds majority.

April 1 Five members of the New York legislature are expelled for being members of the Socialist party. They are reelected, but were again unseated.

April 19 *Missouri v. Holland,* 252 U.S. 416, sustains a treaty between the United States and Canada on migratory bird conservation. Oliver Wendell Holmes, for the majority, argues that treaties are made under the authority of the United States, while acts of Congress are enacted under the authority of the Constitution. This means that the powers of the central government are almost limitless if written into a treaty.

May 5 Nicola Sacco and Bartolomeo Vanzetti, Italian immigrants, are arrested in Braintree, Massachusetts, and charged with the murder of a paymaster and a guard during a payroll robbery.

May 8-14 The Socialist Party Convention nominates Eugene V.

debs for president for the fifth time. Debs conducts his campaign from his Atlanta prison cell.

May 20

Congress declares an end to the world war with Germany and Austria-Hungary. President Wilson vetoes the resolution.

June 1

William L. Frierson becomes solicitor general.

Hawke v. Smith, 253 U.S. 221, 231, holds that Congress has sole discretion in determining the methods of ratification of an amendment to the Constitution.

June 4

The Army Reorganization Act provides for a peacetime force of 298,000 men.

June 5

Under the provisions of the Merchant Marine (Jones) Act the Shipping Board created by statutes of 1916 and 1918, is reorganized in order to dispose of the wartime merchant fleet and to help private parties develop an American mercantile industry.

June 7

In *National Prohibition Cases,* 253 U.S. 350, the Court upholds both the Eighteenth Amendment and the Volstead Act (1919) and rejects the argument that the Eighteenth Amendment is not subject for constitutional provision.

In *Federal Trade Commission v. Gratz,* 253 U.S. 421, the majority holds that desist orders of the commission are void if complaints of unfair competition are unsubstantiated. The real effect of this case is to substitute the judgment of the Court for that of the commission in determining the conclusiveness of the evidence supporting a complaint.

June 10

The Federal Water Power Act authorizes a Federal Power Commission to regulate waterways on public lands and navigable streams and to license the use of dam sites for the generation of electric power.

June 12

Senator Warren G. Harding (Ohio) is nominated by the Republican party for the presidency; Governor Calvin Coolidge (Mass.) is chosen as his running mate.

June 19	The American Federation of Labor's annual convention in Montreal votes to support the League of Nations.
June 28- July 5	The Democratic Party Convention at San Francisco nominates James M. Cox (Ohio) for president and Franklin D. Roosevelt (N.Y.) for vice president.
August 26	The Nineteenth Amendment is ratified and women obtain the right to vote in national elections regardless of state laws.
September 8	Airmail service between New York and San Francisco is inaugurated.
September 16	A bomb explodes in Wall Street in front of the offices of J.P. Morgan and Co. Thirty people are killed and the property loss is estimated at two million dollars.
September 28	Eight members of the Chicago White Sox Baseball Team are indicted on charges of throwing the 1919 World Series.
October 16	A bonus parade is staged in New York City by ex-service-men.
November 2	In the national elections Harding wins by a massive 60.3 percent of the popular vote.
	In California an Alien-Land Tax, to prevent Japanese-Americans from owning farm land, is approved by popular referendum.
	The first national radio service begins when station KDKA in East Pittsburg broadcasts the Harding-Cox election returns.
December 10	President Wilson is awarded the Nobel Peace Prize.
December 13	*Gilbert v. Minnesota,* 254 U.S. 325, sustains a state sedition law because state and federal cooperation in this area is desirable.

1921

January 3   *Duplex Printing Press Co. v. Deering,* 254 U.S. 443, the first test of the Clayton Act, holds that secondary boycotts are enjoinable despite the antiinjunction provisions of the act. This, for the time being, means that labor could not look to the Clayton Act for protection.

January 4   Congress revives the War Finance Corporation, over the President's veto, to relieve economic depression in farm areas.

February 28   *United States v. L. Cohen Grocery Co.,* 255 U.S. 81, invalidates the criminal penalties of the Lever Food Controls Act (1917) because the law fixes no specific standards for guilt.

March 3   President Woodrow Wilson vetoes the Emergency Tariff Bill.

March 4   Harding and Coolidge are inaugurated as president and vice president.

March 5   Harry M. Daugherty assumes the office of attorney general.

March 7   *Milwaukee Publishing Co. v. Burleson,* 255 U.S. 407, approves the postmaster general's authority under the Espionage Act to bar subversive matter from the mails.

March 25   The Soviet government's request that trade relations be resumed is rejected by Secretary of State Charles Evans Hughes.

April 18   In *Block v. Hirsch,* 256 U.S. 135, the majority agrees that the District of Columbia has authority to impose rent controls under emergency conditions.

April 20   The Thompson-Urrutia Treaty, awarding twenty-five million dollars to Columbia for the loss of Panama, is signed.

May 16   *Dillon v. Gloss,* 256 U.S. 368, confirms that Congress has complete discretion in determining the length of time an amendment could remain before the people.

May 19	The Emergency Quota Act restricts immigration for any nationality to three percent of persons of that nationality residing in the United States in 1910. Edward Douglass White, Chief Justice of the Supreme Court, dies in Washington, D.C., at the age of seventy-five.
May 27	In the Emergency Tariff Act Congress raises duties on agricultural products, wool, and sugar, and imposes an embargo on German dyestuffs.
May 31	The administration of naval oil reserves at Teapot Dome, Wyoming is transferred from the Navy Department to the Department of the Interior.
June 1	*Burdeau v. McDowell,* 256 U.S. 465, allows the use of illegally obtained evidence in criminal prosecutions when this evidence was obtained by private parties without the government's knowledge.
June 10	The Budget and Accounting Act establishes the Bureau of the Budget and the General Accounting Office. Charles G. Dawes is appointed the first budget director on June 21.
June 25	Samuel Gompers is elected for the fortieth time president of the American Federation of Labor.
June 30	William Howard Taft is appointed Chief Justice of the Supreme Court by President Harding.
July 1	James M. Beck becomes solicitor general.
July 2	The war with Germany finally ends as President Harding signs a joint resolution of Congress.
July 14	Nicola Sacco and Bartolomeo Vanzetti are convicted of murder, amid worldwide protest.
July 21	General William "Billy" Mitchell demonstrates the superiority of aircraft over ships with the bombing of a

German battleship off the Virigina coast. He is also a strong advocate of a separate air force.

August 9   A U.S. Veterans Bureau is established by Congress.

August 11   The United States invites Great Britain, France, Italy, Japan, Belgium, China, the Netherlands, and Portugal to a conference to discuss the limitation of arms and problems of the Pacific area.

August 15   In the Packers and Stockyards Act Congress provides for the regulation of interstate and foreign commerce in livestock and poultry products.

August 16   The Department of Labor estimates that unemployment has risen to more than five million.

August 24   The Grain Futures Trading Act, designed to control speculation in grain, is invalidated by the Supreme Court in 1922.

August 25   A separate peace treaty with Germany is signed in Berlin. The Senate ratifies the treaty on October 18.

September 14   John Bassett Moore, legal scholar, is elected to the World Court.

September 20   A national conference on unemployment proposes a program to provide jobs.

October 3   Taft is installed as Chief Justice of the Supreme Court. The Taft Court (October 1921-February 1930) includes Justices Louis D. Brandeis, John H. Clarke, William R. Day, Oliver Wendell Holmes, Joseph Rucker Lamar, James C. McReynolds, Mahlon Pitney, and Willis Van Devanter.

November 2   The American Birth Control League, headed by Margaret Sanger, is formed in New York City.

                  Eugene O'Neill's drama, *Anna Christie* is produced in New York City.

November 11   America's Unknown Soldier is buried at Arlington

National Cemetery and President Harding proclaims November 11, Armistice Day, a national holiday.

November 12-
February 6,
1922

A conference for arms limitation is held in Washington, D.C.

November 23

The Sheppard-Towner Maternity and Infancy Act provides funds to the states for maternal and infant welfare. It is widely criticized as an infringement of states' rights.

The Revenue Act repeals some wartime taxes.

December 5

American Steel Foundries v. Trades Council, 257 U.S. 184, invalidates an injunction against picketing, and reaffirms the *Duplex* rule that the antitrust laws circumscribe the rights of organized labor.

December 12

Dahnke-Walker Co. v. Bondurant, 257 U.S. 282, states that when a plaintiff fails to allege his constitutional rights, and the issue is based on state laws reviewed by a state high court, his suit would not be heard by the Supreme Court.

December 13

The Four Power Pacific Treaty, signed by the United States, Great Britain, France, and Japan, guarantees each other's rights to insular possessions in the Pacific Ocean.

December 19

Truax v. Corrigan, 257 U.S. 312, invalidates an Arizona picketing law favorable to labor because it violates the due process and equal protection clauses of the Fourteenth Amendment.

December 22

In the Russian Famine Relief Act Congress authorizes the expenditure of twenty million dollars to purchase seed grain, corn, and preserved milk for Russia.

December 23

President Harding commutes the sentences of Eugene V. Debs and twenty-three others convicted under the Espionage Act.

1922

January 19	Senator William E. Borah (Idaho) calls for the outlawry of war.

January 30   *Cornelius v. Moore,* 257 U.S. 491, rejects as without merit a claim of deprivation of property without due process, where the claimant had acquired interest in liquor in a warehouse but was not permitted to remove it.

February 6   The Nine-Power Treaty which is signed in Washington, D.C., obligates the United States, Great Britain, France, Japan, Italy, the Netherlands, Belgium, and Portugal to respect the sovereignty of China and the Open Door.

February 9   A World War Foreign Debt Commission is established by Congress in order to renegotiate international war debts.

February 18   The Cooperative Marketing Association (Capper-Volstead) Act exempts agricultural cooperatives from antitrust law restrictions. Cooperative buying and selling of agricultural products is also promoted.

February 27   *Terral v. Burke Construction,* 257 U.S. 529, invalidates an Arkansas statute which penalizes foreign (out of state) corporations for using the federal courts in suites within the state.

Leser v. Garnett, 258 U.S. 130, rejects Maryland's contention that the Nineteenth Amendment arbitrarily adds votes to the roles and thus destroys the political balance.

Railroad Commission of Wisconsin v. Chicago, Burlington, and Quincy Railway Co., 257 U.S. 563, denies the right of the Interstate Commerce Commission to regulate intrastate rates where intrastate points are remote from the interstate portion of a carrier's business.

March 24   The Four-Power Treaty is ratified by the Senate.

March 28	New York State prohibits aliens from teaching in the public schools.
April 1–September 4	A major nationwide strike of both soft and hard coal miners breaks out in protest against wage reductions and in support of the union dues checkoff system.
April 7	Secretary of the Interior Albert B. Fall secretly grants a lease without competitive bidding on the Teapot Dome oil reserve to Harry F. Sinclair's Mammoth Oil Co.
May 1	In *Stafford v. Wallace,* 258 U.S. 495, the majority upholds the Packers and Stockyards Act (1921) and also agrees that when livestock are unloaded from interstate carriers, they remain part of the an interstate business transaction.
May 15	In *Hill v. Wallace,* 259 U.S. 44, the Grain Futures Trading Act (1921) is invalidated.
	Bailey v. Drexel Furniture Co., 259 U.S. 20, holds the Child Labor Tax Law (1918) unconstitutional. Thus Congress could not regulate child labor by either the use of the commerce clause (*Hammer v. Dagenhart,* 1918) or the tax power.
May 26	A Narcotics Control Board is established by Congress. Membership on the board consists of the secretaries of state, treasury, and commerce.
May 30	The Lincoln Memorial in Washington, D.C., is dedicated.
June 5	*United Mine Workers v. Coronado Coal Co.,* 259 U.S. 344, unanimously sustains a property damage suit against striking mine workers under the civil liability section of the Sherman Act.
July 1	Railway shopmen strike the railroads to protest the reduction of their wages ordered by the Railroad Labor Board.
July 20	Chile and Peru submit a border dispute (Tacna-Arica) to the president for settlement.

August 2	Alexander Graham Bell, inventor of the telephone, dies in Baddeck, Nova Scotia, at the age of seventy-five.
September 14	The Judicial Conference and Transfer Act authorizes the establishment of a conference of senior judges of the judicial circuits to make a survey of conditions of business in the federal courts and to prepare plans for the assignment and transfer of judges to districts with overcrowded dockets.
September 19	The Fordney-McCumber Tariff Act raises import duties to their highest levels in history.
September 21	The Grain Future Act regulates trading in grain under the interstate commerce power. It replaces a similar act of 1921, found unconstitutional by the Supreme Court.
	Congress in a joint resolution calls for the establishment of a national home for the Jews in Palestine.
September 22	The Cable Act declares that women could no longer lose their U.S. citizenship if they marry aliens.
October 2	Justice George Sutherland succeeds John H. Clarke.
November 7	In the national elections the Republicans lose seventy-six seats in the House of Representatives and eight seats in the Senate, but retain a majority in both houses.
December 11	*United States v. Lanza,* 260 U.S. 377, touches upon an important constitutional issue and holds that protection against double jeopardy applies to a second federal prosecution, and not to separate federal and state prosecutions.

1923

January 2	Justice Pierce Butler succeeds William R. Day.
January 8	*Federal Trade Commission v. Curtis Publishing Co.,* 260 U.S. 568, asserts that the ultimate determination of what constitutes unfair competition under the Federal Trade Commission Act is a judicial matter.

January 10	The American Army of Occupation on the Rhine in Germany is ordered home by President Warren G. Harding.
February 19	Justice Edward Terry Sanford succeeds Mahlon Pitney.
February 28	Under the provisions of the British Debt Refunding Act Great Britain obtains the privilege of repaying her enormous war debt to the United States in semi-annual installments over a period of 62 years with an interest rate of 3.3 percent.
March 4	Secretary Albert B. Fall resigns from the Department of the Interior as the illegal sale of oil leases at Teapot Dome and Elk Hills are being investigated.
March 23	The Agricultural Credits Act provides for twelve Federal Intermediate Credit banks to assist the agricultural and livestock industries.
April 9	In *Adkins v. Children's Hospital,* 261 U.S. 525, the majority rules that the minimum wage law for women in the District of Columbia is unconstitutional as an infringement upon the freedom of contract guaranteed by the Fifth Amendment.
April 16	*Chicago Board of Trade v. Olsen,* 262 U.S. 1, upholds the Grain Futures Trading Act (1922) and asserts that the commerce clause is a more appropriate vehicle for exercising police power than the taxing power of Congress.
April 30	*Cunard Steamship Co. v. Mellon,* 262 U.S. 100, affirms the federal government's right under the Eighteenth Amendment to prohibit the use of liquor on ships within the territorial waters of the United States.
May 21	*S.W. Bell Telephone Co. v. Public Service Commission,* 262 U.S. 276, restricts the power of state commissions to establish utility rates. They could no longer substitute their judgment for the "honest discretion of the company's board of directors" in determining a fair return.

June 3	In *Frothingham v. Mellon* and *Massachusetts v. Mellon,* 262 U.S. 447, jurisdiction over the issue of federal grant-in-aid is denied under the Shepard-Towner Maternity Act (1921) and thus leaves to Congress the subject of federal grants-in-aid in many fields.
June 4	*Meyer v. Nebraska,* 262 U.S. 390, invalidates a state law prohibiting the teaching of foreign languages below the high school level.
June 11	*Wolff Packing Co. v. Court of Industrial Relations,* 262 U.S. 522, unanimously finds unconstitutional a Kansas law which mandates the use of a special tribunal in labor disputes affecting the public interest. William Howard Taft argues for the Court that the public interest could not be arbitrarily attributed by the state, but must depend on surrounding circumstances.
August 2	U.S. Steel adopts the eight-hour day for its workers.
	President Harding dies in San Francisco.
August 3	Calvin Coolidge is sworn in to the presidency by his father, a notary public, in Plymouth, Vermont.
September 15	Governor J.C. Walton (Okla.) places his state under martial law because of Ku Klux Klan activities.
October 25	A U.S. Senate subcommittee investigating the Teapot Dome scandal holds its first meeting under the chairmanship of Thomas J. Walsh (Mont.).
November 6	A patent is issued to Colonel Jacob Schick for the first electric shaver.
December 6	President Coolidge addresses Congress and voices support for the World Court, tax reduction, and prohibition enforcement. He opposes the cancellation of Allied war debts and the payment of a veteran's bonus.
December 8	A treaty of friendship, commerce, and consular rights is signed with Germany in Washington, D.C. The Senate

ratifies the treaty with reservations on February 10, 1925.

December 10 | Robert Andrews Millikan receives the Nobel Prize in physics.

1924

January 7 | *Dayton-Goose Creek Railway Co. v. United States,* 263 U.S. 456, gives the Interstate Commerce Commission the power to evaluate both intrastate and interstate earnings in order to determine railroad rates.

January 16 | The McNary-Haugen Farm Relief Bill that sets prices for products is introduced in Congress, but fails to pass.

February 3 | Woodrow Wilson dies in Washington, D.C.

February 12 | George Gershwin's *Rhapsody in Blue,* a new musical form known as symphonic jazz, is performed for the first time in New York City.

February 27 | The United States signs a treaty with the Dominican Republic which permits American intervention on behalf of political stability.

February 29 | Charles R. Forbes, ex-director of the Veterans' Bureau, is indicted for defrauding the government.

March 1 | The Senate orders the investigation of the administration of Attorney General Harry M. Daugherty. President Coolidge forces Daugherty's resignation on March 28.

April 7 | Harlan F. Stone becomes Attorney General.

April 14 | *Burns Baking Co. v. Bryan,* 264 U.S. 504, invalidates as a denial of due process a law which regulates the weight of bread.

May 19 | A Soldiers' Bonus Bill is passed over the president's veto.

May 21	The theory of evolution is ruled untenable by the General Assembly of the Presbyterian Church at San Antonio, Texas.
May 24	The Foreign Service Act limits the annual quota of immigrants for any country to two percent of the number of individuals both in that country and residing in the United States in 1890. Japanese nationals are totally excluded.
June 2	A child labor amendment to the Constitution is submitted to the states for ratification. Only twenty-six of the necessary thirty-six states ratify it.
	All American Indians who are born in the United States are declared citizens by an act of Congress.
	In the Revenue Act Congress reduces or abolishes most taxes.
June 9	*United States v. New River Co.*, 265 U.S. 533, argues that Courts should not substitute their judgment for the findings and conclusions of the Interstate Commerce Commission when the commission is acting within the scope of its statutory power.
June 10-12	The Republican National Convention meets at Cleveland and nominates Coolidge for president and Charles G. Dawes (Ill.) for vice president.
June 24- July 10	The Democratic party meeting in New York City, nominates John W. Davis (W.Va.) for president and Charles W. Bryan (Neb.) for vice president.
June 30	Albert B. Fall, Harry F. Sinclair, and Edward L. Doheny are indicted for bribery and conspiracy to defraud the government over oil leases in Teapot Dome, Wyoming, and Elk Hills, California.
July 4	A revived Progressive party nominates Senator Robert M. LaFollette (Wis.) for president and Burton K. Wheeler (Mont.) for vice president.
July 11	The Workers' (Communist) party nominates William

Z. Foster (Ill.) for president and Benjamin Gitlow (N.Y.) for vice president.

August 16   The Dawes Plan for the payment of German reparations is accepted by both the Allies and Germany.

August 24   In the Agricultural Credits Act Congress hopes that farm bankruptcies will be curtailed.

September 18   U.S. Marines withdraw from the Dominican Republic.

October 20   *Michaelson v. United States,* 266 U.S. 42, declares that unions can be held in contempt for striking in defiance of a ruling of the Railroad Labor Board.

November 4   In the national elections Coolidge and Dawes receive 382 electoral votes, to 136 for Davis and Bryan, and 13 for LaFollette and Wheeler. The Republicans also retain control of both houses of Congress.

December 13   Samuel Gompers, labor leader and president of the American Federation of Labor, dies in San Antonio, Texas, at the age of seventy-four.

December 19   William Green succeeds Samuel Gompers as president of the American Federation of Labor.

1925

January 5   Mrs. Nellie Ross (Wyo.) becomes the first woman governor in the United States.

February 13   The Judicial Code Revision reduces the number of cases which automatically come to the Supreme Court on appeals by broadening the discretionary power of certiorari; judgments in the Courts of Claims are made final, as well as certain cases in the Circuit Courts of Appeals; and cases in state courts which involve constitutional questions would continue to come before the Supreme Court on writs of error.

February 24   The Purnell Act authorizes funds for economic research at agricultural experiment stations.

March 2	Justice Harlan Fiske Stone succeeds Joseph McKenna on the Supreme Court.

Carroll v. United States, 267 U.S 132, protects the government's right to have agents search without warrant private vehicles suspected of transporting alcoholic beverages.

March 4   Calvin Coolidge and Charles G. Dawes are inaugurated president and vice president.

March 9   President Coolidge argues in favor of Chile in the Tacna-Arica border dispute between Chile and Peru.

March 13   The Tennessee legislature makes it unlawful to teach the theory of evolution in public schools.

March 17   John G. Sargent assumes the office of attorney general.

March 23   The U.S. Senate ratifies a treaty with Cuba which states that the Isle of Pines is Cuban territory.

April 13   Scheduled commercial airplane service between Detroit and Chicago is initiated.

May 13   The Florida legislature passes a measure whereby all public school students are required to read passages from the Bible every day.

May 25   In *Coronado Coal Co. v. United Mine Workers,* 268 U.S. 295, Justice William Howard Taft, speaking for the Court, asserts that a strike which interfers with the interstate shipment of coal is a conspiracy in restraint of trade and therefore subject to prosecution under the Sherman Act (1890).

June 1   *Pierce v. Society of Sisters,* 268 U.S. 510, invalidates an Oregon law which requires all children to attend public schools, therefore prohibiting private education.

William D. Mitchell becomes solicitor general.

June 8   In *Gitlow v. New York,* 268 U.S. 652, although the majority holds that a state could prohibit anarchistic utterances and publications, all the Justices accept the guarantee of free speech under the First Amendment.

June 17   A protocol prohibiting the use of poisonous gases and bacteria is signed by the United States in Geneva, Switzerland.

July 10-21   John T. Scopes, a Tennessee high school teacher, is arrested for teaching evolution in his classes and is defended by Clarence Darrow, but loses the trial and fined $100.

July 26   William Jennings Bryan, a three-time candidate for president, dies.

August 3   American Marines leave Nicaragua after thirteen years of occupation; they return the following year.

August 8   The Ku Klux Klan stages a parade in Washington, D.C., with about 40,000 marching.

September 1   The publication of income tax returns is mandated by the Revenue Act (1924). John D. Rockefeller pays $6,277,699 in personal income tax.

October 16   The Locarno Pact stipulates that the governments of Germany, France, Belgium, Great Britain, and Italy guarantee the peace of western Europe.

October 28-
December 17   "Billy" Mitchell is court-martialed for insubordination since he publicly blamed the War and Navy Departments for neglecting the air forces. He is found guilty and suspended from the army for five years.

November 3   James J. Walker is elected mayor of New York City.

December 8   President Coolidge in a message to Congress urges American Membership in the World Court.

December 10   Vice President Charles G. Dawes receives the Nobel Peace Prize for his work on the Dawes Plan for German economic reorganization and reparations payments.

1926

January 14	The United States and Cuba sign an extradition treaty.
January 27	The Senate, by a vote of 76 to 17, approves with reservations American participation in the Permanent Court of International Justice (World Court) located at The Hague, Netherlands. The reservations are unacceptable to the Court therefore, the United States does not join at this time.
February 26	In the Revenue Act Congress reduces income, surtax, and estate taxes. The income tax publicity clause is also abolished.
March 7	The first transatlantic radio telephone conversation links London and New York City.
March 8	*Weaver v. Palmer Brothers Co.,* 270 U.S. 402, invalidates a Pennsylvania law which forbids the use of certain stuffing materials for bed comforters as an arbitrary use of the public health power.
April 29	A debt-funding agreement between the United States and France is signed. France is to repay her wartime debt to the United States over a period of sixty-two years and over sixty percent of the debt is cancelled.
May 3	In *Colorado v. United States,* 271 U.S. 153, Justice Louis D. Brandeis states the Court's opinion that the Interstate Commerce Commission has authority under the Transportation Act (1920) to judge the merits of requests by railroads to abandon intrastate branches.
May 5	Sinclair Lewis refuses to accept the Pulitzer Prize for his novel *Arrowsmith,* declaring that such prizes makes writers "safe, polite, obedient and sterile."
May 9	Rear Admiral Richard E. Byrd and Floyd Bennett fly over the North Pole.
May 10	The U.S. Marines land in Nicaragua in order to quell an insurrection.

May 20	The Railway Labor Act provides for collective bargaining, union recognition, a grievance procedure, and the arbitration of disputes. It is found to be unconstitutional in *Texas and New Orleans Railway v. Brotherhood of Railway and Steamship Clerks* (1930).
	The Air Commerce Act gives the Department of Commerce extensive power over commercial aviation.
May 24	*Corrigan v. Buckley,* 271 U.S. 323, agrees that restrictive covenants against the sale of real estate to blacks is a private action and not unconstitutional.
May 31	The Philadelphia Sesqui-Centennial Exposition opens.
July 2	The Army Air Corps is established by Congress.
August 5	The first motion picture with a synchronized musical score is shown in New York City.
August 6	Gertrude Ederle, nineteen, becomes the first woman to swim the English Channel.
September 11	The United States Tennis Team wins the Davis Cup for the seventh year in succession.
September 25	Henry Ford introduces the eight-hour day and five-day week at his plants.
September 30	Charles Evans Hughes is appointed a member of the Permanent Court of Arbitration at The Hague by President Coolidge.
October 25	*Myers v. United States,* 272 U.S. 52, invalidates a statute denying the president the right of removing certain postmasters without congressional consent as a improper restraint upon executive power.
November 2	In the national elections Republican majorities in both houses of Congress are reduced.
November 22	*Euclid v. Ambler Realty Co.,* 272 U.S. 365, sustains zoning ordinances which seek to protect residential

districts from encroaching industrialism as a valid exercise of the police power of the state.

1927

January 2	The Hoover Commission, appointed by President Coolidge, proposes the St. Lawrence River as the best waterway route to connect the Great Lakes and the Atlantic Ocean.
January 3	*DiSanto v. Pennsylvania,* 273 U.S. 534, declares unconstitutional a state license tax on travel agents selling steamship tickets for travel abroad.
January 7	Commercial radio service between New York and London is inaugurated.
February 18	Diplomatic relations between the United States and Canada, independent of Great Britain, are˙established.
February 23	The Radio Act asserts public ownership of the airwaves and establishes the Federal Radio Commission for licensing purposes.
February 28	*Tyson Brothers v. Banton,* 273 U.S. 418, invalidates a New York law which regulates the resale of theater tickets. Justice George Sutherland argues for the Court that a business is regulable only when it is "devoted to public use and its use thereby, in effect, granted by the public."
March 3	A Prohibition Bureau in the Treasury Department is established by the Prohibition Reorganization Act.
March 7	*Nixon v. Herndon,* 273 U.S. 536, delcares unconstitutional a Texas law forbidding blacks to vote in primaries.
March 17	Naval oil reserves in Wyoming and California are returned to the control of the Navy Department by executive order.
April 6	Aristide Briand, foreign minister of France, proposes

an agreement between France and the United States to outlaw war.

April 7   For the first time television is successfully demonstrated in New York City.

April 11   *Bedford Stone Co. v. Journeymen Stonecutters,* 274 U.S. 37, undercuts the Clayton Act once again; union efforts to prevent members from finishing products of nonunion labor are defined as "unfair" competition.

May 16   *Whitney v. California,* 274 U.S. 357, upholds, as in *Gitlow v. New York* (1925), a state criminal syndicalism law.

May 20-21   Charles A. Lindbergh makes a nonstop solo flight in the monoplane *Spirit of St. Louis,* from New York to Le Bourget Field, outside of Paris.

June 20-
August 4   The United States, Great Britain, and Japan meet in Geneva, Switzerland, to discuss the limitaton of naval armaments, but the conference fails to achieve any agreements.

July 29   Bellevue Hospital in New York City installs the first electric respirator (iron lung).

August 2   President Coolidge chooses not to run for the presidency in 1928.

August 27   Nicola Sacco and Bartolomeo Vanzetti are executed in Massachusetts.

September   Dwight W. Morrow of J.P. Morgan and Co. is appointed ambassador to Mexico by President Coolidge. His conciliatory efforts help to ease tensions between the United States and Mexico caused by Mexican attempts to limit American ownership of oil leases and land.

September 14   Isadora Duncan, a major contributor to modern dance, dies in Nice, France, at the age of forty-nine.

September 27   Babe Ruth hits his record sixtieth home run at Yankee

Stadium in New York City.

October 6   *The Jazz Singer,* starring Al Jolson, the first film with a sound track, opens.

November 13   The Holland tunnel, the first underwater vehicular tunnel under the Husdon River between Manhattan and New Jersey, is opened to commercial traffic.

December 27   *Show Boat,* a musical comedy by Oscar Hammerstein II and Jerome Kern, opens in New York City.

1928

January 5-
February 20   The Sixth Pan-American Conference is held in Havana, Cuba.

January 31   In the Act Respecting Writs of Error, a long overdue attempt to modernize the federal courts, writs of error are abolished in favor of simple appeals.

February 10   The Bar Association of New York City declares itself against national Prohibition.

February 20   *Delaware, Lackawanna, and Western Railroad Co. v. Morristown,* 276 U.S. 182, invalidates a local ordinance which creates a public taxi stand on the premises of a privately owned railroad terminal. The terminal had leased the stand to a single taxi company.

March 10   The Alien Property Act provides $300 million to compensate Germans for property seized in the United States during World War I.

April 13-18   The Socialist party convention in New York City nominates Norman Thomas (N.Y.) for president and James H. Maurer (Pa.) for vice president.

May 3   Congress again passes the McNary-Haugen Bill which would fix agricultural prices and help alleviate depressed economic conditions in farm areas. President Coolidge once again vetoes the measure.

May 15	Congress appropriates $325 million for flood control in the Mississippi Valley over a period of ten years.
May 22	The Jones-White Merchant Marine Act provides federal subsidies to private shipping concerns to aid an ailing ship industry.
May 28	In *Ribnik v. McBride,* 277 U.S. 350, the majority holds that since the activities of employment agencies do not affect the public interest, they therefore should not be regulated.
June 4	*National Life Insurance Co. v. United States,* 277 U.S. 508, invalidates a section of the Revenue Act (1921) which levies a tax on state and municipal bonds.
June 12-15	The Republican party Convention at Kansas City nominates Secretary of Commerce Herbert Hoover for president and Senator Charles Curtis (Kan.) for vice president.
June 26-29	The Democrats meet at Houston, Texas, and nominate Governor Alfred E. Smith (N.Y.) for president, and Senator Joseph T. Robinson (Ark.) for vice president. Smith is the first Roman Catholic candidate in American history.
July 25	A treaty is signed in Peiping giving the Chinese government complete tariff autonomy.
July 30	The first motion picture in color is demonstrated in Rochester, New York, by George Eastman.
August 25	The Byrd Antarctic Expedition departs from New York.
August 27	The Kellogg-Briand Pact outlawing war is signed in Paris. In all, sixty nations endorsed this pact.
September 8	Charles Evans Hughes succeeds John Bassett Moore as a member of the World Court.
September 27	The United States government recognizes the Nationalist government of China under Chiang Kai-shek.

November 6	In the national elections Herbert Hoover is elected by the electoral vote of 444, to 87 for Smith. Franklin D. Roosevelt is elected governor of New York.
November 19-January 6, 1929	President Hoover embarks on a goodwill tour of eleven Latin American nations.
November 21	Joseph McKenna, Justice of the Supreme Court, dies in Washington, D.C., at the age of eighty-three.
December 17	Undersecretary of State J. Reuben Clark submits a memorandum calling for an end to American intervention in the affairs of Latin American countries. The State Department repudiates the Roosevelt Corollary to the Monroe Doctrine.

1929

January 15	The U.S. Senate ratifies the Kellogg-Briand Pact by a vote of 85 to 1.
February 2	The Federal Reserve Board orders member banks not to make loans for stock speculation or margin.
February 11	Owen D. Young is appointed chairman of a committee to revise the Dawes plan.
February 13	The Cruiser Act provides for the construction of fifteen cruisers and one airplane carrier.
February 14	Seven gangsters are murdered in Chicago (St. Valentine's Day Massacre).
February 18	*Frost v. Corporation Commission,* 278 U.S. 515, curbs the use of state police power by denying the right of Oklahoma to grant a franchise to a cooperative cotton gin in competition with an individual licensee on grounds that the state is impairing a property right it had already granted to the private firm.
March 2	The Jones (Intoxicating Liquor) Act provides more

stringent criminal penalties for those who violate Prohibition.

March 4   Hoover is inaugurated president and Charles Curtis is sworn in as vice president.

William D. Mitchell assumes the office of attorney general.

May 17   President Hoover declares that the Tacna-Arica border dispute between Chile and Peru is finally settled.

May 20   *St. Louis, O'Fallon Railway Co. v. United States,* 279 U.S. 461, substantially reduces the ability of the Interstate Commerce Commission to determine the bases for rate-fixing.

President Hoover appoints George W. Wickersham chairman of a national commission on law observance and enforcement to study prohibition and related problems.

Charles Evans Hughes, Jr., becomes solicitor general.

The Okanogan, Methow, San Poelis, Nespelem, Colville, and Lake Indian Tribes...v. United States, 279 U.S. 655, confirms the right of the president to prevent passage of legislation by the use of the pocket veto.

June 7   The Young Plan supersedes the Dawes Plan for the payment of German reparations and lowers the amount due and extends the time for payment.

June 15   The Agricultural Marketing Act promotes the sale of farm surpluses through a Federal Farm Board and various stabilization corporations. Unfortunately, this legislation does not successfully contain overproduction of farm products.

July 24   The Kellogg-Briand Peace Pact is formally proclaimed in Washington, D.C., by President Hoover.

October 4   Prime Minister J. Ramsay MacDonald of Great Britain arrives in Washington to discuss naval parity.

October 7	Great Britain invites the world's naval powers to a conference in London early in 1930.
October 24-29	The New York Stock Exchange collapses and by November 13, about $30 billion in stock values are wiped out.
October 25	Former Secretary of the Interior Albert B. Fall is found guilty of accepting a bribe of $100,000 in return for an oil lease at the Elk Hills Naval Oil Reserve. He is sentenced to one year in prison and fined $100,000.
November 29	Rear Admiral Richard E. Byrd flies over the South Pole.
December 3	Edsel Ford announces that the minimum wage paid by the Ford Motor Company to its employees would increase from six to seven dollars a day.
	President Hoover voices his conviction before Congress that business confidence has been reestablished.
December 9	The Senate refuses to accept a formula allowing the United States to join the World Court.

1930

January 21- April 22	In the London Naval Conference the United States, Great Britain, and Japan agree to continue limitations on naval armaments.
February 3	Chief Justice William Howard Taft resigns from the Supreme Court because of illness.

PART II

The
Conservative Court

■ ■ ■ ■ ■

*Decisions
and
Documents*

Standard Oil Co. v. United States
221 U.S. 1
1911

The Sherman Anti-Trust Act (1890) was supposed to prevent the growth of monopolies; yet for a number of years it proved an ineffectual weapon against restraint of trade on the part of great businessmen such as John D. Rockefeller and J.P. Morgan. In *United States v. E.C. Knight Co.* (1895), for example, the Court held that the American Sugar Refining Co. had not violated the law, even though it controlled about ninety-eight percent of all sugar refining in the United States. Under President Theodore Roosevelt, however, the prosecution of trusts increased, and there were significant government victories in *Northern Securities Co.* (1904) and in *Swift and Co. v. United States* (1905).

By the end of the decade the Department of Justice had built an impressive record in antitrust cases, one which culminated with a successful prosecution against the Standard Oil Co. Not only was the great oil monopoly found guilty of violating the Sherman Act, but the Court ordered the dissolution of the company. In rendering the Court's decision, Chief Justice Edward Douglas White instituted the "rule of reason," a dictum which meant that "unreasonable" monopolies would be disallowed, while "reasonable" ones, not in restraint of trade, would be found legal. Careful attention should be given to Justice John Marshall Harlan's objections to the "rule of reason" doctrine in his dissent which follows the case.

...It is certain that only one point of concord between the parties is discernable, which is, that the controversy in every aspect is controlled by a correct conception of the meaning of the...Anti-Trust Act....

[W]e shall make our investigation under four separate headings: First. The text of the first and second sections of the act originally considered and its meaning in the light of the common law and the law of this country at the time of its adoption. Second. The contentions of the parties concerning the act, and the scope and effect of the decisions of this court upon which they rely....

In view of the common law and the law in this country as to restraint of trade, which we have reviewed, and the illuminating effect which that history must have under the rule to which we have referred, we think it results:

a. That the context manifests that the statute was drawn in the light of the existing practical conception of the law of restraint of trade, because it groups as within that class, not only contracts which were in restraint of trade in the subjective sense, but all contracts or acts which theoretically were attempts to monopolize, yet which in practice had come to be considered as in restraint of trade in a broad sense.

b. That in view of the many new forms of contracts and combinations which were being evolved from existing economic conditions, it was deemed essential by an all-embracing enumeration to make sure that no form of contract or combination by which an undue restraint of interstate or foreign commerce was brought about could save such restraint from condemnation. The statute under this view evidenced the intent not to restrain the right to make and enforce contracts, whether resulting from combination or otherwise, which did not unduly restrain interstate or foreign commerce, but to protect that commerce from being restrained by methods, whether old or new, which would constitute an interference that is an undue restraint.

c. And as the contracts or acts embraced in the provision were not expressly defined, since the enumeration addressed itself simply to classes of acts, those classes being broad enough to embrace every conceivable contract or combination which could be made concerning trade or commerce or the subjects of such commerce, and thus caused any act done by any of the enumerated methods anywhere in the whole field of human activity to be illegal if in restraint of trade, it inevitably follows that the provision necessarily called for the exercise of judgment which required that some standard should be resorted to for the purpose of determining whether the prohibitions contained in the statute had or had not in any given case been violated. Thus not specifying but indubitably contemplating and requiring a standard, it follows that it was intended that the standard of reason which had been applied at the common law and in this country in dealing with subjects of the character embraced by the statute, was intended to be the measure used for the purpose of determining whether in a given case a particular act had or had not brought about the wrong against which the statute provided. . . .

Mr. Justice Harlan concurring in part, and dissenting in part. . . .

After what has been adjudged, upon full consideration, as to the meaning and scope of the Anti-trust Act, and in view of the usages of this court when attorneys for litigants have attempted to reopen questions that have been deliberately decided, I confess to no little surprise as to what has occurred in the present case. The court says that the previous cases, above cited, "cannot by any possible conception be treated as authoritative without the certitude that *reason* was resorted to for the purpose of deciding them.". . . It is more than once intimated, if not suggested, that if the Anti-trust Act is to be construed as prohibiting *every* contract or combination, of whatever nature, which is in fact in restraint of commerce, regardless of the reasonableness or unreasonableness of such restraint, that fact would show that the court had not proceeded, in its decision, according to "the light of reason," but had disregarded the "rule of reason.". . . . Now this court is asked to do that which it has distinctly declared it could not and would not do, and has now done what it then said it could not constitutionally do. It has, by mere interpretation, modified the act of Congress, and deprived it of practical value as a defensive measure against evils to be remedied. . . . In effect the court says, that it will now, for the first time, bring the discussion under the "light of reason" and apply the "rule of reason" to the questions to be decided. I have the authority of this court for saying that such a course of proceeding on its part would be "judicial legislation."

Still more, what is now done involves a serious departure from the settled usages of this court. Counsel have not ordinarily been allowed to discuss questions already settled by previous decisions. . . .

But my brethren, in their wisdom, have deemed it best to pursue a different course. They have now said to those who condemn our former decisions and who object to all legislative prohibitions of contracts, combinations and trusts in restraint of interstate commerce, "You may *now* restrain such commerce, provided you are reasonable about it; only take care that the restraint is not undue.". . .

It remains for me to refer, more fully than I have heretofore done, to another, and, in my judgment—if we look to the future—the most important aspect of this case. That aspect concerns the usurpation by the judicial branch of the Government of the functions of the legislative department. . . .

I said at the outset that the action of the court in this case might well alarm thoughtful men who revered the Constitution. I meant by this that many things are intimated and said in the court's opinion which will not be regarded otherwise than as sanctioning an invasion by the judiciary of the constitutional domain of Congress—an attempt by interpretation to soften or modify what some regard as a harsh public policy. This court, let me repeat, solemnly adjudged many years ago that it could not, except by *"judicial legislation,"* read words into the Anti-trust Act not put there by Congress, and which, being inserted, give it a meaning which the words of the Act, as passed, if properly interpreted, would not justify. The court has decided that it could not thus change a public policy formulated and declared by Congress; that Congress has paramount authority to regulate interstate commerce, and that it alone can change a policy once inaugurated by legislation. The courts have nothing to do with the wisdom or policy of an act of Congress. Their duty is to ascertain the will of Congress, and if the statute embodying the expression of that will is constitutional, the courts must respect it. They have no function to declare a public policy, nor to *amend* legislative enactments. . . . Nevertheless, if I do not misapprehend its opinion, the court has now read into the act of Congress words which are not to be found there, and has thereby done that which it adjudged in 1896 and 1898 could not be done without violating the Constitution, namely, by interpretation of a statute, changed a public policy declared by the legislative department. . . .

Holmes Gives A Speech
"Law and the Court"
1913

On occasion the Justices of the Supreme Court have made public speeches expressing their views on the law, the courts, and even political matters. At a dinner of the Harvard Law School Association on February 15, 1913, Justice Oliver Wendell Holmes discussed a number of economic and social ideas, defended the role of the Court in reviewing local and national laws, and aired some personal philosophical views. Although Holmes's speech is a typical light after-dinner talk, it gives us some insight into his thinking. [Mark De Wolfe Howe, comp., *The Occasional Speeches of Justice Oliver Wendell Holmes* (Cambridge, Mass. Harvard U.P., 1962), pp. 168-74.]

. . . Vanity is the most philosophical of those feelings that we are taught to despise. For vanity recognizes that if a man is in a minority of one we lock him up, and therefore longs for an assurance from others that one's work has not been in vain. If a man's ambition is the thirst for a power that comes not from office but from within, he never can be sure that any happiness is not a fool's paradise—he never can be sure that he sits on that other bench reserved for the masters of those who know. Then too, at least until one draws near to seventy, one is less likely to hear the trumpets than the rolling fire of the front. I have passed that age, but I still am on the firing line, and it is only in rare moments like this that there comes a pause and for half an hour one feels a trembling hope. They are the rewards of a lifetime's work.

But let me turn to more palpable realities—to that other visible Court to which to ten now accomplished years it has been my opportunity to belong. We are very quiet there, but it is the quiet of a storm center, as we all know. Science has taught the world skepticism and has made it legitimate to put everything to the test of proof. Many beautiful and noble reverences are impaired, but in these days no one can complain if any institution, system, or belief is called on to justify its continuance in life. Of course we are not excepted and have not escaped. Doubts are expressed that go to our very being. Not only are we told than when Marshall pronounced an Act of Congress unconstitutional he usurped a power that the Constitution did not give, but we are told that we are the representatives of a class—a tool of the money power. I get letters, not always anonymous, intimating that we are corrupt. Well, . . . I admit that it makes my heart ache. It is very painful, when one spends all the energies of one's soul in trying to do good work, with no thought but that of solving a problem according to the rules by which one is bound, to know that many see sinister motives and would be glad of evidence that one was consciously bad. But we must take such things philosophically and try to see what we can learn from hatred and distruct and whether behind them there may not be some germ of inarticulate truth.

The attacks upon the Court are merely an expression of the unrest that seems to wonder vaguely whether law and order pay. When the ignorant are taught to doubt they do not know what they may safely believe. And it seems to me that at this time we need education in the obvious more than investigation of the obscure. I do not see so much immediate use in committees on the high cost of living and inquiries how far it is due to the increased production of gold, how far to the narrowing of cattle ranges and the growth of population, how far to the bugaboo, as I do in bringing home to people a few social and economic truths. Most men think dramatically, not quantitatively, a fact that the rich would be wise to remember more than they do. We are apt to contrast the palace with the hovel, the dinner at Sherry's with the working man's pail, and never ask how much or realize how little is withdrawn to make the prizes of success (subordinate prizes—since the only prize much cared for by the powerful is power. The prize of the general is not a bigger tent, but command.). We are apt to think of ownership as a terminus, not as a gateway, and not to realize that except the tax levied for personal consumption large ownership means investment, and investment means the direction of labor towards the production of the greatest returns—returns that so far as they are great show by that very fact that they are not consumed by the man, not alone by the few. If I may ride a hobby for an instant, I should say we need to think things instead of words—to drop ownership, money, etc., and to think of the stream of products; of wheat and cloth and railway travel. When we do it is obvious that the many consume them; that they now as truly have substantially all there is, as if the title were in the United States; that the great body of a property is socially administered now, and that the function of private ownership is to divine in advance the equilibrium of social desires—which socialism equally would have to divine, but which, under the illusion of self-seeking, is more poignantly and shrewdly foreseen.

I should like to see it brought home to the public that the question of fair prices is due to the fact that none of us can have as much as we want of all the things we want; that as less will be produced than the public wants, the question is how much of each products it will have and how much go without; that thus the final competition is between the objects of desire, and therefore between the producers of those objects; that when we oppose labor and capital, labor means the group that is selling its product and capital all the other groups that are buying it. The hated capitalist is simply the mediator, the prophet, the adjuster according to this divination of the future desire. If you could get that believed, the body of the people would have no doubt as to the worth of law.

That is my outside thought on the present discontents. As to the truth embodied in them, in part it cannot be helped. It cannot be helped, it is as it should be, that the law is behind the times. I told a labor leader once that what they asked was favor, and if a decision was against them they called it wicked. The same might be said of their opponents. It means that the law is growing. As law embodies beliefs that have triumphed in the battle of ideas and then have translated themselves into action, while there still is doubt, while opposite convictions still keep a battle front against each other, the time for law has not come; the notion destined to prevail is not yet entitled to the field. It is a misfortune if a judge reads his conscious or unconscious sympathy with one side or the other prematurely into the law, and forgets that what seem to him to be first principles are believed by half his fellow men to be wrong. I think that we have suffered from this misfortune, in State courts at least, and that this is another and very important truth to be extracted from the popular discontent. When twenty years ago a vague terror went over the earth and the word socialism began to be heard, I thought and still think that fear was translated into doctrines that had no proper place in the Constitution or the common law. Judges are apt to be naif, simple-minded men, and they need something of Mephistopheles. We too need education in the obvious—to learn to transcend our own convictions and to leave room for much that we hold dear to be done away with short of revolution by the orderly change of law.

I have no belief in panaceas and almost none in sudden ruin. I believe with Montesquieu that if the chance of a battle—I may add, the passage of a law—has ruined a state, there was a general cause at work that made the state ready to perish by a single battle or law. Hence I am not much interested one way or the other in the nostrums now so strenuously urged. I do not think the United States would come to an end if we lost our power to declare an Act of Congress void. I do think the Union would be imperiled if we could not make that declaration as to the laws of the several States. For one in my place sees how often a local policy prevails with those who are not trained to national views and how often action is taken that embodies what the Commerce Clause was meant to end. But I am not aware that there is any serious desire to limit the Court's power in this regard. For most of the things that properly can be called evils in the present state of law I think the main remedy, as for the evils of public opinion, is for us to grow much civilized.

If I am right it will be a slow business for our people to reach rational views, assuming that we are allowed to work peacably to that end. But as I grow older I grow calm. If I feel what are perhaps an old man's apprehensions, that competition from new races will cut deeper than working men's disputes and will test whether we can hang together and can fight; if I fear that we are running through the world's resources at a pace that we cnnot keep; I do not lose my hopes. I do not pin my dreams for the future to my country or even to my race. I think it probable that civilization somehow will last as long as I care to look ahead—perhaps with smaller numbers, but perhaps also bred to greatness and splendor by science. I think it is not improbable that man, like the grub that prepares a chamber for the winged thing it never has seen but is to be—that man may have cosmic destinies that he does not understand. And so beyond the vision of battling races and an impoverished earth I catch a dreaming glimpse of peace. . . .

Sixteenth Amendment
1913

During the Civil War Congress levied an income tax which was in effect until 1872. This legislation was upheld in *Springer v. United States* (1881) by a unanimous Supreme Court. Eastern liberals and agrarian radicals of the West and South, during the 1880s and 1890s, campaigned for a new income tax law; they wished to eliminate tariffs, which they condemned as a severe burden upon consumers and farmers, as the federal government's chief source of revenue. Surely, the logical sources of income were the new corporate wealth, banks, and rich individuals. It was also commonly accepted that a modern government could not function without strong financial resources; something which tariffs, especially in depressed times, could not guarantee.

In 1894, an income tax of two percent was enacted as part of the Wilson-Gorman Tariff Act. Yet, one year later, in *Pollock v. Farmers' Loan and Trust Co.* the Court struck down the income tax provisions of the act. Obviously, due to the Court's hard and fast position the passage of the Sixteenth Amendment to the Constitution was necessary.

Article XVI.

The Congress shall have power to lay and collect taxes on incomes, from whatever source derived, without apportionment among the several States, and without regard to any census or enumeration. [February 25, 1913.]

Samuel Gompers and the Supreme Court
1913

The sponsors of the Sherman Anti-Trust Act (1890), which outlawed monopolies, intended that the law's restrictions should only cover business enterprises; however, in *Loewe v. Lawlor* (1908) the Supreme Court declared that the Sherman Act was applicable to labor unions engaged in secondary boycotts, and in *Gompers v. Bucks Stove and Range Co.* (1911) the Justices held that it was valid to issue an antitrust order against a union.

In a letter to President Woodrow Wilson, Samuel Gompers, president of the American Federation of Labor, expressed his views about a number of issues important to labor. He was especially concerned about a union movement which faced the possibility of extinction under the onslaught of antitrust litigation, hostile employers, and court injunctions against certain union practices. His message is an eloquent plea for equal treatment for workers. [Arthur S. Link, ed., *The Papers of Woodrow Wilson* (Princeton, N.J.: Princeton University Press, 1978), vol. 27, pp. 182-87.]

. . . It took years to secure relief from the old conspiracy laws which curbed and restricted the workers in protecting and promoting their industrial rights and interests. When at last it seemed that efforts of the toilers were to be rewarded, then the Supreme Court of the United States, by an interpretation which amounted to judicial legislation, applied the Sherman Anti-Trust Law to trade unions in a way which virtually revived the conspiracy laws.

When the court applied the Sherman Anti-Trust law to labor organizations, it created an offense never intended by the makers of that law. As has been repeated again and again, but never refuted, as an investigation of the Congressional Record will prove, the men who drafted the Sherman Anti-Trust Act, Senators Sherman, Edmunds and George, did not intend that it should apply to organizations instituted not for profit. . . .

. . . To classify these combinations, not for profit, and without capital stock, in the same category with corporations, trusts and monopolies, is forcing an indefensible classification and grouping together things not of the same nature.

The associations of working people, commonly known as labor unions, are dealing not with property, material things, but with labor power alone, with lives, happiness, rights and welfare of men, women and children. They are striving for the uplift and conservation of the nation itself.

The corporations, trusts and monopolies aim to create monopoly conditions, to manipulate capital and production to secure monopoly profits. It is most unjust to try to co-ordinate these two inherently different kinds of organizations and to apply to them similar regulations. Justice does not necessarily result from the application of identical provisions to all people. On the contrary, it works injustice if the conditions are dissim[i]lar and the people unequally situated. Theoretical justice only becomes real justice when the men as well as the deeds are taken into consideration.

It is impossible to legislate equitably for labor and capital under the same law. Certainly it is not class legislation to make different provisions for two things inherently different, aiming at different purposes and employing different methods. The provisions of no law will admit of universal indiscriminate application.

This is no "special privilege" or "exemption" that organized labor has been asking. Our demand for justice is that working men and their organizations shall not be prosecuted for entering into any combination or agreement having in view the increasing of wages, the shortening of hours, or the bettering of conditions of labor, or for any act done in furtherance thereof "NOT IN ITSELF UNLAWFUL."

Your attention is respectfully and particularly called to those last four words that have been so persistently and unfairly suppressed by the press and our opponents. We are not seeking to be permitted to do unlawful acts, but are demanding that the rights of which we have been deprived by judicial interpretation be restored to us. We are not asking to be "exempt" from the application of a law of a law [*sic*] which properly applies to labor organizations as well as to other voluntary associations organized not for profit, but we are asking that inherent differences that exist be recognized by the laws and the courts as well as by reason....

Even should the activities of labor organizations be rightfully classified as conspiracies, has not the time come when it must be considered whether these "conspiracies" of organized labor do not do more to further the advancement of humanity and national welfare than the property interests which have been heretofore carefully safeguarded? It is no man of straw that we fear in the application of the Sherman Anti-Trust law to organized labor. While it is unthinkable that the organized labor movement could be crushed out of existence, yet the repression of normal activities, rousing of resentment at injustice among the workers, denial to them of legal methods of redress, would lead to situations and conditions which thoughtful, patriotic citizens could not consider without dread.

This struggle of the working people to secure individual rights and liberty has not been confined to our own country. In England the same problems have been confronted and solved....

Nor is it amiss when I take the liberty of respectfully calling your attention to the declarations of the Democratic party national conventions of 1908 and 1912 upon this, the subject matter under discussion.

My presentation of the cause of organized labor has not been from the legal viewpoint, for I am not a lawyer. But even could I present the legal phrases, I doubt whether that would aid in determining justice for the workers. Often justice is obscured in the mazes of legal theories and technicalities. The law is not an unfailing source of justice, it can only approximate that ideal as it is rendered flexible enough to adjust to new conditions and needs. That is what we ask for in the legislation we week.

As I have already stated, it is not my purpose to present here a legal argument in defense or in furtherance of Labor's position with respect to the principle involved in legislation of this character, nor can I, in this letter, make a sociological or an economic presentation of the subject. My main purpose is that you may give this letter the consideration it deserves at the present time, that you may arrest your final judgment, defer the determination of your course until an opportunity is afforded when you may accord the privilege of a conference in which a more complete and comprehensive presentation of this matter may be made to you.

It is earnestly hoped that your final conclusion upon this entire matter, which is fraught with such far-reaching consequences to the rights and the welfare of the toilers of our country, will be reached only after the most complete consideration of it in all its bearings and all that is involved therein.

I have the honor to remain,

Very respectfully yours,   Saml. Gompers.
                                President
                                American Federation
                                of Labor

Seventeenth Amendment
1913

Article I of the United States Constitution called for a Senate composed of two senators from each state chosen by the state legislatures for six-year terms. The Seventeenth Amendment, which was the result of agitation by progressives and agrarian radicals, replaced this indirect method of choosing senators for direct popular election.

Supporters of the amendment argued that election by state legislatures did not conform to generally recognized principles of democracy; that some senators were greedy corporation lawyers, retired millionaires, or venal machine politicians; and that the Senate too often bowed to the will of the big corporate interests. Most of the opposition to changing the Constitution came from the Senate, where senators were apprehensive about their political security. By 1910, however, the composition of the Senate had changed dramatically with the introduction of state preferential primary laws, which made it possible for voters to express their preference for United States senator. A resolution, calling for an amendment, was passed by Congress in June of 1911, and on May 31, 1913, after ratification by three fourths of the states, the Seventeenth Amendment became part of the Constitution.

Article XVII.

The Senate of the United States shall be composed of two senators from each State, elected by the people thereof, for six years; and each Senator shall have one vote. The electors in each State shall have the qualifications requisite for electors of the most numerous branch of the State legislature.

When vacancies happen in the representation of any State in the Senate, the executive authority of such State shall issue writs of election to fill such vacancies: *Provided,* That the legislature of any State may empower the executive thereof to make temporary appointments until the people fill the vacancies by election as the legislature may direct.

This amendment shall not be so construed as to affect the election or term of any senator chosen before it becomes valid as part of the Constitution. [May 31, 1913.]

Houston and Texas Railroad Co. v. United States
Shreveport Rate Cases
234 U.S. 342
1914

While it was recognized that the Interstate Commerce Commission had the authority to supervise interstate railroads, controversy developed over the power of the commission to control intrastate commerce. In the *Minnesota Rate Cases* (1913) Justice Charles Evans Hughes held that since both interstate and intrastate commerce were inextricably blended, the federal government probably had some power to regulate the latter. The issue finally came to a head in the *Shreveport Rates Cases* in which the Supreme Court ruled that the commission had the authority to regulate intrastate rail rates. Basically the Court, speaking again through Justice Hughes, stated that Congress had paramount powers over interstate commerce and occasionally this might involve some regulation of intrastate commerce. This case demonstrated that the Supreme Court wished to maintain national authority over commerce, even though this might mean the weakening of some rights reserved to the states.

These suits were brought in the Commerce Court. . . to set aside an order of the Interstate Commerce Commission, dated March 11, 1912, upon the ground that it exceeded the Commission's authority. . . .

The gravamen of the complaint, said the Interstate Commerce Commission, was that the carriers made rates out of Dallas and other Texas points into eastern Texas which were much lower than those which they extended into Texas from Shreveport. The situation may be briefly described: Shreveport, Louisiana, is about 40 miles from the Texas state line, and 231 miles from Houston, Texas, on the line of the Houston, East & West Texas and Houston & Shreveport Companies (which are affiliated in interest); it is 189 miles from Dallas, Texas, on the line of the Texas & Pacific. Shreveport competes with both cities for the trade of the intervening territory. The rates on these lines from Dallas and Houston, respectively, eastward to intermediate points in Texas were much less, according to distance, than from Shreveport westward to the same points. It is undisputed that the difference was substantial and injuriously affected the commerce of Shreveport. . . .

The Interstate Commerce Commission found that the interstate class rates out of Shreveport to named Texas points were unreasonable, and it established maximum class rates for this traffic. . . .

The point of the objection to the order is that, as the discrimination found by the Commission to be unjust arises out of the relation of intrastate rates, maintained under state authority, to interstate rates that have been upheld as reasonable, its correction was beyond the Commission's power.... The invalidity of the order in this aspect is challenged upon two grounds:

(1) That Congress is impotent to control the intrastate charges of an interstate carrier even to the extent necessary to prevent injurious discrimination against interstate traffic....

Congress is empowered to regulate,—that is, to provide the law for the government of interstate commerce; to enact 'all appropriate legislation' for its 'protection and advancement' (*The Daniel Ball*, 10 Wall. 557, 564); to adopt measures.... As it is competent for Congress to legislate to these ends, unquestionably it may seek their attainment by requiring that the agencies of interstate commerce shall not be used in such manner as to cripple, retard or destroy it. The fact that carriers are instruments of intrastate commerce, as well as of interstate commerce, does not derogate from the complete and paramount authority of Congress over the latter or preclude the Federal power from being exerted to prevent the intrastate operations of such carriers from being made a means of injury to that which has been confided to Federal care. Wherever the interstate and intrastate transactions of carriers are so related that the government of one involves the control of the other, it is Congress, and not the State, that is entitled to prescribe the final and dominant rule, for otherwise Congress would be denied the exercise of its constitutional authority and the State, and not the Nation, would be supreme within the national field....

...It is for Congress to supply the needed correction where the relation between intrastate and interstate rates presents the evil to be corrected, and this it may do completely by reason of its control over the interstate carrier in all matters having such a close and substantial relation to interstate commerce that it is necessary or appropriate to exercise the control for the effective government of that commerce.

It is also clear that, in removing the injurious discriminations against interstate traffic arising from the relation of intrastate to interstate rates, Congress is not bound to reduce the latter below what it may deem to be a proper standard fair to the carrier and to the public. Otherwise, it could prevent the injury to interstate commerce only by the sacrifice of its judgment as to interstate rates. Congress is entitled to maintain its own standard as to these rates and to forbid any discriminatory action by interstate carriers which will obstruct the freedom of movement of interstate traffic over their lines in accordance with the terms it establishes.

Having this power, Congress could provide for its execution through the aid of a subordinate body; and we conclude that the order of the Commission now in question cannot be held invalid upon the ground that it exceeded the authority which Congress could lawfully confer....

The Brandeis Appointment
1916

When President Woodrow Wilson appointed Louis D. Brandeis to the Supreme Court on January 28, 1916, the announcement caused a furor in the business world and disbelief among conservatives. Brandeis, sometimes called the people's attorney, was a Jewish liberal who had represented labor unions, fought for reform of railroads and utilities and was famous for his highly researched briefs filled with social and economic data.

Although Brandeis faced several months of humiliating hearings before a special subcommittee of the Senate Judiciary Committee and outrageous criticism by public officials, businessmen, jurists, and even several past presidents of the American Bar Association, he was confirmed by the Senate on June 1, 1916 by a vote of 47 to 22.

The following letter by President Wilson to Senator Charles A. Culberson, a member of the Judiciary Committee, outlines his reasons for nominating Brandeis. [Arthur S. Link, ed., *The Papers of Woodrow Wilson* (Princeton, N.J.: Princeton University Press, 1981), vol. 36, pp. 609-11.]

My dear Senator   The White House May 5, 1916

I am very much obliged to you for giving me an opportunity to make clear to the Judiciary Committee my reasons for nominating Mr. Louis D. Brandeis to fill the vacancy in the Supreme Court of the United States created by the death of Mr. Justice Lamar, for I am profoundly interested in the confirmation of the appointment by the Senate.

There is probably no more important duty imposed upon the President in connection with the general administration of the Government than that of naming members of the Supreme Court; and I need hardly tell you that I named Mr. Brandeis as a member of that great tribunal only because I knew him to be singularly qualified by learning, by gifts, and by character for the position.

Many charges have been made against Mr. Brandeis: the report of your sub-committee has already made it plain to you and to the country at large how unfounded those charges were. They threw a great deal more light upon the character and motives of those with whom they originated than upon the qualifications of Mr. Brandeis. I myself looked into them three years ago when I desired to make Mr. Brandeis a member of my Cabinet and found that they proceeded for the most part from those who hated Mr. Brandeis because he had refused to be serviceable to them in the promotion of their own selfish interests, and from those whem they had prejudiced and misled.

The propaganda in this matter has been very extraordinary and very distressing to those who love fairness and value the dignity of the great professions.

I perceived from the first that the charges were intrinsically incredible by anyone who had really known Mr. Brandeis. I have known him. I have tested him by seeking his advice upon some of them most difficult and perplexing public questions about which it was necessary for me to form a judgment. I have dealt with him in matters where nice questions of honor and fair play, as well as large questions of justice and the public benefit, were involved. In every matter in which I have made test of his judgment and point of view I have received from him counsel singularly enlightening, singularly clear-sighted and judicial, and, above all, full of moral stimulation. He is a friend of all just men and a lover of the right; and he knows more than how to talk about the right,—he knows how to set it forward in the face of its enemies. I knew from direct personal knowledge of the man what I was doing when I named him for the highest and most responsible tribunal of the nation.

Of his extraordinary ability as a lawyer no man who is competent to judge can speak with anything but the highest admiration. You will remember that in the opinion of the late Chief Justice Fuller he was the ablest man who ever appeared before the Supreme Court of the United States. "He is also," the Chief Justice added, "absolutely fearless in the discharge of his duties."

Those who have resorted to him for assistance in settling great industrial disputes can testify to his fairness and love of justice. In the troublesome controversies between the garment workers and manufacturers of New York City, for example, he gave a truly remarkable proof of his judicial temperament and had what must have been the great satisfaction of rendering decisions which both sides were willing to accept as disinterested and evenhanded.

Mr. Brandeis has rendered many notable services to the city and state with which his professional life has been identified. He successfully directed the difficult campaign which resulted in obtaining cheaper gas for the City of Boston. It was chiefly under his guidance and through his efforts that legislation was secured in Massachusetts which authorized savings banks to issue insurance policies for small sums at much reduced rates. And some gentlemen who tried very hard to obtain control by the Boston Elevated Railway Company of the subways of the city for a period of ninety-nine years can probably testify as to his ability as the people's advocate when public interests call for an effective champion. He rendered these services without compensation and earned, whether he got it or not, the gratitude of every citizen of the state and city he served. These are but a few of the services of this kind he has freely rendered. It will hearten friends of the community and public rights throughout the country to see his quality signally recognized by his elevation to the Supreme Bench. For the whole country is aware of his quality and is interested in this appointment.

I did not in making choice of Mr. Brandeis ask for or depend upon "endorsements." I acted upon public knowledge and personal acquaintance with the man, and preferred to name a lawyer for this great office whose abilities and character were so widely recognized that he needed no endorsement. I did, however, personally consult many men in whose judgment I had great confidence, and am happy to say was supported in my selection by the voluntary recommendation of the Attorney General of the United States, who urged Mr. Brandeis upon my consideration independently of any suggestion from me.

Let me say by way of summing up, my dear Senator, that I nominated Mr. Brandeis for the Supreme Court because it was, and is, my deliberate judgment that, of all the men now at the bar whom it has been my privilege to observe, test, and know, he is exceptionally qualified. I cannot speak too highly of his impartial, impersonal, orderly, and constructive mind, his rate analytical powers, his deep human sympathy, his profound acquaintance with the historical roots of our institutions and insight into their spirit, or of the many evidences he has given of being imbued to the very heart with our American ideals of justice and equality of opportunity; of his knowledge of modern economic conditions and of the way they bear upon the masses of the people, or of his genius in getting persons to unite in common and harmonious action and look with frank and kindly eyes into each other's minds, who had before been heated antagonists. This friend of justice and of men will ornament the high court of which we are all so justly proud. I am glad to have had the opportunity to pay him this tribute of admiration and of confidence, and I beg that your Committee will accept this nomination as coming from me quick with a sense of public obligation and responsibility.

With warmest regard,

Cordially and sincerely yours,   Woodrow Wilson

Wilson v. New
243 U.S. 332
1917

During the summer of 1916, President Woodrow Wilson persuaded Congress to pass the Adamson Act which averted a strike by establishing an eight-hour day for railroad workers. The statute, which became law on September 3, 1916, also provided for a three-man commission to study the operation and effects of the eight-hour day, and to report its findings to the President. Shortly after the passage of the act, the United States District Court for Western Missouri found the law unconstitutional. The federal government immediately appealed the decision to the Supreme Court.

In *Wilson v. New* the Court by a 5-4 majority reversed the District Court and thus upheld the Adamson Act. Chief Justice Edward Douglas White's opinion noted the public character of rail transporation, the right of public regulation, and the emergency character of the statute. While the act also had in effect fixed wages, White argued that this was temporary and had only been adopted after the parties had not been able to come to any agreement prior to government intervention. Justices William R. Day, Mahlon Pitney, Willis Van Devanter, and James C. McReynolds vigorously dissented; their contention was that the law violated due process and did not properly regulate interstate commerce.

Was there power in Congress under the circumstances existing to deal with the hours of work and wages of railroad employees engaged in interstate commerce, is the principal question here to be considered....

All the propositions relied upon and arguments advanced ultimately come to two questions: First, the entire want of constitutional power to deal with the subjects embraced by the statute, and second, such abuse of the power if possessed as rendered its exercise unconstitutional. We will consider these subjects under distinct propositions separately.

I. *The entire want of constitutional power to deal with the subjects embraced by the statute....*

...Concretely stated, therefore, the question is this: Did Congress have power under the circumstances stated, that is, in dealing with the dispute between the employers and employees as to wages, to provide a permanent eight-hour standard and to create by legislative action a standard of wages to be operative upon the employers and employees for such reasonable time as it deemed necessary to afford an opportunity for the meeting of the minds of employers and employees on the subject of wages? Or, in other words, did it have the power in order to prevent the interruption of interstate commerce to exert its will to supply the absence of a wage scale resulting from the disagreement as to wages between the employers and employees and to make its will on that subject controlling for the limited period provided for?

Coming to the general considerations by which both subjects must be controlled, to simplify the analysis for the purpose of considering the question of inherent power, we put the question as to the eight-hour standard entirely out of view on the ground that the authority to permanently establish it is so clearly sustained as to render the subject not disputable....

...That the business of common carriers by rail is in a sense a public business because of the interest of society in the continued operation and rightful conduct of such business and that the public interest begets a public right of regulation to the full extent necessary to secure and protect it, is settled by so many decisions, state and federal, and is illustrated by such a continuous exertion of state and federal legislative power as to leave no room for question on the subject. It is also equally true that as the right to fix by agreement between the carrier and its employees a standard of wages to control their relations is primarily private, the establishment and giving effect to such agreed on standard is not subject to be controlled or prevented by public authority. But taking all these propositions as undoubted, if the situation which we have described and with which the act of Congress dealt be taken into view, that is, the dispute between the employers and employees as to a standard of wages, their failure to agree, the resulting absence of such standard, the entire interruption of interstate commerce which was threatened, and the infinite injury to the public interest which was imminent, it would seem inevitably to result that the power to regulate necessarily obtained and was subject to be applied to the extent necessary to provide a remedy for the situation, which included the power to deal with the dispute, to provide by appropriate action for a standard of wages to fill the want of one caused by the failure to exert the private right on the subject and to give effect by appropriate legislation to the regulations thus adopted. This must be unless it can be said that the right to so regulate as to save and protect the public interest did not apply to a case where the destruction of the public right was imminent as the result of a dispute between the parties and their consequent failure to establish by private agreement the standard of wages which was essential; in other words that the existence of the public right and the public power to preserve it was wholly under the control of the private right to establish a standard by agreement. Nor is it an answer to this view to suggest that the situation was one of emergency and that emergency cannot be made the source of power. *Ex parte Milligan,* 4 Wall. 2. The proposition begs the question, since although an emergency may not call into life a power which has never lived, nevertheless emergency may afford a reason for the exertion of a living power already enjoyed....

...[L]et us come to briefly recapitulate some of the more important of the regulations which have been enacted in the past in order to show how necessarily the exertion of the power to enact them manifests the existence of the legislative authority to ordain the regulation now before us, and how completely the whole system of regulations adopted in the past would be frustrated or rendered unavailing if the power to regulate under the conditions stated which was exerted by the act before us was not possessed. . . .

In the presence of this vast body of acknowledged powers there would seem to be no ground for disputing the power which was exercised in the act which is before us . . . to exert the legislative will for the purpose of settling the dispute and bind both parties to the duty of acceptance and compliance to the end that no individual dispute or difference might bring ruin to the vast interests concerned in the movement of interstate commerce, for the express purpose of protecting and preserving which the plenary legislative authority granted to Congress was reposed. . . .

We are of opinion that the reasons stated conclusively establish that from the point of view of inherent power the act which is before us was clearly within the legislative power of Congress to adopt, and that in substance and effect it amounted to an exertion of its authority under the circumstances disclosed to compulsorily arbitrate the dispute between the parties by establishing as to the subject matter of that dispute a legislative standard of wages operative and binding as a matter of law upon the parties,—a power none the less efficaciously exerted because exercised by direct legislative act instead of by the enactment of other and appropriate means providing for the bringing about of such result. If it be conceded that the power to enact the statute was in effect the exercise of the right to fix wages where by reason of the dispute there had been a failure to fix by agreement, it would simply serve to show the nature and character of the regulation essential to protect the public right and safeguard the movement of interstate commerce not involving any denial of the authority to adopt it. . . .

. . . [W]e conclude that the court below erred in holding the statute was not within the power of Congress to enact and in restraining its enforcement and its decree therefore must be and it is reversed and the cause remanded with directions to dismiss the bill. And it is so ordered.

Walter Lippman on Shorter Hours
1916

An Oregon statute established a maximum ten-hour workday for both men and women; prohibited employees from working more than three hours of overtime per day; and provided overtime pay rates of one and a half times the regular wage. When the law was appealed to the Supreme Court, a number of voices were heard in its support. One of these belonged to Walter Lippman, a young political commentator, who would become by the middle of the century the unchallenged Dean of American journalists. [Walter Lippman, *Early Writings* (New York: Liveright, 1970), pp. 253-54.]

Oregon has a law which says that "it is the public policy of the state of Oregon that no person shall be hired or permitted to work for wages, under any conditions or terms, for longer hours or days of service than is consistent with his health and physical wellbeing and ability to promote the general welfare by his increasing usefulness as a healthy and intelligent citizen. It is hereby declared that the working of any person more than ten hours in one day, in any mill, factory, or manufacturing establishment is injurious to the physical health and wellbeing of such person, and tends to prevent him from acquiring that degree of intelligence that is necessary to make him and useful and desirable citizen of the state." The Oregon Supreme Court has declared this statute constitutional. It is now before the Supreme Court of the United States. The question is, does the police power cover such legislation or is it a violation of "liberty" under the Fourteenth Amendment? It is the first time that the court has had to deal with the working hours of men since the Lochner case in 1905, when a ten-hour law applying to bakers in New York was annulled. The court reasoned then that it had not been convinced that baking is a "dangerous occupation." Thus as matters stand now it is constitutional to limit the hours of women, but of men only in certain accepted dangerous trades. In this so-called Bunting case which comes from Oregon, the attempt will be made to secure a decision extending the right to limit men's hours in all trades.

The argument is that practically any trade becomes a dangerous trade if the hours are overlong. To prove it the state of Oregon has submitted a brief about a thousand pages long which is an exhaustive collection of all the available facts and opinions, medical, economic, moral, drawn from the whole world, which bear upon the question of overwork. It was prepared by Miss Josephine Goldmark of the National Consumers' League in consultation with Mr. Louis D. Brandeis, who was to have argued the case, but of course had to withdraw when he was nominated for the Supreme Court. At the invitation of Attorney-General Brown of Oregon, Professor Felix Frankfurter of the Harvard Law School was invited to take Mr. Brandeis's place. Miss Goldmark's brief has more than a passing interest. It is more than a bit of argument. It is really an authoritative treatise on the effect of fatigue, as applied to men as well as women. It carries on her masterly work now published under the title *Fatigue and Efficiency*. It contains more honest and illuminated research than has ever before been brought to the support of a piece of American labor legislation. For this brief is not only an argument to a court, it is a scientific demonstration of the need for shorter working hours, and it will be used for a long time by legislators, trade unionists, and by enlightened employers as a book of reference and authority.

Bunting v. Oregon
243 U.S. 426
1917

When *Bunting v. Oregon* came before the Court, its staunchest supporter, Justice Louis Brandeis, had to disqualify himself since he had earlier helped to prepare the brief submitted by the Consumers' League. Considering the unfriendly attitude of the Court toward labor, it was somewhat remarkable that the Justices found the statute constitutional. The suit alleged that the law controlled wages and so violated due process. Justice Joseph McKenna, speaking for five members of the Court, argued that the law did not regulate wages, only overtime rates, and so was only a maximum-hours statute similar to those found in many other states. Thus, the legislature of Oregon had exercised its police power in a reasonable manner.

. . . The consonance of the Oregon law with the Fourteenth Amendment is the question in the case, and this depends upon whether it is a proper exercise of the police power of the State, as the Supreme Court of the State decided that it is.

That the police power extends to health regulations is not denied, but it is denied that the law has such purpose or justification. It is contended that it is a wage law, not a health regulation, and takes the property of plaintiff in error without due process. . . .

There is a certain verbal plausibility in the contention that it was intended to permit 13 hours' work if there by 15½ hours' pay, but the plausibility disappears upon reflection. The provision for overtime is permissive, in the same sense that any penalty may be said to be permissive. Its purpose is to deter by its burden and its adequacy for this was a matter of legislative judgment under the particular circumstances. . . .

We cannot know all of the conditions that impelled the law or its particular form. The Supreme Court, nearer to them, describes the law as follows: "It is clear that the intent of the law is to make 10 hours a regular day's labor in the occupations to which reference is made. Apparently the provisions for permitted labor for the overtime on express conditions were made in order to facilitate the enforcement of the law, and in the nature of a mild penalty for employing one not more than three hours overtime. It might be regarded as more difficult to detect violations of the law by an employment for a shorter time than for a longer time. This penalty also goes to the employee in case the employer avails himself of the overtime clause.". . .

But passing general considerations and coming back to our immediate concern, which is the validity of the particular exertion of power in the Oregon law, our judgment of it is that it does not transcend constitutional limits. . . .

There is a contention made that the law, even regarded as regulating hours of service, is not either necessary or useful "for preservation of the health of the employees in mills, factories and manufacturing establishments." The record contains no facts to support the contention, and against it is the judgment of the legislature and the Supreme Court, which said: "In view of the well-known fact that the custom in our industries does not sanction a longer service than 10 hours per day, it cannot be held, as a matter of law, that the legislative requirement is unreasonable or arbitrary as to hours of labor. Statistics show that the average daily working time among workingmen in different countries is, in Australia, 8 hours; in Great Britain, 9; in the United States, 9¾; in Denmark, 9¾; in Norway, 10; Sweden, France, and Switzerland, 10½; Germany, 10¼; Belgium, Italy, and Austria, 11; and in Russia, 12 hours." . . .

Hammer v. Dagenhart
247 U.S. 251
1918

After many years of hard campaigning progressives were able to persuade Congress in 1916, to pass legislation prohibiting certain forms of child labor. The authors of the Keating-Owen Child Labor Law hoped to eliminate the exploitation of underage children by prohibiting the interstate shipment of any goods which had been manufactured with the assistance of child labor, and thus make profit improbable. Congress, for some time, had employed the commerce clause of the Constitution to attack other social evils such as the sale of impure food and harmful drugs, and prostitution.

The Supreme Court generally had supported such congressional concern; for example, in *Hoke v. United States* (1913) the Justices ruled favorably upon the constitutionality of the Mann (White Slave) Act (1910). By 1918, however, attitudes changes and in *Hammer v. Dagenhart* Justice William R. Day, speaking for the Court, voided the Child Labor Law on the ground that the statute was not a regulation of commerce but an outright prohibition. In *Hammer,* a deeply divided Court reversed a series of precedents which supported the national government's attempts to regulate the health, welfare, and morals of the people. Justices Oliver Wendell Holmes, Louis D. Brandeis, Joseph McKenna, and John H. Clarke objected to the majority reasoning. Holmes was especially bitter since he was convinced that child labor was an unmitigated evil.

. . . The attack upon the act rests upon three propositions: First: It is not a regulation of interstate and foreign commerce; Second: It contravenes the Tenth Amendment to the Constitution; Third: It conflicts with the Fifth Amendment to the Constitution.

The controlling question for decision is: Is it within the authority of Congress in regulating commerce among the States to prohibit the transporation in interstate commerce of manufactured goods, the product of a factory in which, within thirty days prior to their removal therefrom, children under the age of fourteen have been employed or permitted to work, or children between the ages of fourteen and sixteen years have been employed or permitted to work more than eight hours in any day, or more than six days in any week, or after the hour of seven o'clock P.M. or before the hour of 6 o'clock A.M.?

The power essential to the passage of this act, the Government contends, is found in the commerce clause of the Constitution which authorizes Congress to regulate commerce with foreign nations and among the States....

... But it is insisted that adjudged cases in this court establish the doctrine that the power to regulate given to Congress incidentally includes the authority to prohibit the movement of ordinary commodities and therefore that the subject is not open for discussion. The cases demonstrate the contrary. They rest upon the character of the particular subjects dealt with and the fact that the scope of governmental authority, state of national, possessed over them is such that the authority to prohibit is as to them but the exertion of the power to regulate.

The first of these cases is *Champion v. Ames,* 188 U.S. 321, the so-called *Lottery Case,* in which it was held that Congress might pass a law having the effect to keep the channels of commerce free from use in the transporation of tickets used in the promotion of lottery schemes. In *Hipolite Egg Co. v. United States,* ... this court sustained the power of Congress to pass the Pure Food and Drug Act which prohibited the introduction into the States by means of interstate commerce of impure foods and drugs. In *Hoke v. United States,* ... this court sustained the constitutionality of the so-called "White Slave Traffic Act" whereby the transportation of a woman in interstate commerce for the purpose of prostitution was forbidden....

In each of these instances the use of interstate transportation was necessary to the accomplishment of harmful results. In other words, although the power over interstate transportation was to regulate, that could only be accomplished by prohibiting the use of the facilities of interstate commerce to effect the evil intended.

This element is wanting in the present case. The thing intended to be accomplished by this statute is the denial of the facilities of interstate commerce to those manufacturers in the States who employ children within the prohibited ages. The act in its effect does not regulate transportation among the States, but aims to standardize the ages at which children may be employed in mining and manufacturing within the States. The goods shipped are of themselves harmless. The act permits them to be freely shipped after thirty days from the time of their removal from the factory. When offered for shipment, and before transportation begins, the labor of their production is over, and the mere fact that they were intended for interstate commerce transportation does not make their production subject to federal control under the commerce power.

Commerce "consists of intercourse and traffic...and includes the transportation of persons and property, as well as the purchase, sale and exchange of commodities." The making of goods and the mining of coal are not commerce, nor does the fact that these things are to be afterwards shipped or used in interstate commerce, make their production a part thereof. *Delaware, Lackawanna & Western R.R. Co. v. Yurkonis,* 238 U.S. 439.

Over interstate transportation, or its incidents, the regulatory power of Congress is ample, but the production of articles, intended for interstate commerce, is a matter of local regulation....

... If it were otherwise, all manufacture intended for interstate shipment would be brought under federal control to the practical exclusion of the authority of the States, a result certainly not contemplated by the framers of the Constitution when they vested in Congress the authority to regulate commerce among the States. *Kidd v. Pearson,* 128 U.S. 1, 21.

It is further contended that the authority of Congress may be exerted to control interstate commerce in the shipment of child-made goods because of the effect of the circulation of such goods in other States where the evil of this class of labor has been recognized by local legislation, and the right to thus employ child labor has been more rigorously restrained than in the State of production. In other words, that the unfair competition, thus engendered, may be controlled by closing the channels of interstate commerce to manufacturers in those States where the local laws do not meet what Congress deems to be the more just standard of other States.

There is no power vested in Congress to require the States to exercise their police power so as to prevent possible unfair competition. Many causes may cooperate to give one State, by reason of local laws or conditions, an economic advantage over others. The Commerce Clause was not intended to give to Congress a general authority to equalize such conditions. In some of the States laws have been passed fixing minimum wages for women, in others the local law regulates the hours of labor of women in various employments. Business done in such States may be at an economic disadvantage when compared with States which have no such regulations; surely, this fact does not give Congress the power to deny transportation in interstate commerce to those who carry on business where the hours of labor and the rate of compensation for women have not been fixed by a standard in use in other States and approved by Congress.

The grant of power to Congress over the subject of interstate commerce was to enable it to regulate such commerce, and not to give it authority to control the States in their exercise of the police power over local trade and manufacture.

The grant of authority over a purely federal matter was not intended to destroy the local power always existing and carefully reserved to the States in the Tenth Amendment to the Constitution....

That there should be limitations upon the right to employ children in mines and factories in the interest of their own and the public welfare, all will admit. That such employment is generally deemed to require regulation is shown by the fact that the brief of counsel states that every State in the Union has a law upon the subject, limiting the right to thus employ children. In North Carolina, the State wherein is located the factory in which the employment was had in the present case, no child under twelve years of age is permitted to work.

It may be desirable that such laws be uniform, but our Federal Goverment is one of enumerated powers. . . .

. . . To sustain this statute would not be in our judgement a recognition of the lawful exertion of congressional authority over interstate commerce, but would sanction an invasion by the federal power of the control of a matter purely local in its character, and over which no authority has been delegated to Congress in conferring the power to regulate commerce among the States. . . .

In our view the necessary effect of this act is, by means of a prohibition against the movement in interstate commerce of ordinary commercial commodities, to regulate the hours of labor of children in factories and mines within the States, a purely state authority. Thus the act in a twofold sense is repugnant to the Constitution. It not only transcends the authority delegated to Congress over commerce but also exerts a power as to a purely local matter to which the federal authority does not extend. The far reaching result of upholding the act cannot be more plainly indicated than by pointing out that if Cngress can thus regulate matters entrusted to local authority by prohibition of the movement of commodities in interstate commerce, all freedom of commerce will be at an end, and the power of the States over local matters may be eliminated, and thus our system of government be practically destroyed.

For these reasons we hold that this law exceeds the constitutional authority of Congress. It follows that the decree of the District Court must be affirmed.

Mr. Justice Holmes, dissenting.

The single question in this case is whether Congress has power to prohibit the shipment in interstate or foreign commerce of any product of a cotton mill situated in the United States, in which within thirty days before the removal of the product children under fourteen have been employed, or children between fourteen and sixteen have been employed more than eight hours in a day, or more than six days in any week, or between seven in the evening and six in the morning. The objection urged against the power is that the States have exclusive control over their methods of production and that Congress cannot meddle with them, and taking the proposition in the sense of direct intermeddling I agree to it and suppose that no one denies it. But if an act is within the powers specifically conferred upon Congress, it seems to me that it is not made any less constitutional because of the indirect effects that it may have, however obvious it may be that it will have those effects, and that we are not at liberty upon such grounds to hold it void.

The first step in my argument is to make plain what no one is likely to dispute—that the statute in question is within the power expressly given to Congress if considered only as to its immediate effects and that if invalid it is so only upon some collateral ground. The statute confines itself to prohibiting the carriage of certain goods in interstate or foreign commerce. Congress is given power to regulate such commerce in unqualified terms. It would not be argued today that the power to regulate does not include the power to prohibit. Regulation means the prohibition of something, and when interstate commerce is the matter to be regulated, I cannot doubt that the regulation may prohibit any part of such commerce that Congress sees fit to forbid. At all events it is established by the *Lottery Case* and others that have followed it that a law is not beyond the regulative power of Congress merely because it prohibits certain transportation out and out. *Champion v. Ames,* 188 U.S. 321, 355, 359, *et seq.* So I repeat that this statute in its immediate operation is clearly within the Congress's constitutional power.

The question then is narrowed to whether the exercise of its otherwise constitutional power by Congress can be pronounced unconstitutional because of its possible reaction upon the conduct of the States in a matter upon which I have admitted that they are free from direct control. I should have thought that that matter had been disposed of so fully as to leave no room for doubt. I should have thought that the most conspicuous decisions of this Court had made it clear that the power to regulate commerce and other constitutional powers could not be cut down or qualified by the fact that it might interfere with the carrying out of the domestic policy of any State.

The manufacture of oleomargarine is as much a matter of state regulation as the manufacture of cotton cloth. Congress levied a tax upon the compound when colored so as to resemble butter that was so great as obviously to prohibit the manufacture and sale. In a very elaborate discussion the present Chief Justice excluded any inquiry into the purpose of an act which apart from that purpose was within the power of Congress. *McCray v. United States,* 195 U.S. 27.... Fifty years ago a tax on state banks, the obvious purpose and actual effect of which was to drive them, or at least their circulation, out of existence, was sustained, although the result was one that Congress had no constitutional power to require. The Court made short work of the argument as to the purpose of the act. "The judicial cannot prescribe to the legislative department of the government limitations upon the exercise of its acknowledged powers." *Veazie Bank v. Fenno,* 8 Wall. 533. So it well might have been argued that the corporation tax was intended under the guise of a revenue measure to secure a control not otherwise belonging to Congress, but the tax was sustained, and the objection so far as noticed was disposed of by citing *McCray v. United States. Flint v. Stone Tracy Co.,*.... And to come to cases upon interstate commerce, notwithstanding *United States v. E.C. Knight Co.,* 156 U.S. 1, the Sherman Act has been made an instrument for the breaking up of combinations in restraint of trade and monopolies, using the power to regulate commerce as a foothold, but not proceeding because that commerce was the end actually in mind. The objection that the control of the States over

production was interfered with was urged again and again but always in vain.
. . .

The Pure Food and Drug Act which was sustained in *Hipolite Egg Co. v. United States,* . . . with the intimation that "no trade can be carried on between the States to which it [the power of Congress to regulate commcerce] does not extend," applies not merely to articles that the changing opinions of the time condemn as intrinsically harmful but to others innocent in themselves, simply on the ground that the order for them was induced by a preliminary fraud. *Weeks v. United States,* 245 U.S. 618. It does not matter whether the supposed evil precedes or follows the transportation. It is enough that in the opinion of Congress the transportation encourages the evil. . . .

The notion that prohibition is any less prohibition when applied to things now thought evil I do not understand. But if there is any matter upon which civilized countries have agreed—far more unanimously than they have with regard to intoxicants and some other matters over which is country is now emotionally aroused—it is the evil of premature and excessive child labor. I should have thought that if we were to introduce our own moral conceptions where in my opinion they do not belong, this was preeminently a case for upholding thc cxcrcisc of all its powers by the United States.

But I had thought that the propriety of the exercise of a power admitted to exist in some cases was for the consideration of Congress alone and that this Court always had disavowed the right to intrude its judgment upon questions of policy or morals. It is not for this Court to pronounce when prohibition is necessary to regulation if it ever may be necessary—to say that it is permissible as against strong drink but not as against the product of ruined lives.

The act does not meddle with anything belonging to the States. They may regulate their internal affairs and their domestic commerce as they like. But when they seek to send their products across the state line they are no longer within their rights. If there were no Constitution and no Congress their power to cross the line would depend upon their neighbors. Under the Constitution such commerce belongs not the the States but to Congress to regulate.. It may carry out its views of public policy whatever indirect effect they may have upon the activities of the States. Instead of being encountered by a prohibitive tariff at her boundaries the State encounters the public policy of the United States which it is for Congress to express. The public policy of the United States is shaped with a view to the benefit of the nation as a whole. If, as has been the case within the memory of men still living, a States should take a different view of the propriety of sustaining a lottery from that which generally prevails, I cannot believe that the fact would require a different decision from that reached in *Champion v. Ames.* Yet in that case it would be said with quite as much force as in this that Congress was attempting to intermeddle with the State's domestic affairs. The national welfare as understood by Congress may require a different attitude within its sphere from that of some self-seeking State. It seems to me entirely constitutional for Congress to enforce its understanding by all the means at its command.

Mr. Justice McKenna, Mr. Justice Brandeis and Mr. Justice Clarke concur in this opinion.

Socialism and the Court
1918

During the years between the turn of the century and the end of the First World War, socialism in America became both a political and a moral force. Such socialist leaders as Eugene V. Debs, Victor L. Berger, and Morris Hillquit were national figures and numerous party candidates won election at the local and federal levels. Victor L. Berger (Wis.) and Meyer London (N.Y.) joined the rank and file of the House of Representatives, and in 1912, Eugene V. Debs received almost one million votes in the presidental election.

On June 16, 1918, Debs gave a speech in Nimisilla Park, Canton, Ohio, protesting American involvement in the world war. He also took the opportunity to criticize a recent action of the Supreme Court; the Justices had voided the Keating-Owen Child Labor Law (1916). Most socialists believed that the Court was a retrogressive institution which hindered the development of democracy. In 1912, the Socialist party platform called for the right of the "people" to question the constitutionality of national laws instead of the Supreme Court. [Ronald Radosh, ed., *Debs* (Englewood Cliffs, N.J.: Prentice-Hall, 1971), pp. 69-70. *Proceedings of the National Convention of the Socialist Party, 1912* (Chicago: The Socialist Party, 1912), p. 198.]

. . . Who appoints our federal judges? The people? In all the history of the country, the working class have never named a federal judge. There are 121 of these judges and every solitary one holds his position, his tenure, through the influence and power of corporate capital. The corporations and trusts dictate their appointment. And when they go to the bench, they go, not to serve the people, but to serve the interests that place them and keep them where they are.

Why, the other day, by a vote of five to four—a kind of craps game—come seven, come 'leven—they declared the child labor law unconstitutional—a law secured after twenty years of education and agitation on the part of all kinds of people. And yet, by a majority of one, the Supreme Court, a body of corporation lawyers, with just one exception, wiped that law from the statute books, and this in our so-called Democracy, so that we may continue to grind the flesh and blood and bones of puny little children into profits for the junkers of Wall Street. And this in a country that boasts of fighting to make the world safe for democracy! The history of this country is being written in the blood of the childhood the industrial lords have murdered. . . .

Socialist Party Platform, 1912

h. The abolition of the power usurped by the Supreme Court of the United Statess to pass upon the constitutionality of the legislation enacted by Congress. National laws to be repealed only by act of Congress or by a referendum vote of the whole people.

Eighteenth Amendment
1919

The Prohibition movement, going back to pre-Civil War days, has had a long history in the United States. However, it was not until 1900, that the movement began to make significant gains. By 1916, nineteen states were entirely dry, and many sections of the others were dry under local-option laws. Congress had also passed the Webb-Kenyon Act in 1913, which forbade the shipment of liquor in interstate commerce into dry states. In *Clark Distilling Co. v. Western Maryland Railway Co.* (1917) the Supreme Court upheld this law.

The First World War greatly aided the Prohibitionists because of the nation's need for food: the Lever Act (1917) prohibited the use of grain in the manufacture of alcoholic beverages. Finally, in December of 1917, Congress passed a resolution calling for an amendment to the Constitution which would outlaw the manufacture, transportation, and sale of intoxicating liquors. Because of great political pressure and the enthusiasm of progressive reformers, the amendment was quickly ratified and became part of the Constitution. The Volstead Act, which provided for federal enforcement of the amendment, became law on October 28, 1919.

The "noble" experiment now commenced. Although the consumption of alcohol declined, the law was widely violated by millions of citizens; America's desire for drink encouraged a criminal element which established an illicit liquor trade. Most importantly, Prohibition produced serious rifts in the social fabric of the country.

Article XVII.

After one year from the ratification of this article, the manufacture, sale, or transportation of intoxicating liquors within, the importation thereof into, or the exportation thereof from the United States and all territory subject to the jurisdiction thereof for beverage purposes is hereby prohibited.

The Congress and the several States shall have concurrent power to enforce this article by appropriate legislation.

This article shall be inoperative unless it shall have been ratified as an amendment to the Constitution by the legislatures of the several States, as provided in the Constitution, within seven years from the date of the submission thereof to the States by Congress. [January 29, 1919.]

Schenck v. United States
249 U.S. 47
1919

During World War I—as is most wars—civil liberties came under severe pressure. Congress, for example, passed the Espionage Act in the spring of 1917, which authorized the postmaster general to suppress any material which *he* considered treasonable or seditious. Many publications, including popular weeklys such as the *Saturday Evening Post* as well as radical periodicals and newspapers, were banned temporarily from the mails. Since a great many journals and newspapers relied on mail subscriptions, the postmaster general could actually determine the financial future of these publications.

While the provisions of the Espionage Act were both constitutional and popular, writers and publishers certainly had the right to protest against alleged abuses in the courts. In *Schenck v. United States,* which involved an appeal from a conviction in the lower federal courts on a charge of circulating antidraft leaflets, the Supreme Court unanimously ruled that the Espionage Act was constitutional. Oliver Wendell Holmes, speaking for the Court, declared that the right of free speech was never an absolute one, in peace or in war. "Free speech," he stated in his famous illustration, "would not protect a man in falsely shouting fire in a theatre, and causing a panic." Therefore, if there was a "clear and present danger" that a particular statement would threaten the nation, it could be suppressed.

This is an indictment in three counts. The first charges a conspiracy to violate the Espionage Act of June 15, 1917...by causing and attempting to cause insubordination, &c., in the military and naval forces of the United States, and to obstruct the recruiting and enlistment service of the United States, when the United States was at war with the German Empire, to-wit, that the defendants wilfully conspired to have printed and circulated to men who had been called and accepted for military service under the Act of May 18, 1917, a document set forth and alleged to be calculated to cause such insubordination and obstruction. The count alleges overt acts in pursuance of the conspiracy, ending in the distribution of the document set forth....

It is argued that the evidence, if admissible, was not sufficient to prove that the defendant Schenck was concerned in sending the documents. According to the testimony Schenck said he was general secretary of the Socialist party and had charge of the Socialist headquarters from which the documents were sent. He identified a book found there as the minutes of the Executive

Committee of the party. The book showed a resolution of August 13, 1917, that 15,000 leaflets should be printed on the other side of one of them in use, to be mailed to men who had passed exemption boards, and for distribution. Schenck personally attended to the printing. On August 20 the general secretary's report said, "Obtained new leaflets from printer and started work addressing envelopes" &c.; and there was a resolve that Comrade Schenck be allowed $125 for sending leaflets through the mail. He said that he had about fifteen or sixteen thousand printed. There were files of the circular in question in the inner office which he said were printed on the other side of the one sided circular and were there for distribution. Other copies were proved to have been sent through the mails to drafted men. Without going into confirmatory details that were proved, no reasonable man could doubt that the defendant Schenck was largely instrumental in sending the circulars about....

The document in question upon its first printed side recited the... Thirteenth Amendment, said that the idea embodied in it was violated by the Conscription Act and that a conscript is little better than a convict. In impassioned language it intimated that conscription was despotism in its worst form and a monstrous wrong against humanity in the interest of Wall Street's chosen few. It said "Do not submit to intimidation," but in form at least confined itself to peaceful measures such as a petition for the repeal of the act. The other and later printed side of the sheet was headed "Assert Your Rights." It stated reasons for alleging that any one violated the Constitution when he refused to recognize "your right to assert your opposition to the draft," and went on "If you do not assert and support your rights, you are helping to deny or disparage rights which it is the solemn duty of all citizens and residents of the United States to retain." It described the arguments on the other side as coming from cunning politicians and a mercenary capitalist press, and even silent consent to the conscription law as helping to support an infamous conspiracy. It denied the power to send our citizens away to foreign shores to shoot up the people of other lands, and added that words could not express the condemnation such cold-blooded ruthlessness deserves, &c., &c., winding up "You must do your share to maintain, support and uphold the rights of the people of this country." Of course the document would not have been sent unless it had been intended to have some effect, and we do not see what effect it could be expected to have upon persons subject to the draft except to influence them to obstruct the carrying of it out. The defendants do not deny that the jury might find against them on this point.

But it is said, suppose that that was the tendency of this circular, it is protected by the First Amendment to the Constitution.... We admit that in many places and in ordinary times the defendants in saying all that was said in the circular would have been within their constitutional rights. But the character of every act depends upon the circumstances in which it is done. *Aikens v. Wisconsin,* 195 U.S. 194, 205, 206. The most stringent protection of free speech would not protect a man in falsely shouting fire in a theatre and causing a panic. It does not even protect a man from an injunction against uttering words that may have all the effect of force. *Gompers v. Bucks Stove & Range Co.,* 221 U.S. 418, 439. The question in every case is whether the words used are used in such circumstances and are of such a nature as to create a clear and present danger that they will bring about the substantive evils that Congress has a right to prevent. It is a question of proximity and degree. When a nation is at war many things that might be said in time of peace are such a hindrance to its effort that their utterance will not be endured so long as men fight and that no Court could regard them as protected by any constitutional right. . . .

Abrams v. United States
250 U.S. 616
1919

In May of 1918, Congress, under pressure from both the military and the public, passed the Sedition Act, which made it a crime to "incite mutiny or insubordination in the ranks of the armed forces," and to "disrupt or discourage recruiting or enlistment service, or utter, print, or publish disloyal, profane, scurrilous, or abusive language about the form of government, the Constitution, soldiers and sailors, flag, or uniform of the armed forces...." This law, like the far more infamous Sedition Act of 1798, threatened to penalize all criticism of the government and its symbols of sovereignty during wartime.

In *Abrams v. United States* the Court reviewed a conviction of appellants who were charged with printing and distributing pamphlets attacking the United States's expeditionary force in Russia. The majority of the Justices upheld the conviction and the statute; it was now possible for the government to suppress all discussion of the merits and methods of the war. Oliver Wendell Holmes's dissent, often considered one of the great statements on freedom of speech follows. For Holmes free speech was essential to a republican society unless it threatened to interfere with the lawful and pressing purposes of the law.

This indictment is founded wholly upon the publication of two leaflets which I shall describe in a moment. The first count charges a conspiracy pending the war with Germany to publish abusive language about the form of government of the United States, laying the preparation and publishing of the first leaflet as overt acts. The second count charges a conspiracy pending the war to publish language intended to bring the form of government into contempt, laying the preparation and publishing of the two leaflets as overt acts. The third count alleges a conspiracy to encourage resistance to the United States in the same war and to attempt to effectuate the purpose by publishing the same leaflets. The fourth count lays a conspiracy to incite curtailment of production of things necessary to the prosecution of the war and to attempt to accomplish it by publishing the second leaflet to which I have referred....

No argument seems to me necessary to show that these pronunciamentos in no way attack the form of government of the United States, or that they do not support either of the first two counts. What little I have to say about the third count may be postponed until I have considered the fourth. With regard to that it seems too plain to be denied that the suggestion to workers in the ammunition factories that they are producing bullets to murder their dearest, and the further advocacy of a general strike, both in the second leaflet, do urge curtailment of production of things necessary to the prosecution of the war within the meaning of the Act of May 16, 1918...amending...the earlier Act of 1917. But to make the conduct criminal that statue requires that it should be "with intent by such curtailment to cripple or hinder the United States in the prosecution of the war." It seems to me that no such intent is proved.

I am aware of course that the word intent as vaguely used in ordinary legal discussion means no more than knowledge at the time of the act that the consequences said to be intended will ensue. Even less than that will satisfy the general principle of civil and criminal liability. A man may have to pay damages, may be sent to prison, at common law might be hanged, if at the time of his act he knew facts from which common experience showed that the consequences would follow, whether he individually could foresee them or not. But, when words are used exactly, a deed is not done with intent to produce a consequence unless that consequence is the aim of the deed. It may be obvious, and obvious to the actor, that the consequence will follow, and he may be liable for it even if he regrets it, but he does not do the act with intent to produce it unless the aim to produce it is the proximate motive of the specific act, although there may be some deeper motive behind....

I do not see how anyone can find the intent required by the statute in any of the defendants' words. The second leaflet is the only one that affords even a foundation for the charge, and there, without invoking the hatred of German militarism expressed in the former one, it is evident from the beginning to the end that the only object of the paper is to help Russia and stop American intervention there against the popular goverment—not to impede the United States in the war that it was carrying on. To say that two phrases taken literally might import a suggestion of conduct that would have interference with the war as an indirect and probably undesired effect seems to me by no means enough to show an attempt to produce that effect....

In this case sentences of twenty years imprisonment have been imposed for the publishing of two leaflets that I believe the defendants had as much right to publish as the Government has to publish the Constitution of the United States now vainly invoked by them. Even if I am technically wrong and enough can be squeezed from these poor and puny anonymities to turn the color of legal litmus paper; I will add, even if what I think the necessary intent were shown; the most nominal punishment seems to me all that possibly could be inflicted, unless the defendants are to be made to suffer not for what the indictment alleges but for the creed that they avow—a creed that I believe to be the creed of ignorance and immaturity when honestly held, as I see no reason to doubt that it was held here, but which, although made the subject of examination at the trial, no one has a right even to consider in dealing with the charges before the Court.

Persecution for the expression of opinions seems to me perfectly logical. If you have no doubt of your premise or your power and want a certain result with all your heart you naturally express your wishes in law and sweep away all opposition. To allow opposition by speech seems to indicate that you think the speech impotent, as when a man says that he has squared the circle, or that you do not care whole-heartedly for the result, or that you doubt either your power or your premises. But when men have realized that time has upset many fighting faiths, they may come to believe even more than they believe the very foundations of their own conduct that the ultimate good desired is better reached by free trade in ideas—that the best test of truth is the power of the thought to get itself accepted in the competition of the market, and that truth is the only ground upon which their wishes safely can be carried out. That at any rate is the theory of our Constitution. It is an experiment, as all life is an experiment. Every year if not every day we have to wager our salvation upon some prophecy based upon imperfect knowledge. While that experiment is part of our system, I think that we should be eternally vigilant against attempts to check the expression of opinions that we loathe and believe to be fraught with death, unless they so imminently threaten immediate interference with the lawful and pressing purposes of the law that an immediate check is required to save the country. I wholly disagree with the argument of the Government that the First Amendment left the common law as to seditious libel in force. History seems to me against the notion. I had conceived that the United States through many years had shown its repentance for the Sedition Act of 1798, by repaying fines that it imposed. Only the emergency that makes it immediately dangerous to leave the correction of evil counsels to time warrants making any exception to the sweeping command, "Congress shall make no law...abridging the freedom of speech." Of course I am speaking only of expression of opinion and exhortations, which were all that were uttered here, but I regret that I cannot put into more impressive words my belief that in their conviction upon this indictment the defendants were deprived of their rights under the Constitution of the United States.

Missouri v. Holland
252 U.S. 416
1920

In this case the Supreme Court made a powerful statement of the doctrine of national supremacy; seven Justices declared that there were virtually no limits to federal authority, if exercised in pursuance of the treaty-making power of the Constitution.

The case involved the validity of the Migratory Bird Act (1918) and a treaty of 1916, between Great Britain and the United States for the protection of migratory birds. The two countries had agreed by treaty and by statute to establish closed seasons on several species of birds migrating annually between the United States and Canada. The state of Missouri argued that such actions went beyond the powers of the federal government, undermined the powers of the states and violated the Tenth Amendment. Justice Oliver Wendell Holmes, speaking for the Court, declared that the treaty power was broader than the enumerated powers of Congress; he also defended broad authority on the grounds of national welfare and public necessity. In short, a treaty could accomplish anything so long as its substance related to the general welfare.

This is a bill in equity brought by the State of Missouri to prevent a game warden of the United States from attempting to enforce the Migratory Bird Treaty Act of July3 , 1918...and the regulations made by the Secretary of Agriculture in pursuance of the same. The ground of the bill is that the statute is an unconstitutional interference with the rights reserved to the States by the Tenth Amendment, and that the acts of the defendant done and threatened under that authority invade the sovereign right of the State and contravene its will manifested in statutes. The State also alleges a pecuniary interest, as owner of the wild birds within its borders....

On December 8, 1916, a treaty between the United States and Great Britain was proclaimed by the President. It recited that many species of birds in their annual migrations traversed certain parts of the United States and of Canada, that they were of great value as a source of food and in destroying insects injurious to vegetation, but were in danger of extermination through lack of adequate protection. It therefore provided for specified closed seasons and protection in other forms, and agreed that the two powers would take or propose to their law-making bodies the necessary measures for carrying the treaty out.... The above mentioned Act of July 3, 1918, entitled an act to give effect to the convention, prohibited the killing, capturing or selling any of the migratory birds included in the terms of the treaty except as permitted by regulations compatible with those terms, to be made by the Secretary of Agriculture. Regulations were proclaimed on July 31, and October 25, 1918. ... It is unnecessary to go into any details, because, as we have said, the question raised is the general one whether the treaty and statute are void as an interference with the rights reserved to the States.

To answer this question it is not enough to refer to the Tenth Amendment, reserving the powers not delegated to the United States, because by Article II ...the power to make treaties is delegated expressly, and by Article VI treaties made under the authority of the Uited States, along with the Constitution and laws of the United States made in pursuance thereof, are declared the supreme law of the land. If the treaty is valid there can be no dispute about the validity of the statute under Article I,. . . as a necessary and proper means to execute the powers of the Government. The language of the Constitution as to the supremacy of treaties being general, the question before us is narrowed to an inquiry into the ground upon which the present supposed exception is placed.

It is said that a treaty cannot be valid if it infringes the Constitution, that there are limits, therefore, to the treaty-making power, and that one such limit is that what an act of Congress could not do unaided, in derogation of the powers reserved to the States, a treaty cannot do. An earlier act of Congress that attempted by itself and not in pursuance of a treaty to regulate the killing of migratory birds within the States had been held bad in the District Court. United States v. Shauver, 214 Fed. Rep. 154. *United States v. McCullagh,* 221 Fed. Rep. 288. Those decisions were supported by arguments that migratory birds were owned by the States in their soverign capacity for the benefit of their people, and that under cases like *Geer v. Connecticut,* 161 U.S. 519, this control was one that Congress had no power to displace. The same argument is supposed to apply now with equal force.

Whether the two cases cited were decided rightly or not they cannot be accepted as a test of the treaty power. Acts of Congress are the supreme law of the land only when made in pursuance of the Constitution, while treaties are declared to be so when made under the authority of the United States. It is open to question whether the authority of the United States means more than the formal acts prescribed to make the convention. We do not mean to imply that there are no qualifications to the treaty-making power; but they must be ascertained in a different way. It is obvious that there may be matters of the sharpest exigency for the national well being that an act of Congress could not deal with but that a treaty followed by such an act could, and it is not light to be assumed that, in matters requirng national action, "a power which must belong to and somewhere reside in every civilized government" is not to be found. *Andrews v. Andrews,* 188 U.S. 14, 33. What was said in that case with regard to the powers of the States applies with equal force to the powers of the nation in cases where the States individually are incompetent to act. We are not yet discussing the particular case before us but only are considering the validity of the test proposed. With regard to that we may add that when we are dealing with words that also are a constituent act, like the Constitution of the United States, we must realize that they have called into life a being the development of which could not have been foreseen completely by the most gifted of its begetters. It was enough for them to realize or to hope that they created a nation. The case before us must be considered in the light of our whole experience and not merely in that of what was said a hundred years ago. The treaty in question does not contravene any prohibitory words to be found in the Constitution. The only question is whether it is forbidden by some invisible radiation from the general terms of the Tenth Amendment. We must consider what this country has become in deciding what that Amendment has reserved.

The State as we have intimated founds its claim of exclusive authority upon an assertion of title to migratory birds, an assertion that is embodied in statute. No doubt it is true that as between a State and its inhabitants the State may regulate the killing and sale of such birds, but it does not follow that its authority is excluisve of paramount powers. To put the claim of the State upon title is to lean upon a slender reed. Wild birds are not in the possession of anyone; and possession is the beginning of ownership. The whole foundation of the State's rights is the presence within their jurisidction of birds that yesterday had not arrived, tomorrow may be in another State and in a week a thousand miles away. If we are to be accurate we cannot put the case of the State upon higher ground than that the treaty deals with creatures that for the moment are within the state borders, that it must be carried out by officers of the United States within the same territory, and that but for the treaty the State would be free to regulate this subject itself.

As most of the laws of the United States are carried out within the States and as many of them deal with matters which in the silence of such laws the State might regulate, such general grounds are not enough to support Missouri's claim. Valid treaties of course "are as binding within the territorial limits of the States as they are elsewhere throughout the dominion of the United States." *Baldwin v. Franks,* 120 U.S. 678, 683. No doubt the great body of private relations uusually fall within the control of the State, but a treaty may override its power. . . .

Here a national interest of very nearly the first magnitude is involved. It can be protected only by national action in concert with that of another power. The subject-matter is only transitorily within the State and has no permanent habitat therein. But for the treaty and the statute there soon might be no birds for any powers to deal with. We see nothing in the Constitution that compels the Government to sit by while a food supply is cut off and the protectors of our forests and our crops are destroyed. It is not sufficient to rely upon the States. The reliance is vain, and were it otherwise, the question is whether the United States is forbidden to act. We are of the opinion that the treaty and statute must be upheld.

Nineteenth Amendment
1920

Gaining the vote for women was perhaps the greatest of the great victories for reformers during the Progressive Era. It had been a long and hard battle; the first skirmish having taken place back in the 1830s. Nineteenth-century suffragettes were sharply criticized, ridiculed, and abused yet by the turn of the century, they had already achieved some gains. For example, after several states gave women the franchise male politicians were forced to take the movement seriously. When Theodore Roosevelt in 1912, and Charles Evans Hughes in 1916, campaigned for the presidency, they openly supported an amendment to the Constitution grainting women the vote. Although President Wilson was personally hostile—largely to keep morale high and the war effort strong—he urged Congress to pass a resolution calling for an amendment. After much agitation on the part of women and their male supporters, the amendment was passed by Congress on June 4, 1919; it was ratified by the states little more than a year later. In 1920, some political commentators argued that the vote for women would have an enormous impact on the political process, yet over the years the effect has been slight. Perhaps the reason for this is that women have the same political interests and make the same political mistakes as men.

Article XIX.

The right of citizens of the United States to vote shall not be denied or abridged by the United States or by any State on account of sex.

The Congress shall have power by appropriate legislation to enforce the provisions of this article. [August 26, 1920.]

National Prohibition Cases
253 U.S. 350
1920

The Supreme Court consolidated seven cases which involved the constitutionality of the Volstead Act (1919) and the validity of the Eighteenth Amendment. Speaking through Justice Willis Van Devanter, the Court declared that Congress had the authority to limit the alcohol content in beverages. Moreover, the Eighteenth Amendment was lawfully proposed and ratified by the states, and therefore must be respected. It is of some importance to note that for the first time in the history of the Supreme Court the Justices stated their opinion on a question of constitutional law without giving their reasoning. Chief Justice Edward Douglas White concurred in the opinion, but regretted the Court's decision to only voice its conclusions.

. . . The cases have been elaborately argued at the bar and in printed briefs; and the arguments have been attentively considered, with the result that we reach and announce the following conclusions on the questions involved:

1. The adoption by both houses of Congress, each by a two-thirds vote, of a joint resolution proposing an amendment to the Constitution sufficiently shows that the proposal was deemed necessary by all who voted for it. An express declaration that they regarded it as necessary is not essential. None of the resolutions whereby prior amendments were proposed contained such a declaration.

2. The two-thirds vote in each house which is required in proposing an amendment is a vote of two-thirds of the members present—assuming the presence of a quorum—and not a vote of two-thrids of the entire membership, present and absent. *Missouri Pacific Ry. Co. v. Kansas,* 248 U.S. 276.

3. The referendum provisions of state constitutions and statutes cannot be applied, consistently with the Constitution of the United States, in the ratification or rejection of amendments to it. *Hawke v. Smith, ante,* 221.

4. The prohibition of the manufacture, sale, transportation, importation and exportation of intoxicating liquors for beverage purposes, as embodied in the Eighteenth Amendment, is within the power to amend reserved by Article V of the Constitution.

5. That Amendment, by lawful proposal and ratification, has become a part of the Constitution, and must be respected and given effect the same as other provisions of that instrument.

6. The. . . section of the Amendment—the one embodying the prohibi-

tion—is operative throughout the entire territorial limits of the United States, binds all legislative bodies, courts, public officers and individuals within those limits, and of its own force invalidates every legislative act—whether by Congress, by a state legislature, or by a territorial assembly—which authorizes or sanctions what the section prohibits.

7. The...section of the Amendment—the one declaring "The Congress and the several States shall have concurrent power to enforce this article by appropriate legislation"—does not enable Congress or the several States to defeat or thwart the prohibition, but only to enforce it by appropriate means.

8. The words "concurrent power" in that section do not mean joint power, or require that legislation thereunder by Congress, to be effective, shall be approved or sanctioned by the several States or any of them; nor do they mean that the power to enforce is divided between Congress and the several States along the lines which separate or distinguish foreign and interstate commerce from intrastate affairs.

9. The power confided to Congress by that section, while not exclusive, is territorially coextensive with the prohibition of the first section, embraces manufacture and other intrastate transactions as well as importation, exportation and interstate traffic, and is in no wise dependent on or affected by action or inaction on the part of the several States or any of them.

10. That power may be exerted against the disposal for beverage purposes of liquors manufactured before the Amendment became effective just as it may be against subsequent manufacture for those purposes. In either case it is a constitutional mandate or prohibition that is being enforced.

11. While recognizing that there are limits beyond which Congress cannot go in treating beverages as within its power of enforcement, we think those limits are not transcended by the provision of the Volstead Act...wherein liquors containing as much as one-half of one per cent of alcohol by volume and fit for use for beverage purposes are treated as within that power. *Jacob Ruppert v. Caffey,* 215 U.S. 264....

Mr. Chief Justice White, concurring.

I profoundly regret that in a case of this magnitude, affecting as it does an amendment to the Constitution dealing with the powers and duties of the national and state governments, and intimately concerning the welfare of the whole people, the court has deemed it proper to state only ultimate conclusions without an exposition of the reasoning by which they have been reached....

Duplex Printing Press Co. v. Deering
254 U.S. 443
1921

Several provisions of the Clayton Anti-Trust Act (1914) exempted labor unions from the antitrust laws and protected workers from the use of injunctions in labor disputes. It was not until 1921, however, that those provisions, particularly the use of the labor injunction, were challenged before the high court. The primary issue involved the use of secondary boycotts by a labor union by which workers attempted to coerce third parties, not concerned with the dispute in question, to break business relations with an employer. In *Duplex Printing Press Co. v. Deering* Justice Mahlon Pitney, arguing for the Court, held that secondary boycotts constituted an unlawful practice which interfered with interstate commerce; their use by unions was enjoinable under the antitrust laws. Moreover, Pitney stated that the restriction upon the use of the injunction only applied to the immediate parties concerned in a dispute, a labor union and the employer. The effect of *Duplex* was to minimize the protection afforded by the Clayton Act. Labor was severely weakened in its dealings with unyielding employers and during the 1920s, injunction proceedings and prosecutions against labor unions increased enormously.

This was a suit in equity brought by appellant in the District Court for the Southern District of New York for an injunction to restrain a course of conduct carried on by defendants in that District and vicinity in maintaining a boycott against the products of complainant's factory, in furtherance of a conspiracy to enjure and destroy its good will, trade, and business— especially to obstruct and destroy its interstate trade....

...The suit was begun before but brought to hearing after the passage of the Clayton Act of October 15, 1914,... Both parties invoked the provisions of the latter act, and both courts treated them as applicable. Complainant relied also upon the common law; but we shall deal first with the effect of the acts of Congress.

The facts...may be summarized as follows. Complainant conducts its business on the "open shop" policy, without discrimination against either union or non-union men. The individual defendants and the local organizations of which they are the representatives are affiliated with the International Association of Machinists, an unincorporated association having a membership of more than 60,000; and are united in a combination, to which the International Association also is a party, having the object of compelling complainant to unionize its favtory and enforce the "closed shop," the eighthour day, and the union scale of wages, by means of interfering with and restraining its interstate trade in the products of the factory.... In August, 1913... the International Association called a strike at complainant's factory in Battle Creek, as a result of which union machinists to the number of about eleven in the factory and three who supervised the erection of presses in the field left complainant's employ. But the defection of so small a number did not materially interfere with the operation of the factory, and sales and shipments in interstate commerce continued. The acts complained of made up the details of an elaborate programme adopted and carried out by defendants and ther organizations in and about the City of New York as part of a country-wide programme adopted by the International Association, for the purpose of enforcing a boycott of complainant's product.... All the judges of the Circuit Court of Appeals concurred in the view that defendants' conduct consisted essentially of efforts to render it impossible for complainant to carry on any commerce in printing presses between Michigan and New York; and that defendants had agreed to do and were endeavoring to accomplish the very thing pronounced unlawful by this court in *Loewe v. Lawlor,* 208 U.S.274; 235 U.S. 522. The judges also agreed that the interference with interstate commerce was such as ought to be enjoined, unless the Clayton Act of October 15, 1914, forbade such injunction....

That... complainant has sustained substantial damage to its interstate trade, and is threatened with further and irreparable loss and damage in the future; is proved by clear and undisputed evidence. Hence the right to an injunction is clear if the threatened loss is due to a violation of the Sherman Act as amended by the Clayton Act.

The substance of the matters here complained of is an interference with complainant's interstate trade, intended to have coercive effect upon complainant, and produced by what is commonly known as a "secondary boycott," that is, a combination not merely to refrain from dealing with complainant, or to advice or by peaceful means persuade complainant's customers to refrain ("primary boycott"), but to exercise coercive pressure upon such customers, actual or prospective, in order to cause them to withhold or withdraw patronage from complainant through fear of loss or damage to themselves should they deal with it.

As we shall see, the recognized distinction between a primary and a secondary boycott is material to be considered upon the question of the proper construction of the Clayton Act.... The principal reliance is upon § 20.... [It] declares that "no *such* restraining order or injunction" shall prohibit certain conduct specified—manifestly still referring to a "case between an employer and employees,...involving, or growing out of, a dispute concerning terms or conditions of employment,"...It is very clear that the restriction upon the use of the injunction is in favor only of those concerned as parties to such a dispute as is described....

The majority of the Circuit Court of Appeals appear to have entertianed the view that the words "employers and employees,"...should be treated as referring to "the business class or clan to which the parties litigant respectly belong"; and that, as there had been a dispute at complainant's factory in Michigan concerning the conditions of employment there—a dispute created, it is said, if it did not exist before, by the act of the Machinists' Union in calling a strike at the factory—...operated to permit members of the Machinists' Union elsewhere—some 60,000 in number—although standing in no relation of employment under complainant, past, present, or prospective, to make that dispute their own and proceed to instigate sympathetic strikes, picketing, and boycotting against employers wholly unconnected with complainant's factory and having relations with complainant only in the way of purchasing its product in the ordinary course of interstate commerce—and this where there was no dispute between such employers and their employees respecting terms or conditions of employment.

We deem this construction altogether inadmissible....

...The emphasis placed on the words "lawful" and "lawfully," "peaceful" and "peacefully," and the references to the dispute and the parties to it, strongly rebut a legislative intent to confer a general immunity for conduct violative of the anti-trust laws, or otherwise unlawful. The subject of the boycott is dealt with specifically in the "ceasing to patronize" provision, and by the clear force of the language employed the exemption is limited to pressure exerted upon a "party to such dispute" by means of "peaceful and *lawful*" influence upon neutrals. There is nothing here to justify defendants or the organizations they represent in using either threats or persuasion to bring about strikes or a cessation of work on the part of employees of complainant's customers or prospective customers, or of the trucking company employed by the customers, with the object of compelling such customers to withdraw or refrain from commercial relations with complainant, and of thereby constraining complainant to yield the matter in dispute. To instigate a sympathetic strike in aid of a secondary boycott cannot be deemed "peaceful and lawful" persuasion. In essence it is a threat to inflict damage upon the immediate employer, between whom and his employees no dispute exists, in order to bring him against his will into a concerted plan to inflict damage upon another employer who is in dispute with his employees.
. . .

...The question whether...[a] bill legalized the secondary boycott having been raised, it was emphatically and unequivocally answered...in the negative. The subject...was under consideration when the bill was framed, and the section as reported was carefully prepared with the settled purpose of excluding the secondary boycott and confining boycotting to the parties to the dispute, allowing parties to cease to patronize and to ask others to cease to patronize a party to the dispute; it was the opinion of the committee that it did not legalize the secondary boycott, it was not their purpose to authorize such a boycott, not a member of the committee would vote to do so; clarifying amendment was unnecessary; the section as reported expressed the real purpose so well that it could not be tortured into a meaning authorizing the secondary boycott. . . .

There should be an injunction against defendants and the associations represented by them. . . .

Mr. Chief Justice Taft

1921

William Howard Taft assumed the high office of Chief Justice of the Supreme Court on June 30, 1921. Although he had been at one time associated with the Progressive Movement, he was no social reformer. Actually, Taft had become a staunch conservative, who looked upon Courts as the best instruments for preserving the *status quo.* While on the high bench, he would attempt to restrain all impulses for radical change and to defend private property with great zeal. The following *New Republic* editorial first questioned Taft's qualifications yet, recognizing the important role of the Justices in determining social policy, argued that the only safeguard against the great powers of the Supreme Court was to be critical of its work. The editors of the *New Republic* were essentially putting the Taft Court on notice that it would monitor and interpret the Conservative Court's work from its own liberal perspective. "Mr. Chief Justice Taft," *The New Republic,* 27 (July 27, 1921): 230-31.

If Mr. Taft had been named Chief Justice of the Supreme Court in 1913, is there any doubt that an outburst of liberal criticism would have greeted the appointment? The very Progressivism which President Taft provoked would uncompromisingly have resented Chief Justice Taft. This Progressive opposition would not have been a mere partisan expression, but the manifestation of sound political instinct, namely, that the forces, conscious or unconscious, which make a man either a conservative or a liberal in the White House, are fundamentally the same forces which determine his decisions on the Supreme Court. To the Progressives of 1913, the William Howard Taft, with his lack of liberal convictions as to conservation, would have been the same William Howard Taft at the other end of Pennsylvania Avenue.

Today this opposition seems to have melted away. The press greets Mr. Taft's appointment with almost universal acclaim. Only the N.Y. Herald speaks out,—possibly a hang-over of Mr. Munsey's Progressive days with Goerge W. Perkins. The Senate confirms the nomination pell-mell, in its eagerness to testify to the general approval. Of the Progressive group only Borah, Johnson and LaFollette recall the ancient days and frankly challenge Mr. Taft's fitness. The rest is silence.

Whence the change from Taft, the target of the Progressives, to Taft, their acclaimed? Surely it's the same Mr. Taft. True, during the war there was discernible in him a slight interlude, due partly to the general wooing of

Labor, and partly to Mr. Taft's genial submissiveness to the constant stimulus of Frank Walsh. But it was only an interlude. The same stand-pat pieties and timidity which led Mr. Taft to denounce Roosevelt for "laying the axe at the root of the tree" and "profaning the Ark of the Covenant" have inevitably made him an easy prey to post-war fears and hysteria. When Mitchell Palmer was running amuck and law officers and courts were indulging in tyrannous and lawless conduct, Secretary Hughes and Senator Beveridge spoke out bravely in behalf of the Constitution which Mr. Taft professes to revere; but never a word from Mr. Taft. And while in the abstract favoring trade-unionism as a social necessity, he has joined the prevalent denunciation of Labor and supported the present majority view of the Supreme Court in making the courts partisans in the economic struggle.

Why, then, the change of attitude toward Mr. Taft,—this silencing of opposition? There are many reasons. Mr. Taft's personality accounts for much. He was a bad President, but a good sport. His customary geniality arouses a pervasively lazy good nature towards him. There is also a widespread assumption as to his judicial competence. Partly, he is the beneficiary of an unconscious law of compensation; he was very bad as President, therefore he must be great as a judge. From a slight foundation in fact, reiteration and this law of compensation have gradually built up Mr. Taft's judicial competence into a myth of judicial greatness. He was a good judge; one of the good judges of a Court—the Sixth Circuit—of rigorous traditions. But, surely, informed professional opinion would not think of him in the same class with such judges as Baker, Cardozo or Learned Hand. Moreover, such aptitudes and judicial habits as Mr. Taft had, had been unused for twenty years. During all his years as professor of law at Yale, Mr. Taft contributed practically nothing to legal thought; when he has written on legal matters it has been largely in the lay press, in a spirit of partisanship and with irresponsible inaccuracy.

Two causes deeper than Mr. Taft's personality make for acquiescence in his appointment. First, the recurring failure on the part of the public to grasp the real significance of the Supreme Court in the political life of the nation, to appreciate that when members of the Court decide the Hitchman case, or the Duplex case, they move in the field of statesmanship. In such cases—and it is cases like these which matter in the work of the Court—the justices are not merely passive interpreters of ready-made law; they adjust conflicting interests, and by so doing enforce, consciously or unconsciously, varying conceptions of public policy. The New York Tribune expresses the naive hope that "With Justice Taft as moderator, it is probable that not a few asperities that mar the harmony of the celestial chamber, the consulting room, will be softened and that not quite so often in the future will the court divide five and four." Such simple-mindedness as this betrays a complete ignorance of the Court's history. Divisions in the Court are not attributable to want of "fact and good humor" in the "moderator," nor will they be effaced by smiles. A gentler spirit, a more twinkling humor and a more accommodating mind probably never presided over the Supreme Court than during the period of Chief Justice Fuller. Yet divided opinions on crucial public questions were plentiful during his time, as they were during the time of Chief Justice White, and as they will be during the time of Chief Justice Taft. The reason is that divided opinions are the result of real differences of opinion as to policy, and not mere differences in interpreting fixed rules of "law."

But the greatest significance of the widespread popular approval of Mr. Taft's appointment lies in the fact that it mesures the present temporary triumph of reaction. Labor is cowed, liberalism is confused, and the country's thinking generally is done in the storm-cellar. The New Republic does not begrudge Mr. Taft this outpoor of goodwill. But the Chief Justiceship of the Supreme Court is not a subject for mere good-nature. The moment of jubilation will quickly pass for years of litigation on fundamental issues. Cases involving the social control allowed the states under the fourteenth amendment, or the exercise of federal power for police purposes, such as the Child Labor law, will soon again call forth a clash of differing conceptions of policy and of the proper scope of the Court's ultimate veto power. Mr. Taft, even before he was one of its members, has been rather obsessed by the notion that the Supreme Court is a sacred priesthood immune from profane criticism. He is not likely to be more hospitable to criticism as the presiding Justice of the Court. But the New Republic cannot emphasize too often that the only safeguard against the terrible powers vested in the Supreme Court lies in continuous, informed and responsible criticism of the work of the Court. Only thus will it be able to function as a living organ of the national will and not as an obstructive force of scholastic legalism.

Truax v. Corrigan
257 U.S. 312
1921

During the 1920s, the Supreme Court demonstrated a strong inclination to support all business enterprise, but especially those which were having problems with labor. A good example of this is *Truax v. Corrigan* where the Court declared unconstitutional an Arizona statute which prevented local courts from issuing injunctions against picketing. Chief Justice William Howard Taft, speaking for the majority, argued that the law violated due process and the equal protection clause of the Fourteenth Amendment because it singled out property (a business enterprise) involved in a labor dispute for exposure to wrongful injury. During the 1930s, labor organizations would argue successfully that the Fourteenth Amendment gave workers the right to peacefully picket struck companies. In the meantime unions could only cite Justice Oliver Wendell Holmes for encouragement; his dissent showed great disdain for Taft's reasoning.

Essentially, the Court was not only protecting private enterprise, but also was reflecting its bias toward laissez-faire economic philosophy. The conservative Justices invalidated numerous state statutes favoring labor or consumers on the grounds that they imposed "arbitrary" or "unreasonable" restrictions upon private property.

...The complaint further averred that the defendants were relying for immunity on...the Revised Statutes of Arizona, 1913, which is in part as follows:

"No restraining order or injunction shall be granted by any court of this state, or a judge or the judges thereof, in any case between an employer and employees, or between employers and employees, or between employees, or between persons employed and persons seeking employment, involving or growing out of a dispute concerning terms or conditions of employment, unless necessary to prevent irreparable injury to property or to a property right of the party making the application, for which injury there is no adequate remedy at law, and such property or property right must be described with particularity in the application, which must be in writing and sworn to by the applicant or by his agent or attorney.

"And no such restraining order or injunction shall prohibit any person or persons from terminating any relation of employment, or from ceasing to perform any work or labor, or from recommending, advising, or persuading others by peaceful means so to do; or from attending at or near a house or place where any person resides or works, or carries on business, or happens to be for the purpose of peacefully obtaining or communicating information, or of peacefully persuading any person to work or to abstain from working; or from ceasing to patronize or to employ any party to such dispute; or from recommending, advising, or persuading others by peaceful means so to do; . . ."

The plaintiffs alleged that this paragraph if it made lawful defendants' acts contravened the Fourteenth Amendment to the Constitution of the United States by depriving plaintiffs of their property without due process of law, and by denying to plaintiffs the equal protection of the laws, and was, therefore, void and of no effect. Upon the case thus stated the plaintiffs asked a temporary, and a permanent injunction. . . .

The Superior Court for Cochise County sustained the demurrer and dismissed the complaint, and this judgment was affirmed by the Supreme Court of Arizona. . . .

The effect of this ruling is that, under the statute, loss may be inflicted upon the plaintiff's property and business by "picketing" in any form if violence be not used, and that, because no violence was shown or claimed, the campaign carried on, as described in the complaint and exhibits, did not unlawfully invade complainant's rights. . . .

The complaint and its exhibits make this case:

The defendants conspired to injure and destroy plaintiffs' business by inducing their theretofore willing patrons and would-be patrons not to patronize them. . . .

The result of this campaign was to reduce the business of the plaintiffs from more than $55,000 a year to one of $12,000.

Plaintiffs' business is a property right (*Duplex Printing Press Co. v. Deering,* 254 U.S. 443, 465) and free access for employees, owner and customers to his place of business is incident to such right. Intentional injury caused to either right or both by a conspiracy is a tort. . . .

A law which operates to make lawful such a wrong as is described in plaintiffs' complaint deprives the owner of the business and the premises of his property without due process, and can not be held valid under the Fourteenth Amendment. . . .

If, however, contrary to the construction which we put on the opinion of the Supreme Court of Arizona, it does not withhold from the plaintiffs all remedy for the wrongs they suffered but only the equitable relief of injunction, there still remains the question whether they are thus denied the equal protection of the laws. . . .

. . .[t]he plaintiffs in error would have had the right to an injunction against such a campaign as that conducted by the defendants in error, if it had been directed against the plaintiff's business and property in any kind of a controversy which was not a dispute between employer and former employees. . . .

This brings us to consider the effect in this case of that provision of the Fourteenth Amendment which forbids any State to deny to any person the equal protection of the laws. The clause is associated in the Amendment with the due process clause and it is customary to consider them together.. . .

The guaranty was aimed at undue favor and individual or class privilege, on the one hand, and at hostile discrimination or the oppression of inequality, on the other. It sought an equality of treatment of all persons, even though all enjoyed the protection of due process. Mr. Justice Field, delivering the opinion of this court in *Barbier v. Connolly,* 113 U.S. 27, 32, of the equality clause, said—"Class legislation, discriminating against some and favoring others, is prohibited, but legislation which, in carrying out a public purpose, is limited in its application, if within the sphere of its operation it affects alike all persons similarly situated, is not within the amendment.". . .

Mr. Justice Matthews, in *Yick Wo v. Hopkins,* 118 U.S. 356, 369, speaking for the court of both the due process and the equality clause of the Fourteenth Amendment, said:

"These provisions are universal in their application, to all persons within the territorial jurisdiction, without regard to any differences of race, of color, or of nationality; *and the equal protection of the laws is a pledge of the protection of equal laws."*. . .

With these views of the meaning of the equality clause, it does not seem possible to escape the conclusion that by. . . the Revised Statutes of Arizona, here relied on by the defendants, as construed by its Supreme Court, the plaintiffs have been deprived of the equal protection of the law.. . .

. . . Here is a direct invasion of the ordinary business and property rights of a person, unlawful when committed by any one, and remediable because of its otherwise irreparable character by equitable process, except when committed by ex-employees of the injured person. If this is not a denial of the equal protection of the laws, then it is hard to conceive what would be.. . .

. . . Classification is the most inveterate of our reasoning processes. We can scarcely think or speak without consciously or unconsciously exercising it. It must therefore obtain in and determine legislation; but it must regard real resemblances and real differences between things, and persons, and class them in accordance with their pertinence to the purpose in hand. Classificaiton like the one with which we are here dealing is said to be the development of the philosophic thought of the world and is opening the door to legalized experiment. When fundamental rights are thus attempted to be taken away, however, we may well subject such experiment to attentive judgment. The Constitution was intended, its very purpose was, to prevent experimentation with the fundamental rights of the individual. We said through Mr. Justice Brewer, in *Muller v. Oregon,* 208 U.S. 412, that "it is the peculiar value of a written constitution that it places in unchanging form limitations upon legislative action, and thus gives a permanence and stability to popular government which otherwise would be lacking.". . .

We conclude that the demurrer in this case should have been overruled, the defendants required to answer, and that if the evidence sustained the averments of the complaint, an injunction should issue as prayed.... The judgment of the Supreme Court of Arizona is reversed.

Mr. Justice Holmes, dissenting.

The dangers of a delusive exactness in the application of the Fourteenth Amendment have been adverted to... Delusive exactness is a source of fallacy throughout the law. By calling a business "property" you make it seem like land, and lead up to the conclusion that a statute cannot substantially cut down the advantages of ownership existing before the statute was passed. An established business no doubt may have pecuniary value and commonly is protected by law against various unjustified injuries. But you cannot give it definiteness of contour by calling it a thing. It is a course of conduct and like other conduct is subject to substantial modificaiton according to time and circumstances both in itself and in regard to what shall justify doing it a harm. I cannot understand the notion that it would be unconstitutional to authorize boycotts and the like in aid of the employees' or the employers' interest by statute when the same result has been reached constitutionally without statute by Courts with Whom I agree. See *The Hamilton*, 207 U.S. 398, 404. In this case it does not even appear that the business was not created under the laws as they now are. *Denny v. Bennett*, 128 U.S. 489.

I think further that the selection of the class of employers and employees for special treatment, dealing with both sides alike, is beyond criticism on principles often asserted by this Court. And especially I think that without legalizing the conduct complained of the extraordinary relief by injunction may be denied to the class. Legislation may begin where an evil begins. If, as many intelligent people believe, there is more danger that the injunction will be abused in labor cases than elsewhere I can feel no doubt of the power of the legislature to deny it in such cases....

I must add one general consideration. There is nothing that I more deprecate than the use of the Fourteenth Amendment beyond the absolute compulsion of its words to prevent the making of social experiments that an important part of the community desires, in the insulated chambers afforded by the several States, even though the experiments may seem futile or even noxious to me and to those whose judgment I most respect. I agree with the more elaborate expositions of my brothers Pitney and Brandies and in their conclusion that the judgment should be affirmed.

Taft and Court Reform
1922

Although Chief Justice William Howard Taft was a staunch conservative on economic and social issues, he came to the Supreme Court intent on radically reforming the federal courts. He wished to modernize the system by eliminating outmoded procedures, automatic appeals to the Supreme Court, and clogged dockets. In order to promote his program he made numerous speeches across the nation, wrote articles in legal journals, and gave testimony on behalf of court reform before the House and Senate Judiciary committees. In a speech before the Bar Association of Chicago, "Three Needed Steps of Progress," he outlined his plan in great detail and pled for assistance in gaining passage of legislation which would accomplish his aims. William Howard Taft, "Three Needed Steps of Progress," *American Bar Association Journal* 8 (January 1922): 34-36.

. . . I would like to say something on three steps of progress which I hope may be taken in the near future to make the administration of justice in the Federal Courts more expeditious, and therefore more useful. In what I say, I speak for myself only and not for my colleagues. I presume it is a compliment to the Federal Courts for Congress and the people to seek to increase their jurisdiction. Whatever be the motive, it is certain that their jurisdiction has been vastly enlarged. Dormant powers of the Federal Government under the Constitution have been made active, and the Federal Government has poked its nose into a great many fields where it was not known before, for lack of Congressional initiation. In the first place, the giving to the Federal trial courts jurisdiction of suits involving federal questions without regard to citizenship was one addition. Then the enactment of the Interstate Commerce law and the casting upon Federal Courts the revisory power over the action of the Interstate Commerce Commission was another. Then, the Anti Trust Law, the Railroad Safety Appliance Law, the Adamson Law, the Federal Trade Commission Law, the Clayton Act, the Federal Employers' Liability Law, the Pure Food Law, the Narcotic Law, the White Slave Law and other acts, and finally the Eighteenth Amendment and the Volsted Act, have expanded the civil and criminal jurisdiction of the Federal Courts of first instance to such an extent that unless something is done, they are likely to be swamped, and delay is a denial of justice. Examination of the statistics of cases brought and tried and personal conference with judges leave no doubt that an increase of the judges of first instance in the Federal system is absolutely necessary. The existing arrangement of courts and districts in nine circuits is a matter of long standing. The arrangement has really been outgrown, and ought to be changed. But it is of such age, and the country has grown so used to it, that a re-arrangement would involve much discussion and arouse much opposition. If the needed increase of the judiciary were to be halted until that was settled, it would involve much delay and imperil immediate relief.

It seems likely that the two bills will result in a compromise, that the number of district judges at large will be reduced to perhaps half the original number, and that the fixed district judges will also be reduced.

The bills are alike in what seems to me to be a most important new feature in the Federal Judiciary. Provision is made for annual or more frequent meetings at the call of the Chief Justice, of the senior circuit judges of the nine circuits, in Washington or some other convenient place, to take up the question from year to year of the arrears of business, and after conference to agree and recommend a plan, thereafter to be carried out in the discretion of those in authority, for the massing of the extra judicial force at strategic points, and thus overcoming the enemy known as "arrears in business."

You in Chicago have had your city courts under some such organization as this, and I understand that it has worked well. There is not the slightest reason why into judicial work we should not introduce some simple and primary principles of business dispatch. When we have too much work in one district and too little in another, we should use the judge whose work is done, to help out the man in the other district whose work is too heavy for him to get through. Judges should be independent in their judgments, but they should be subject to some executive direction as to the use of their services, and somebody should be made responsible for the whole business of the United States. This council of the Chief Justice and the senior circuit judges of the nine circuits is as well adapted to do this work as anybody that can be suggested. I think the country is thoroughly imbued with the idea that there must be some measures adopted, and that an increase in the judges is essential. So far as I can observe, both Houses are in accord as to the suggestion of some kind of executive administration with reference to putting the judges of the country where they can do the most good.

The second step that should be taken is a simplification of the procedure in all cases in the Federal trial courts. We still retain in those courts the distinction between suits at law, suits in equity and suits in admiralty. The Constitution refers specifically to them, and in deference to that separation in the Constitution, the distinction is preserved in the Federal practice. It seems to me that there is no reason why this distinction, so far as actual practice is concerned, should not be wholly abolished, and what are now suits in law, in equity and in admiralty, should not be conducted in the form of one civil action, just as is done in the code states. Of course it will be necessary in such a system to preserve the substantial differences in procedure and right which are insured by the Constitution and are of the utmost value in the administration of justice. Of course the right of jury trial secured by the Constitution in civil cases involving over $20 must be preserved and can be without difficulty, and can be reconciled with the right of a man under equity procedure to certain forms of more satisfactory remedy, preventive and otherwise. What can be done has been done in Great Britain, and the simplicity of the practice there reflects on the enterprise of lawyers on this side of the water. They have accomplished what they have done on that side by laying down certain general principles and then vesting the courts of justice with the power by rules to prescribe the details of the procedure. This is done now with us in courts of admiralty and courts of equity, in which the framing of the rules is entrusted to the Supreme Court. All that is needed is to vest the same power in the Supreme Court with reference to the rules at common law and then to give that court the power to blend them into a code, which shall make the procedure the same in all and as simple as possible....

It is thought that to introduce a new system would make it awkward for lawyers and litigants used to a particular state procedure. This I conceive is not a sound objection, because the plan is to make the system so simple that it needs no special knowledge to master it. It is for the plaintiff to write a letter to the court and state his case, and if he has not amplified it enough to make the case, to give him the opportunity in the course of the proceeding to put in the facts which are lacking, if he can do so.

It is not a delegation of great power to the Supreme Court. The court in formulating the rules will of course consult a committee of the Bar and committee of the trial judges. Congress can lay down the fundamental principles that should govern and then the court can fill out the details. The procedure in the Federal Courts should be a model for all other courts. The administration of justice has been under attack and subjected to proper criticism. The legislatures have been largely to blame and not the judges engaged in carrying out what the legislatures have put into the statutes. Reforms of this character should begin in Congress and the state legislatures, and I am glad to say that I think Congress is ready to undertake the reform, if it be clearly outlined.

The third step to be taken is a change in the jurisdiction of the Supreme Court. In the first place, the jurisdiction of the Supreme Court is defined in a great many different statutes and special acts, and it has really become almost a trap to catch the unwary. Some of us are working on a proposed bill to simplify the statement of the jurisdiction of the Supreme Court and have it embraced in one statute.

The second and the moving cause of the proposed reform is the feeling that many have, that there must be some method adopted by which the cases brought before that Court shall be reduced in number, and yet the Court may retain full jurisdiction to pronounce the last word on every important issue under the Constitution and the statutes of the United States and on all important questions of general law with respect to which there is a lack of uniformity in the intermediate Federal courts of appeal. Much has already been done in this way by reducing the number of cases in which a writ of error or appeal in the Supreme Court is a matter of right, and by submitting other cases to the preliminary selection by the Court of those which it should hear. A Supreme Court where there are intermediate courts of appeal is not a tribunal constituted to secure, as its ultimate end, justice to the immediate parties. They have had all that they have a right to claim when they have had two courts in which to have adjudicated their controversy. The use of the Supreme Court is merely to maintain uniformity of decision for the various courts of appeal, to pass on constitutional and other important questions for the purpose of making the law clearer for the general public. Litigants, therefore, can not complain where they have had their two chances that there should be reserved to the discretion of the Supreme Court to say whether the issue between them is of sufficient importance to justify a hearing of it in the Supreme Court. The Supreme Court already has a wide jurisdiction by certiorari. That Court considers carefully the character of each case in which a certiorari is applied for. The examination of records for this purpose is part of the hard work of the Court, and the Bar ought not to suppose when a motion for certiorari is submitted that the Court does not give the motion the most careful consideration. This power enables the Court to get rid of a very large mass of cases that have but little importance save as between the parties, some of which are frivolous, many of which involve no principle that needs settlement by the court of final appeal because already well settled. . . .

The three reforms, therefore, to which I invite your attention are, first, an increase in the judicial force in the trial Federal courts, and an organization and effective distribution of the force by a council of judges; second, simplicity of procedure in the trial Federal courts; and, third, a reduction in the obligatory jurisdiction of the Supreme Court and an increse in the field of its discretionary jurisdiction by certiorari. It thus will remain the supreme revisory tribunal, but will be given sufficient control of the number and character of the cases which come before it, to enable it to remain the one Supreme Court and to keep up with its work. I venture to ask the members of the Bar of the United States and of this important Bar to aid the cause of justice by promoting the legislation which I have attempted to describe.

There is no field of governmental action so important to the people as our courts, and there is nothing in those courts so essential to the doing of justice as the prompt dispatch of buisiness and the elimination from procedure of such requirements as will defeat the ends of justice through technicality and delay. While the Bar and the Bench are really much less responsible for delays in legal procedure than the public are likely to think, the very fact that they are popularly supposed to be responsible should make us act with energy to justify the existence of our profession and the maintenance of courts.

Railroad Commission of Wisconsin v. Chicago, Burlington, and Quincy Railway Co.
257 U.S. 563
1922

The Transportation Act (1920) returned the railroads to private ownership and operation after three years of wartime government control. It also created a Railroad Labor Board to handle labor problems and to strengthen the Interstate Commerce Commission's power to set rates and oversee railroad financing. The statute, particularly the right of the commission to regulate intrastate rates, was immediately challenged. Chief Justice William Howard Taft, speaking for the Court, upheld the constitutionality of the act and argued that it was valid for the Interstate Commerce Commission to make sure that the railroads obtained a fair income. Thus when low intrastate rates, even when not in direct competition with interstate rates, undermined profits, it was necessary for the Commission to revise intrastate rates upward. This meant that for all intents and purposes the commission could fix all railroad rates, and the Court recognized, once again, the right of the national government to control virtually all aspects of commerce.

The Commission's order, interference with which was enjoined by the District Court, effects the removal of the unjust discrimination found to exist against persons in interstate commerce, and against interstate commerce, by fixing a minimum for intrastate passenger fares in Wisconsin at 3.6 cents per mile per passenger....

We have two questions to decide.

First. Do the intrastate passenger fares work undue prejudice against persons in interstate commerce, such as to justify a horizontal increase to them all?

Second. Are these intrastate fares an undue discrimination against interstate commerce as a whole which it is the duty of the Commission to remove?...

The order in this case...is much wider than the orders made in the proceeding following the *Shreveport* and *Illinois Central Cases*. There, as here, the report of the Commission showed discrimination against persons and localities at border points, and the orders were extended to include all rates or fares from all points in the State to border points. But this order is not so restricted. It includes fares between all interior points although neither may be near the border and the fares between them may not work a discrimination against interstate travellers at all. Nothing in the precedents cited justifies an order affecting all rates of a general description when it is clear that this would include many rates not within the proper class or the reason of the order....

Intrastate rates and the income from them must play a most important part in maintaining an adequate national railway system. Twenty per cent of the gross freight receipts of the railroads of the country are from intrastate traffic, and fifty per cent of the passenger receipts. The ratio of the gross intrastate revenue to the interstate revenue is a little less than one to three. If the rates, on which such receipts are based, are to be fixed at a substantially lower level than in interstate traffic, the share which the intrastate traffic will contribute will be proportionately less....

It is objected here, as it was in the *Shreveport Case,* that orders of the Commission which raise the intrastate rates to a level of the interstate structure violate the specific proviso of the original Interstate Commerce Act repeated in the amending acts, that the Commission is not to regulate traffic wholly within a State. To this, the same answer must be made as was made in the *Shreveport Case* (234 U.S. 342, 358), that such orders as to intrastate traffic are merely incidental to the regulation of interstate commerce and necessary to its efficiency. Effective control of the one must embrace some control over the other in view of the blending of both in actual operation. The same rails and the same cars carry both. The same men conduct them. Commerce is a unit and does not regard state lines, and while, under the Constitution, interstate and intrastate commerce are ordinarily subject to regulation by different sovereignties, yet when they are so mingled together that the supreme authority, the Nation, cannot exercise complete effective control over interstate commerce without incidental regulation of intrastate commerce, such incidental regulation is not an invasion of state authority or a violation of the proviso....

...Congress in its control of its interstate commerce system is seeking in the Transportation Act to make the system adequate to the needs of the country by securing for it a reasonable compensatory return for all the work it does. The States are seeking to use that same system for intrastate traffic. That entails large duties and expenditures on the interstate commerce system which may burden it unless compensation is received for the intrastate business reasonably proportionate to that for the interstate business. Congress as the dominant controller of interstate commerce may, therefore, restrain undue limitation of the earning power of the interstate commerce system in doing state work. The affirmative power of Congress in developing interstate commerce agencies is clear.... In such development, it can impose any reasonable condition on a State's use of interstate carriers for intrastate commerce it deems necessary or desirable. This is because of the supremacy of the national power in this field.

Bailey v. Drexel Furniture Co.
259 U.S. 20
1922

The Keating-Owen Child Labor Law (1916) was struck down by the Supreme Court in *Hammer v. Dagenhart* (1918) because the movement of products manufactured by child labor could not be prohibited in interstate commerce. Congress therefore enacted a second Child Labor Law based on the federal government's taxing power instead of the commerce clause of the Constitution. The law laid a tax of ten percent upon the net profits of any business enterprise employing child labor.

Proponents of antichild labor legislation were disappointed for a second time when, in *Bailey v. Drexel Furniture Co.,* the Court voided the second act. Chief Justice William Howard Taft, speaking for the majority, declared that both congressional actions had attempted to regulate a matter reserved to the states; while the first act had abused the commerce power, the second had violated the taxing power. In short, Taft found that it was proper to use taxation for the purpose of regulation, even though there were numerous federal precedents in taxes imposed on state bank notes, oleomargarine, and narcotics.

. . . The law is attacked on the ground that it is a regulation of the employment of child labor in the States—an exclusively state function under the Federal Constitution and within the reservations of the Tenth Amendment. It is defended on the ground that it is a mere excise tax levied by the Congress of the United States under its broad power of taxation conferred by . . . Article I, of the Federal Constitution. We must construe the law and interpret the intent and meaning of Congress from the language of the act. The words are to be given their ordinary meaning unless the context shows that they are differently used. Does this law impose a tax with only that incidental restraint and regulation which a tax must inevitably involve? Or does it regulate by the use of the so-called tax as a penalty? If a tax, it is clearly an excise. If it were an excise on a commodity or other thing of value we might not be permitted under previous decisions of this court to infer solely from its heavy burden that the act intends a prohibtion instead of a tax. But this act is more. It provides a heavy exaction for a departure from a detailed and specified course of conduct in business. That course of business is that employers shall employ in mines and quarries, children of an age greater than sixteen years; in mills and factories, children of an age greater than fourteen years, and shall prevent children of less than sixteen years in mills and factories from working more than eight hours a day or six days in the week. If an employer departs from this prescribed course of business, he is to pay to the Government one-tenth of his entire net income in the business for a full year. The amount is not to be proportioned in any degree to the extent or frequency of the departures, but is to be paid by the employer in full measure whether he employs five hundred children for a year, or employes only one for a day. Moreover, if he does not know the child is within the named age limit, he is not to pay; that is to say, it is only where he knowingly departs from the prescribed course that payment is to be exacted.... In the light of these features of the act, a court must be blind not to see that the so-called tax is imposed to stop the employment of children within the age limits prescribed. Its prohibitory and regulatory effect and purpose are palpable. All others can see and understands this. How can we properly shut our minds to it?

It is the high duty and function of this court in cases regularly brought to its bar to decline to recognize or enforce seeming laws of Congress, dealing with subjects not entrusted to Congress but left or committed by the supreme law of the land to the control of the States. We can not avoid the duty even though it require us to refuse to give effect to legislation designed to promote the highest good. The good sought in unconstitutional legislation is an insidious feature because it leads citizens and legislators of good purpose to promote it without thought of the serious breach it will make in the ark of our covenant or the harm which will come from breaking down recognized standards. In the maintenance of local self government, on the one hand, and the national power, on the other, our country has been able to endure and prosper for near a century and a half.

Out of a proper respect for the acts of a coordinate branch of the Government, this court has gone far to sustain taxing acts as such, even though there has been ground for suspecting from the weight of the tax it was intended to destroy its subject. But, in the act before us, the presumption of validity cannot prevail, because the proof of the contrary is found on the very face of its provisions. Grant the validity of this law, and all that Congress would need to do, hereafter, in seeking to take over to its control any one of the great number of subjects of public interest, jurisdiction of which the States have never parted with, and which are reserved to them by the Tenth Amendment, would be to enact a detailed measure of complete regulation of the subject and enforce it by a so-called tax upon departures from it. To give such magic to the word "tax" would be to break down all constitutional limitations of the powers of Congress and completely wipe out the sovereignty of the States....

For the reasons given, we must hold the Child Labor Tax Law invalid and the judgment of the District Court is affirmed.

Pierce Butler:
Friend of Intolerance
1922

When Pierce Butler, a railroad attorney, was nominated to the Supreme Court in 1922, liberals were deeply concerned about the position he would take in valuation cases stemming from the Federal Railroad Valuation Act (1913). Equally troubling was his part in the dismissal of several University of Minnesota professors. Butler, who was famous for his defense of railroads in the Supreme Court, was also successful in saving them money by convincing the Interstate Commerce Commission to raise the legal value of railroad property so that his clients could charge higher rates. While holding the office of regent at the University of Minnesota he attacked the faculty on numerous occasions, and during the First World War he had several professors discharged because of their work on railroad valuations, the promotion of municipal ownership of street railways and alleged pro-German sympathies. Progressive senators such as George Norris and Robert LaFollette voiced their disaproval of Butler's nomination and Samuel Gompers, president of the American Federation of Labor, asserted that Butler was a reactionary who should not be sent to the high court. In the following article, we see some of the liberal animus directed toward Butler in his roles of corporation lawyer and university regent. M.H. Hedges, "Pierce Butler: Friend of Intolerance," *The Nation* 115 (December 13, 1922): 660-61.

News of Pierce Butler's nomination to the Supreme Court of the United States caught him in a characteristic posture. With a number of associates he had just filed a brief before the State Supreme Court asking dismissal of a contempt case brought by the city of Minneapolis against officers and directors of the Minneapolis Street Railway Company. The aim of the city, when the lower court decided in its favor, was to get certain records to show what the officers had done with a mysterious $227,000 spent for alleged political purposes. Dispatches from Washington said that Butler had been chosen by the President because he was a "Democrat and a man of liberal views."

Be it said at the outset that Butler has never been put in a class with Attorney General Daugherty, another unpopular appointment of President Harding, even by his most outspoken critics. He has never been a lobbyist for corporations, and though he has been known as the attorney for the Great Northern Railway for years,he has never been on a salary. He is admitted even by his enemies to be the foremost corporation lawyer of the Northwest. What is it, then, that has drawn the fire of all kinds of people against him? It is a quality that endears him to his friends and makes him not so much hated by, as hateful to, his victims—a kind of intellectual brutality. Pierce Butler is a man physically big, and a burly man intellectually, and he carries this quality into all human relations. He has not done the work of corporations any more thoroughly than other men but he has done it with more consuming zeal. As a regent of the University of Minnesota he has not used the whip and gag with more rigor than others of his colleagues, but here gain he has applied them with an inquisitorial intolerance that has made men unforgetting when they were the recipients of his attentions. And it is this peculiar attribute that men consider unbecoming the judicial mind. A professor at the university, in a letter to Senator Ladd, protesting against his confirmation by the Senate, declared: "Everything seems to indicate that we have here a personality of intense and unmitigated prejudices, accustomed to permitting these prejudices a free and unchecked expression in word and deed, even to the point of offensiveness in manner and attitude."

The "American Bar," the Who's Who of the legal profession, lists the firm of Butler, Mitchell, and Doherty, St. Paul, thus: "Firm is counsel for St. Paul Gas Light Company; Capital National Bank; St. Paul Fire and Marine Insurance Company; Providence Life and Trust Company; Canadian Northern; New York Central Lines." In all his long career it is not recorded that Butler ever championed an unpaying or vicarious cause. His usual fee is reputed to be $1,000 a day. He has the distinction of exacting through court procedure the largest bill for damages from the street-car company ever recorded, about 10 years ago—that is all. His other achievements as a lawyer overshadow this. He represented the Great Northern Railroad and other Hill lines before the Interstate Comerce Commission, which hearing resulted in the present enormous valuation of nineteen billion dollars for the railroads of the nation. He represented Northwestern railroads in 1907, in the famous Minnesota rate cases, involving the State's right to regulate intra-State traffic. He represented the Minneapolis Gas Light Company in 1920 when that company went into technical receivership on plea of a subsidiary of the United Gas Company of Philadelphia of which the local gas company is also a subsidiary. The receivership wiped out a contract favorable to the city and boosted rates from 80 cents to $1.31 per unit. When the Minneapolis Steel and Machinery Company, during the war, refused to abide by the decision of the War Labor Board and grant a wage adjustment to its workers, Butler defended the corporation. And finally when John Meintz, an old farmer of Luverne, Minnesota, a stockholder in a Nonpartisan League weekly newspaper, was seized by thirty business men and delivered across the State's border to a mob, where he was tarred and feathered, it was Butler who defended the thirty respectable citizens with the plea that they were seeking to protect the old farmer.

This legal record throws into eclipse the work he has done for the Canadian Government in evaluating the Grand Trunk lines, or the shadowy service he performed for Taft in prosecuting the packers. The man in the street says today: "Yes, Butler is a trust-buster just as Kellogg is a trust-buster."

This corporation lawyer has come into contact with the public chiefly as a member of the board of regents of the University of Minnesota. He has held office through three administrations, and it is a known fact that his relations with each of the three presidents were strained. Butler as regent incarnates the spirit of private ownership of public institutions. He is credited with treating university presidents and deans as his particular employees, responsible to him personally for conduct of the various schools. It is reported that Dr. L.D. Coffman, the present president, resigned recently for a brief period when Butler sought to preempt his power to appoint instructors. Professor William Schaper, a national authority in the field of political science, relieved of his professorship during the war on the charge of pro-Germanism, went to Washington to protest against the Senate's confirmation of Butler's appointment. Professor Schaper was a believer in municipal ownership of public utilities. When he was dismissed Butler refused him hearing. Stanley Rypins, a Rhodes scholar, a popular instructor in English, also credits Butler with his discharge. Rypins was a member of the State branch of the Committee of Forty-eight. At regent meetings Butler with peculiar zest inquires into the qualifications of prospective instructors, prying into their political views, "Are they generally sound?" is the formula he and his colleagues use. A.W. Rankin, professor of education, retired, announced publicly that he would not oppose Butler's appointment because he was so glad to see him off the board of regents.

Before the news of his appointment reached Minnesota, liberal members of the new legislature were preparing to refuse him confirmation as regent if Governor Preus should send his name forward for approval. The Minneapolis City Council passed a resolution protesting against Butler's appointment to the bench on the ground that he would, as justice, decide against the city cases which he fought in lower courts in behalf of corporations.

In a few days it may be that the doors of the Supreme Court chamber will close behind Associate Justice Butler. He is fifty-five years old. Is it likely that the mere donning of judicial robes will change the inquisitorial zeal with which he has opposed the opinions of others, or change the intellectual habits of a lifetime formed in the service of corporations?

Adkins v. Children's Hospital
261 U.S. 525
1923

By 1917, most states had placed limitations on the hours of women industrial workers, and about ten states mandated minimum wages for women. Congress also enacted a law in 1918, for women workers in the District of Columbia which established, through a District Wage Board, a maximum on hours and a minimum on wages. The Supreme Court, however, in a 5-3 opinion, declared the federal statute void as a violation of due process and the Fifth Amendment. Justice George Sutherland, speaking for the Court, stressed that minimum wage laws interfered with the freedom of contract, except in those cases where businesses were affected with a public interest. He also implied that the Nineteenth Amendment, granting the vote to women, had nullified the constitutional basis for special legislation for women and generally attacked minimum wage legislation as economically and socially unsound. Both William Howard Taft and Oliver Wendell Holmes wrote vigorous dissents in *Adkins v. Children's Hospital* and, curiously, Taft more bitterly attacked Sutherland; he particularly protested against the majority's inclination to strike down acts which did not coincide with the economic beliefs of the Justices. *Adkins* was an important precedent for other Conservative Court attacks on labor and social legislation until the 1930s.

The question presented for determination by these appeals is the constitutionality of the Act of September 19, 1918, providing for the fixing of minimum wages for women and children in the District of Columbia. . . .

. . .[I]t is declared that the purposes of the act are "to protect the women and minors of the District from conditions detrimental to their health and morals, resulting from wages which are inadequate to maintain decent standards of living; and the Act in each of its provisions and in its entirety shall be interpreted to effectuate these purposes.". . .

The statute now under consideration is attacked upon the ground that it authorizes an unconstitutional interference with the freedom of contract included within the guaranties of the due process clause of the Fifth Amendment. That the right to contract about one's affairs is a part of the liberty of the individual protected by this clause, is settled by the decisions of this Court and is no longer open to question. . . .

Within this liberty are contracts of employment of labor. In making such contracts, generally speaking, the parties have an equal right to obtain from each other the best thems they can as the result of private bargaining. . . .

There is, of course, no such thing as absolute freedom of contract. It is subject to a great variety of restraints. But freedom of contract is, nevertheless, the general rule and restraint the exception; and the exercise of legislative authority to abridge it can be justified only by the existence of exceptional circumstances. Whether these circumstances exist in the present case constitutes the question to be answered. It will be helpful to this end to review some of the decisions where the interference has been upheld and consider the grounds upon which they rest.

(1) *Those dealing with statutes fixing rates and charges to be exacted by businesses impressed with a public interest.* There are many cases, but it is sufficient to cite *Munn v. Illinois,* 94 U.S. 113. The power here rests upon the ground that where property is devoted to a public use the owner thereby, in effect, grants to the public an interest in the use which may be controlled by the public for the common good to the extent of the interest thus created. It is upon this theory that these statutes have been upheld and, it may be noted in passing, so upheld even in respect of their incidental and injurious or destructive effect upon preexisting contracts. See *Louisville & Nashville R.R. Co. v. Mottley,* 219 U.S. 467. In the case at bar the statute does not depend upon the existence of a public interest in any business to be affected, and this class of cases may be laid aside as inapplicable.

(2) *Statutes relating to contracts for the performance of public work.* Atkin v. Kansas, 191 U.S. 207; Heim v. McCall, 239 U.S. 175; Ellis v. United States, 206 U.S. 246. These cases sustain such statutes as depending, not upon the right to condition private contracts, but upon the right of the government to prescribe the conditions upon which it will permit work of a public character to be done for it, or, in the case of a State, for its municipalities. We may, therefore, in like manner, dismiss these decisions from consideration as inapplicable.

(3) *Statutes prescribing the character, methods and time for payment of wages.* Under this head may be included *McLean v. Arkansas,* 211 U.S. 539, sustaining a state statute requiring coal to be measured for payment of miners' wages before screening; *Knoxville Iron Co. v. Harbison,* 183 U.S. 13, sustaining a Tennessee statute requiring the redemption in cash of store orders issued in payment of wages; *Erie R.R. Co. v. Williams,* 233 U.S. 685, upholding a statute regulating the time within which wages shall be paid to employees in certain specified industries; and other cases sustaining statutes of like import and effect. In none of the statutes thus sustained, was the liberty of employer or employee to fix the amount of wages the one was willing to pay and the other willing to receive interfered with. Their tendency and purpose was to prevent unfair and perhaps fraudulent methods in the payment of wages and in no sense can they be said to be, or to furnish a precedent for, wage-fixing statutes.

(4) *Statutes fixing hours of labor.* It is upon this class that the gratest

emphasis is laid in argument and therefore, and because such cases approach most nearly the line of principle applicable to the statute here involved, we shall consider them more at length. In some instances the statute limited the hours of labor for men in certain occupations and in others it was confined in its application to women. No statute has thus far been brought to the attention of this Court which by its terms, applied to all occupations. In *Holden v. Hardy,* 169 U.S. 366, the Court considered an act of the Utah legislature, restricting the hours of labor in mines and smelters. This statute was sustained as a legitimate exercise of the police power, on the ground that the legislature had determined that these particular employments, when too long pursued, were injurious to the health of the employees, and that, as there were reasonable grounds for supporting this determination on the part of the legislature, its decision in that respect was beyond the reviewing power of the federal courts.

That this constituted the basis of the decisions is emphasized by the subsequent decision in *Lochner v. New York,* 198 U.S. 45, reviewing a state statute which restricted the employment of all persons in bakeries to ten hours in any one day. The Court referred to *Holden v. Hardy, supra,* and, declaring it to be inapplicable, held the statute unconstitutional as an unreasonable, unnecessary and arbitrary interference with the liberty of contract and therefore void under the Constitution....

If now, in the light furnished by the foregoing exceptions to the general rule forbidding legislative interference with freedom of contract, we examine and analyze the statute in question, we shall see that it differs from them in every material respect. It is not a law dealing with any business charged with a public interest or with public work, or to meet and tide over a temporary emergency. It has nothing to do with the character, methods or periods of wage payments. It does not prescribe hours of labor or conditions under which labor is to be done. It is not for the protection of persons under legal disability or for the prevention of fraud. It is simply and exclusively a price-fixing law, confined to adult women (for we are not now considering the provisions relating to minors), who are legally as capable of contracting for themselves as men. It forbids two parties having lawful capacity—under penalties as to the employer—to freely contract with one another in respect of the price for which one shall render service to the other private employment where both are willing, perhaps anxious, to agree, even though the consequence may be to oblige one to surrender a desirable engagement and the other to dispense with the services of a desirable employee. The price fixed by the board need have no relation to the capacity or earning power of the employee, the number of hours which may happen to constitute the day's work, the character of the place where the work is to. be done, or the circumstances or surroundings of the employment; and, while it has no other basis to support its validity than the assumed necessities of the employee, it takes no account of any independent resources she may have. It is based wholly on the opinions of the members of the board and their advissers—perhaps an average of their opinions, if they do not precisely agree—as to what will be necessary to provide a living for a woman, keep her in health and preserve her morals. It applies to any and every occupation in the District, without regard to its nature or the character of the work.

The standard furnished by the statute for the guidance of the board is so vague as to be impossible of practical application with any reasonable degree of accuracy. What is sufficient to supply the necessary cost of living for a woman worker and maintain her in good health and protect her morals is obviously not a precise or unvarying sum—not even approximately so. The amount will depend upon a variety of circumstances: the individual temperament, habits of thirft, care, ability to buy necessaries intelligently, and whether the woman live alone or with her family. To those who practice economy, a given sum will afford comfort, while to those of contrary habit the same sum will be wholly inadequate. The cooperative economies of the family group are not taken into account though they constitute an important consideration in estimating the cost of living, for it is obvious that the individual expense will be less in the case of a member of a family than in the case of one living alone. The relation between earnings and morals is not capable of standardization. It cannot be shown that well paid women safeguard their morals more carefully than those who are poorly paid. Morality rests upon other considerations than wages; and there is, certainly, no such prevalent connection between the two as to justify a broad attempt to adjust the latter with reference to the former. As a means of safeguarding morals the attempted classification, in our opinion, is without reeasonable basis. No distinction can be made between women who work for others and those who do not; nor is there ground for distinction between women and men, for, certainly, if women require a minimum wage to preserve their morals men require it to preserve their honesty. For these reasons, and others which might be stated, the inquiry in respect of the necessary cost of living and of the income necessary to preserve health and morals, presents an individual and not a composite question, and must be answered for each individual considered by herself and not by a general formula prescribed by a statutory bureau....

The law takes account of the necessities of only one party to the contract. It ignores the necessities of the employer by compelling him to pay not less than a certain sum, not only whether the employee is capable of earning it, but irrespective of the ability of his business to sustain the burden, generously leaving him, of course, the privilege of abandoning his business as an alternative for going on at a loss. Within the limits of the minimum sum, he is precluded, under penalty of fine and imprisonment, from adjusting compensaiton to the differing merits of his employees. It compels him to pay at least the sum fixed in any event, because the employee needs it, but requires no service of equivalent value from the employee. It therefore undertakes to solve but one-half of the problem. The other half is the establishment of a corresponding standard of efficiency, and this forms no part of the policy of the legislation, although in practice the former half without the latter must lead to ultimate failure, in accordance with the inexorable law that no one can continue indefinitely to take our more than he puts in without ultimately exhausting the supply. The law is not confined to the great and powerful employers but embraces those whose bargaining power may be as weak as that of the employee. It takes no account of periods of stress and business depression, of crippling losses, which may leave the employer himself without adequate means of livelihood. To the extent that the sum fixed exceeds the fair value of the services rendered, it amounts to a compulsory exaction from the employer for the support of a partially indigent person, for whose condition there rests upon him no peculiar responsibility, and therefore, in effect, arbitrarily shifts to his shoulders a burden which, if it belongs to anybody, belongs to society as a whole.

The feature of this statute which, perhaps more than any other, puts upon it the stamp of invalidity is that it exacts from the employer an arbitrary payment for a purpose and upon a basis having no causal connection with his business, or the contract or the work the employee engages to do. The declared basis, as already pointed out, is not the value of the service rendered, but the extraneous circumstance that the employee needs to get a prescribed sum of money to insure her subsistence, health and morals. The ethical right of every worker, man or woman, to a living wage may be conceded. One of the declared and important purposes of trade organizations is to secure it. And with that principle and with every legitimate effort to realize it in fact, no one can quarrel; but the fallacy of the proposed method of attaining it is that it assumes that every employer is bound at all events to furnish it. . . .

It is said that great benefits have resulted from the operation of such statutes, not alone in the District of Columbia but in the several States, where they have been in force. A mass of reports, opinions of special observers and students of the subject, and the like, has been brought before us in support of this statement, all of which we have found interesting but only mildly persuasive. . . .

Finally, it may be said that if, in the interest of the public welfare, the police power may be invoked to justify the fixing of a minimum wage, it may, when the public welfare is thought to require it, be invoked to justify a maximum wage. The power to fix high wages connotes, by like course of reasoning, the power to fix low wages. If, in the face of the guaranties of the Fifth Amendment, this form of legislation shall be legally justified, the field for the operation of the police power will have been widened to a great and dangerous degree. If, for example, in the opinion of future lawmakers, wages in the building trades shall become so high as to preclude people of ordinary means from building and owning homes, an authority which sustains the minimum wage will be invoked to support a maximum wage for building laborers and artisans, and the same argument which has been here urged to strip the employer of his constitutional liberty of contract in one direction will be utilized to strip the employee of his constitutional liberty of contract in the opposite direction. A wrong decision does not end with itself: it is a precedent, and, with the swing of sentiment, its bad influence may run from one extremity of the arc to the other.

It has been said that legislation of the kind now under review is required in the interest of social justice, for whose ends freedom of contract may lawfully be subjected to restraint. The liberty of the individual to do as he pleases, even in innocent matters, is not absolute. It must frequently yield to the common good, and the line beyond which the power of interference may not be pressed is neither definite nor unalterable but may be made to move, within limits not well defined, with changing need and circumstance. Any attempt to fix a rigid boundary would be unwise as well as futile. But, nevertheless, there are limits to the power, and when these have been passed, it becomes the plain duty of the courts in the proper exercise of their authority to so declare. To sustain the individual freedom of action contemplated by the Constitution, is not to strike down the common good but to exalt it; for surely the good of society as a whole cannot be better served than by the preservation against arbitrary restraint of the liberties of its constituent members.

It follows from what has been said that the act in question passes the limit prescribed by the Constitution, and, accordingly, the decrees of the court below are affirmed.

Mr. Justice Brandies took no part in the consideration or decision of these cases.

Mr. Chief Justice Taft, dissenting. . . .

Legislatures in limiting freedom of contract between employee and employer by a minimum wage proceed on the assumption that employees, in the class receiving least pay, are not upon a full level of equality of choice with their employer and in their necessitous circumstances are prone to accept pretty much anything that is offered. They are peculiarly subject to the overreaching of the harsh and greedy employer. The evils of the sweating system and of the long hours and low wages which are characteristic of it are well known. Now, I agree that it is a disputable question in the field of political economy how far a statuory requirement of maximum hours or minimum wages may be a useful remedy for these evils, and whether it may not make the case of the oppressed employee worse than it was before. But it is not the function of this Court to hold congressional acts invalid simply because they are passed to carry out economic views which the Court believes to be unwise or unsound. . . .

The right of the legislature under the Fifth and Fourteenth Amendments to limit the hours of employment on the score of health of the employee, it seems to me, has been firmly established. As to that, one would think the line had been pricked out so that it has become a well formulated rule....

However, the opinion herein does not overrule the *Bunting Case* in express terms, and therefore I assume that the conclusion in this case rests on the distinction between a minimum of wages and a maximum of hours in the limiting of liberty to contract. I regret to be at variance with the Court as to the substance of this distinction....

If it be said that long hours of labor have a more direct effect upon the health of the employee than the low wage, there is very respectable authority from close observers, disclosed in the record and in the literature on the subject quoted at length in the briefs, that they are equally harmful in this regard. Congress took this view and we can not say it was not warranted in so doing....

I am authorized to say that Mr. Justice Sanford concurs in this opinion.

Mr. Justice Holmes, dissenting.

The question in this case is the broad one, Whether Congress can establish minimum rates of wages for women in the District of Columbia with due provision for special circumstances, or whether we must say that Congress has no power to meddle with the matter at all. To me, notwithstanding the deference due to the prevailing judgment of the Court, the power of Congress seems absolutely free from doubt. The end, to remove conditions leading to ill health, immorality and the deterioration of the race, no one would deny to be within the scope of constitutional legislation. The means are means that have the approval of Congress, of many States, and of those governments from which we have learned our greatest lessons. When so many intelligent persons, who have studied the matter more than any of us can, have thought that the means are effective and are worth the price, it seems to me impossible to deny that the belief reasonably may be held by reasonable men. If the law encountered no other objection than that the means bore no relation to the end or that they cost too much I do not suppose that anyone would venture to say that it was bad. I agree, of course, that a law answering the foregoing requirements might be invalidated by specific provisions of the Constitution. For instance it might take private property without just compensation. But in the present instance the only objection that can be urged is found within the vague contours of the Fifth Amendment, prohibiting the depriving any person of liberty or property without due process of law. To that I turn.

The earlier decisions upon the same words in the Fourteenth Amendment began within our memory and went no farther than an unpretentious assertion of the liberty to follow the ordinary callings. Later that innocuous generality was expanded into the dogma, Liberty of Contract. Contract is not specially mentioned in the text that we have to construe. It is merely an example of doing what you want to do, embodied in the word liberty. But pretty much all law consists in forbidding men to do some things that they want to do, and contract is no more exempt from law than other acts.. . .

The criterion of constitutionality is not whether we believe the law to be for the public good. We certainly cannot be prepared to deny that a reasonable man reasonably might have that belief in view of the legislation of Great Britain, Victoria, and a number of the States of this Union. The belief is fortified by a very remarkable collection of documents submitted on behalf of the appellants, material here, I conceive, only as showing that the belief reasonably may be held. In Australia the power to fix a minimum for wages in the case of industrial disputes extending beyond the limits of any one State was given to a Court, and its President wrote a most interesting account of its operation. . . . If a legislature should adopt what he thinks the doctrine of modern economists of all schools, that "freedom of contract is a misnomer as applied to a contract between an employer and an ordinary individual employee,". . . I could not pronounce an opinion with which I agree impossible to be entertained by reasonable men. If the same legislature should acept his further opinion that industrial peace was best attained by the device of a Court having the above powers, I should not feel myself able to contradict it, or to deny that the end justified restrictive legislation quite as adcquately as beliefs concerning Sunday or exploded theories about usury. I should have my doubts, as I have them about this statute—but they would be whether the bill that has to be paid for every gain, although hidden as interstitial detriments, was not greater than the gain was worth: a matter that it is not for me to decide.

I am of opinion that the statute is valid and that the decree should be reversed.

Wolff Packing Co. v.
Court of Industrial Relations of Kansas
262 U.S. 522
1923

Since the 1870s, the Supreme Court had struggled with the difficult job of defining what constituted "public interest." Some Justices believed that the monopolist nature of certain businesses made them "special" enterprises subject to public regulation, but others justified federal action merely by the discovery of a "broad and definite public interest."

In *Wolff Packing Co. v. Court of Industrial Relations of Kansas* the Court concerned itself with the monopoly conception of public interest; the Justices invalidated a Kansas statute which declared that food, clothing, fuel, transportation, and public utility businesses were subject to regulation since they were affected with a public interest. Chief Justice William Howard Taft, speaking for a unanimous Court, argued that the state could not classify certain economic areas as subject to the principle of public interest by simply declaring that such an interest existed. He declared that a business was affected with a public interest when it was indispensable to the community, and if not regulated, the public could be subject to arbitrary treatment and exorbitant charges. In short, Taft's conception of the public interest suggested that public utilities were the only enterprises subject to public scrutiny.

The necessary postulate of the Industrial Court Act is that the State, representing the people, is so much interested in their peace, health and comfort that it may compel those engaged in the manufacture of food, and clothing, and the production of fuel, whether owners or workers, to continue in their business and employment on terms fixed by an agency of the State if they can not agree. Under the construction adopted by the State Supreme Court the act gives the Industrial Court authority to permit the owner or employer to go out of the business, if he shows that he can only continue on the terms fixed at such heavy loss that collapse will follow; but this privilege under the circumstances is generally illusory. *Block v. Hirsh,* 256 U.S. 135, 157. A laborer dissatisfied with his wages is permitted to quit, but he may not agree with his fellows to quit or combine with others to induce them to quit.

These qualifications do not change the essence of the act. It curtails the right of the employer on the one hand, and of the employee on the other, to contract about his affairs. This is part of the liberty of the individual protected by the guaranty of the due process clause of the Fourteenth Amendment.......

It is manifest from an examination of the cases cited...that the mere declaration by a legislature that a business is affected with a public interest is not conclusive of the question whether its attempted regulation on that ground is justified. The circumstances of its alleged change from the status of a private business and its freedom from regulation into one in which the public have come to have an interest are always a subject of judicial inquiry.
. . .

It has never been supposed, since the adoption of the Constitution, that the business of the butcher, or the baker, the tailor, the wood chopper, the mining operator or the miner was clothed with such a public interest that the price of his product or his wages could be fixed by State regulation....

To say that a business is clothed with a public interest, is not to detrmine what regulation may be permissible in view of the private rights of the owner. The extent to which an inn or a cab system may be regulated may differ widely from that allowable as to a railroad or other common carrier. It is not a matter of legislative discretion solely. It depends on the nature of the business, on the feature which touches the public, and on the abuses reasonably to be feared. To say that a business is clothed with a public interest is not to import that the public may take over its entire management and run it at the expense of the owner. The extent to which regulation may reasonably go varies with different kinds of business. The regulation of rates to avoid monopoly is one thing. The regulation of wages is another. A business may be of such character that only the first is permissible, while another may involve such a possible danger of monopoly on the one hand, and such disaster from stoppage on the other, that both come within the public concern and power of regulation.

If, as, in effect, contended by counsel for the State, the common callings are clothed with a public interest by a mere legislative declaration, which necessarily authorizes full and comprehensive regulation within legislative discretion, there must be a revolution in the relation of government to general business. This will be running the public interest argument into the ground, to use a phrase of Mr. Justice Bradley when characterizing a similarly extreme contention. *Civil Rights Cases,* 109 U.S. 3, 24. It will be impossible to reconcile such result with the freedom of contract and of labor secured by the Fourteenth Amendment.

This brings us to the nature and purpose of the regulation under the Industrial Court Act. The avowed object is continuity of food, clothing and fuel supply.... [R]easonable continuity and efficiency of the industries specified are declared to be necessary for the public peace, health, and general welfare, and all are forbidden to hinder, limit or suspend them.... [T]he Industrial Court power, in case of controversy [is given] between employers and workers which may endanger the continuity or efficiency of service, to bring the employer and employees before it and, after hearing and investigation, to fix the terms and conditions between them. The employer is bound by this act to pay the wages fixed and, while the worker is not required to work, at the wages fixed, he is forbidden, on penalty of fine and imprisonment, to strike against them, and thus is compelled to give up that means of putting himself on an equality with his employer which action in concert with his fellows gives him. . . .

The minutely detailed government supervision, including that of their relations to their employees, to which the railroads of the country have been gradually subjected by Congress through its power over interstate commerce, furnishes no precedent for regulation of the business of the plaintiff in error whose classification as public is at the best doubtful. It is not too much to say that the ruling in *Wilson v. New* went to the border line, although it concerned an interstate common carrier in the presence of a nation-wide emergency and the possibility of great disaster. Certainly there is nothing to justify extending the drastic regulation sustained in that exceptional case to the one before us.

We think the Industrial Court Act, in so far as it permits the fixing of wages in plaintiff in error's packing house, is in conflict with the Fourteenth Amendment and deprives it of its property and liberty of contract without due process of law.

The judgment of the court below must be reversed.

Dayton-Goose Creek Railway Co.
v. United States
263 U.S. 456
1924

As in *Railroad Commission of Wisconsin v. Chicago, Burlington, and Quincy Railway Co.* (1922), the Supreme Court upheld in *Dayton-Goose Creek Railway Co. v. United States* the federal government's supreme power to regulate commerce. In the former case the Justices ruled that the Interstate Commerce Commission had the authority to fix intrastate rail rates when they threatened to undermine a fair return for a railroad company involved in interstate commerce. In the latter case, they validated the recapture provisions of the Transportation Act (1920). As a result, while a business which was affected with a public interest should receive a fair income, it could not expect unusually high profits. Chief Justice William Howard Taft, a staunch conservative who consistently sought to protect private property, contended in affirming the decree of the District Court that railroads were utilities and thus subject to restraints so that the public would not be treated in an arbitrary manner.

The main question in this case is whether the so-called "recapture" paragraphs of the Transportation Act of 1920...are constitutional....

This Court has recently had occasion to construe the Transportation Act. ...

...[I]t was pointed out that the Transportation Act adds a new and important object to previous interstate commerce legislation, which was designed primarily to prevent unreasonable or discriminatory rates against persons and localities. The new act seeks affirmatively to build up a system of railways prepared to handle promptly all the interstate traffic of the country. It aims to give the owners of the railways an opportunity to earn enough to maintain their properties and equipment in such a state of efficiency that they can carry well this burden. To achieve this great purpose, it puts the railroad systems of the country more completely than ever under the fostering guardianship and control of the Commission, which is to supervise their issue of securities, their car supply and distribution, their joint use of terminals, their construction of new lines, their abandonment of old lines, and by a proper division of joint rates, and by fixing adequate rates for interstate commerce, and in case of discrimination, for intrastate commerce, to secure a fair return upon the properties of the carriers engaged....

We have been greatly pressed with the argument that the cutting down of income actually received by the carrier for its service to a so-called fair return is a plain appropriation of its property without any compensation, that the income it receives for the use of its property is as much protected by the Fifth Amendment as the property itself. The statute declares the carrier to be only a trustee for the excess over a fair return received by it. Though in its possession, the excess never becomes its property and it accepts custody of the product of all the rates with this understanding. It is clear, therefore, that the carrier never has such a title to the excess as to render the recapture of it by the Government a taking without due process.

It is then objected that the Government has no right to retain one-half of the excess, since, if it does not belong to the carrier, it belongs to the shippers and should be returned to them. If it were valid, it is an objection which the carrier can not be heard to make. It would be soon enough to consider such a claim when made by the shipper. But it is not valid. The rates are reasonable from the standpoint of the shipper as we have shown, though their net product furnishes more than a fair return for the carrier. The excess caused by the discrepancy between the standard of reasonableness for the shipper and that for the carrier due to the necessity of maintaining uniform rates to be charged to shippers, may properly be appropriated by the Government for public uses because the appropriation takes away nothing which equitably belongs either to the shiper or to the carrier. . . .

The third question for our consideration is whether the recapture clause, by reducing the net income from intrastate rates, invades the reserved power of the States and is in conflict with the Tenth Amendment. In solving the problem of maintaining the efficiency of an interstate commerce railway system which serves both the States and the Nation, Congress is dealing with a unit in which state and interstate operations are often inextricably commingled. When the adequate maintenance of interstate commerce involves and makes necessary on this account the incidental and partial control of intrastate commerce, the power of Congress to exercise such control has been clearly established. . . . The combination of uniform rates with the recapture clauses is necessary to the better development of the country's interstate transportation system as Congress has planned it. The control of the excess profit due to the level of the whole body of rates is the heart of the plan. To divide that excess and attempt to distribute one part to interstate traffic and the other to intrastate traffic would be impracticable and defeat the plan. . . .

Pierce v. Society of Sisters
268 U.S. 510
1925

While the Supreme Court was most intensely concerned with the protection of property rights during the 1920s, it also showed an interest in personal liberty and freedom. This was especially true when property rights were also involved. A fine example of this approach came when an Oregon statute required children between the ages of eight and sixteen to attend public schools, an order which threatened to eliminate private education from the state. The Court in *Pierce v. Society of Sisters* voided the statute; Justice James C. McReynolds, speaking for the Justices, argued that the law violated property rights and denied parents the right to rear their children as they saw fit.

These appeals are from decrees...which granted preliminary orders restraining appellants from threatening or attempting to enforce the Compulsory Education Act adopted November 7, 1922, under the initiative provision of her Constitution by the voters of Oregon....

The challenged Act, effective September 1, 1926, requires every parent, guardian or other person having control or charge or custody of a child between eight and sixteen years to send him "to a public school for the period of time a public school shall be held during the current year" in the district where the child resides; and failure so to do is declared a misdemeanor....

The manifest purpose is to compel general attendance at public schools by normal children, between eighth and sixteen, who have not completed the eighth grade. And without doubt enforcement of the statute would seriously impair, perhaps destroy, the profitable features of appellees' business and greatly diminish the value of their property.

Appellee, the Society of Sisters, is an Oregon corporation, organized in 1880, with power to care for orphans, educate and instruct the youth, establish and maintain academies or schools, and acquire necessary real and personal property.... It conducts interdependent primary and high schools and junior colleges, and maintains orphanages for the custody and control of children between eight and sixteen. In its primary schools many children between those ages are taught the subjects usually pursued in Oregon public schools during the first eight years. Systematic religious instruction and moral training according to the tenets of the Roman Catholic Church are also regularly provided. All courses of study, both temporal and religious, contemplate continuity of training under appellee's charge; the primary schools are essential to the system and the most profitable. It owns valuable buildings, especially constructed and equipped for school purposes. The business is remunerative—the annual income from primary schools exceeds thirty thousand dollars—and the successful conduct of this requires long time contracts with teachers and parents. The Compulsory Education Act of 1922 has already caused the withdrawal from its schools of children who would otherwise continue, and their income has steadily declined....

. . .[T]he Society's bill alleges that the enactment conflicts with the right of parents to choose schools where their children will receive appropriate mental and religious training, the right of the child to influence the parents' choice of a school, the right of schools and teachers therein to engage in a useful business or profession, and is accordingly repugnant to the Constitution and void. And, further, that unless enforcement of the measure is enjoined the corporation's business and property will suffer irreparable injury....

No question is raised concerning the power of the State reasonably to regulate all schools, to inspect, supervise and examine them, their teachers and pupils; to require that all children of proper age attend some school, that teachers shall be of good moral character and patriotic disposition, that certain studies plainly essential to good citizenship must be taught, and that nothing be taught which is manifestly inimical to the public welfare.

The inevitable practical result of enforcing the Act under consideration would be destruction of appellees' primary schools, and perhaps all other private primary schools for normal children within the State of Oregon. These parties are engaged in a kind of undertaking not inherently harmful, but long regarded as useful and meritorious. Certainly there is nothing in the present records to indicate that they have failed to discharge their obligations to patrons, students or the State. And there are no peculiar circumstances or present emergencies which demand extraordinary measures relative to primary education.

Under the doctrine of *Meyer v. Nebraska,* 262 U.S. 390, we think it entirely plain that the Act of 1922 unreasonably interferes with the liberty of parents and guardians to direct the upbringing and education of children under their control. As often heretofore pointed out, rights guaranteed by the Constitution may not be abridged by legislation which has no reasonable relation to some purpose within the competency of the State. The fundamental theory of liberty upon which all governments in this Union repose excludes any general power of the State to standardize its children by forcing them to accept instruction from public teachers only. The child is not the mere creature of the State; those who nurture him and direct his destiny have the right, coupled with the high duty, to recognize and prepare him for additional obligations....

The suits were not premature. The injury to appellees was present and very real, not a mere possibility in the remote future. If no relief had been possible prior to the effective date of the Act, the injury would have become irreparable. Prevention of impending injury by unlawful action is a well recognized function of courts of equity.

The decrees below are affirmed.

Gitlow v. New York
268 U.S. 652
1925

Starting in 1925, the Supreme Court heard a number of significant cases which dealt with the questions of free speech and freedom of the press. In *Gitlow v. New York* the Justices reviewed a state criminal anarchy statute which outlawed any call for the violent overthrow of organized government. Justice Edward Terry Sanford, speaking for the Court, declared that the fundamental rights guaranteed by the First Amendment were also protected from impairment by the states through the due process clause of the Fourteenth Amendment. Thereupon, he upheld the statute and thus affirmed New York's restrictions upon freedom of speech and of the press. In *Gitlow,* the Court took a narrow view of freedom of speech, yet it did extend the scope of the Fourteenth Amendment so that the First Amendment not only bound the federal government, but also became a limitation upon the states. Predictably enough, neither Justice Oliver Wendell Holmes nor Justice Louis D. Brandies were convinced by the majority opinion; their dissent is included.

Benjamin Gitlow was indicted in the Supreme Court of New York, with three others, for the statutory crime of criminal anarchy. New York Penal Laws,... He was separately tried, convicted, and sentenced to imprisonment. The judgment was affirmed by the Appellate Division and by the Court of Appeals.... The case is here on writ of error to the Supreme Court, to which the record was remitted. 260 U.S. 703.

"§ 161. *Advocacy of criminal anarchy.* Any person who:

"1. By word of mouth or writing advocates, advises or teaches the duty, necessity or propriety of overthrowing or overturning organized government by force or violence, or by assassination of the executive head or of any of the executive officials of government, or by any unlawful means; or,

"2. Prints, publishes, edits, issues or knowingly circulates, sells, distributes or publicly displays any book, paper, document, or written or printed matter in any form, containing or advocating, advising or teaching the doctrine that organized government should be overthrown by force, violence or any unlawful means...,

"Is quilty of a felony and punishable" by imprisonment or fine, or both.

The indictment was in two counts. The first charged that the defendant had advocated, advised and taught the duty, necessity and propriety of overthrowing and overturning organized government by force, violence and unlawful means, by certain writings therein set forth entitled "The Left Wing Manifesto"; the second that he had printed, published and knowingly circulated and distributed a certain paper called "The Revolutionary Age," containing the writings set forth in the first count advocating, advising and teaching the doctrine that organized government should be overthrown by force, violence and unlawful means.. . .

There was no evidence of any effect resulting from the publication and circulation of the Manifesto.

No witnesses were offered in behalf of the defendant.

Extracts from the Manifesto are set forth in the margin. Coupled with a review of the rise of Socialism, it condemned the dominant "moderate Socialism" for its recognition of the necessity of the democratic parliamentary state; repudiated its policy of introducing Socialism by legislative measures; and advocated, in plain and unequivocal language, the necessity of accomplishing the "Communist Revolution" by a militant and "revolutionary Socialism," based on "the class struggle" and mobilizing the "power of the preletariat in action," through mass industrial revolts developing into mass political strikes and "revolutionary mass action," for the purpose of conquering and destroying the parliamentary state and establishing in its place, through a "revolutionary dictatorship of the proletariat," the system of Communist Socialism. The then recent strikes in Seattle and Winnipeg were cited as instances of a development already verging on revolutionary action and suggestive of proletarian dictatorship, in which the strike-workers were "trying to usurp the functions of municipal government"; and revolutionary Socialism, it was urged, must use these mass industrial revolts to broaden the strike, make it general and militant, and develop it into mass political strikes and revolutionary mass action for the annihilation of the parliamentary state.. . .

The sole contention here is, essentially, that as there was no evidence of any concrete result flowing from the publication of the Manifesto or of circumstances showing the likelihood of such result, the state as construed and applied by the trial court penalizes the mere utterance, as such, of "doctrine" having no quality of incitement, without regard either to the circumstances of its utterance or to the likelihood of unlawful sequences; and that, as the exercise of the right of free expression with relation to government is only punishable "in circumstances involving likelihood of substantive evil," the statute contravenes the due process clause of the Fourteenth mendment. The argument in support of this contention rests primarily upon the following propositions: 1st, That the "liberty" protected by the Fourteenth Amendment includes the liberty of speech and of the press; and 2nd, That while liberty of expression "is not absolute," it may be restrained "only in circumstances where its exercise bears a causal relation with some substantive evil, consummated, attempted or likely," and as the statute "takes no account of circumstances," it unduly restrains this liberty and is therefore unconstitutional.

The precise question presented, and the only question which we can consider under this writ of error, then is, whether the statute, as construed and applied in this case by the state courts, deprived the defendant of his liberty of expression in violation of the due process clause of the Fourteenth Amendment.

The statute does not penalize the utterance or publication of abstract "doctrine" or academic discussion having no quality of incitement to any concrete action. It is not aimed against mere historical or philosophical essays. It does not restrain the advocacy of changes in the form of government by constitutional and lawful means. What it prohibits is language advocating, advising or teaching the overthrow of organized government by unlawful means. . . .

The Manifesto, plainly, is neither the statement of abstract doctrine nor, as suggested by counsel, mere prediction that industrial disturbances and revolutionary mass strikes will result spontaneously in an inevitable process of evolution in the economic system. It advocates and urges in fervent language mass action which shall progressively foment industrial disturbances and through political mass strikes and revolutionary mass action overthrow and destroy organized parliamentary government. It concludes with a call to action in these words: "The proletariat revolution and the Communist reconstruction of society—*the struggle for these*—is now indispensable. . . . The Communist International calls the proletariat of the world to the final struggle!" This is not the expression of philosophical abstraction, the mere prediction of future events; it is the language of direct incitement.

The means advocated for bringing about the destruction of organized parliamentary government, namely, mass industrial revolts usurping the functions of municipal government, political mass strikes directed against the parliamentary state, and revolutionary mass action for its final destruction, necessarily imply the use of force and violence, and in their essential nature are inherently unlawful in a constitutional government of law and order. That the jury were warranted in finding that the Manifesto advocated not merely the abstract doctrine of overthrowing organized government by force, violence and unlawful means, but action to that end, is clear.

For present purposes we may and do assume that fredom of speech and of the press—which are protected by the First Amendment from abridgment by Congress—are among the fundamental personal rights and "liberties" protected by the due process clause of the Fourteenth Amendment from impairment by the States. We do not regard the incidental statement in *Prudential Ins. Co. v. Cheek,* 259 U.S. 530, 543, that the Fourteenth Amendment imposes no restrictions on the States concerning freedom of speech, as determinative of this question.

It is a fundamental principle, long established, that the freedom of speech and of the press which is secured by the Constitution does not confer an absolute right to speak or publish, without responsibility, whatever one may choose, or an unrestricted and unbridled license that gives immunity for every possible use of language and prevents the punishment of those who abuse this freedom. . . .

That a State in the exercise of its police power may punish those who abuse this freedom by utterances inimical to the public welfare, tending to corrupt public morals, incite to crime, or disturb the public peace, is not open to question. . . . Thus it was held by this Court in the *Fox Case,* that a State may punish publications advocating and encouraging a breach of its criminal laws; and, in the *Gilbert Case,* that a State may punish utterances teaching or advocating that its citizens should not assist the United States in prosecuting or carrying on war with its public enemies.

And, for yet more imperative reasons, a state may punish utterances endangering the foundations of organized government and threatening its overthrow by unlawful means. These imperil its own existence as a constitutional State. Freedom of speech and press, said Story (*supra*) does not protect disturbances to the public peace or the attempt to subvert the government. It does not protect publications or teachings which tend to subvert or imperil the government or to impede or hinder it in the performance of its governmental duties. . . .

By enacting the present statute the State has determined, through its legislative body, that utterances advocating the overthrow of organized government by force, violence and unlawful means, are so inimical to the general welfare and involve such danger of substantive evil that they may be penalized in the exercise of its police power. That determination must be given great weight. Every presumption is to be indulged in favor of the validity of the statute. *Mugler v. Kansas,* 123 U.S. 623, 661. And the case is to be considered "in the light of the principle that the State is primarily the judge of regulations required in the interest of public safety and welfare"; and that its police "statutes may only be declared unconstitutional where they are arbitrary or unreasonable attempts to exercise authority vested in the State in the public interst." *Great Northern Ry. v. Clara City,* 246 U.S. 434, 439. That utterances inciting to the overthrow of organized government by unlawful means, present a sufficient danger of substantive evil to bring their punishment within the rage of legislative discretion, is clear. Such utterances, by their very nature, involve danger to the public peace and to the security of the State. They threaten breaches of the peace and ultimate revolution. And the immediage danger is none the less real and substantial, because the effecct of a given utterance cannot be accurately foreseen. The State cannot reasonably be required to measure the danger from every such utterance in the nice balance of a jeweler's scale. A single revolutionary spark may kindle a fire that, smouldering for a time, may burst into a sweeping and destructive conflagration. It cannot be said that the State is acting arbitrarily or unreasonably when in the exercise of its judgment as to the measures necessary to protect the public peace and safety, it seeks to extinguish the spark without waiting until it has enkindled the flame or blazed into the conflagration. It cannot reasonably be required to defer the adoption of measures for its own peace and safety until the revolutionary utterances lead to actual disturbances of the public peace or imminent and immediate danger of its own destruction; but it may, in the exercise of its judgment, suppress the threatened danger in its incipiency. In *People v. Lloyd, supra,* . . . it was aptly said: "Manifestly, the legislature has authority to forbid the advocacy of a doctrine designed and intended to overthrow the government without waiting until there is a present and imminent danger of the success of the plan advocated. If the State were compelled to wait until the apprehended danger became certain, then its right to protect itself would come into being simultaneously with the overthrow of the government, when there would be neither prosecuting officers nor courts for the enforcement of the law."

We cannot hold that the present statute is an arbitrary or unreasonable exercise of the police power of the State unwarrantably infringing the freedom of speech or press; and we must and do sustain its constitutionality.

This being so it may be applied to every utterance—not too trivial to be beneath the notice of the law—which is of such a character and used with such intent and purpose as to bring it within the prohibition of the statute. . . . In other words, when the legislative body has determined generally, in the constitutional exercise of its discretion, that utterances of a certain kind involve such danger of substantive evil that they may be punished, the question whether any specific utterance coming within the prohibited class is likely, in and of itself, to bring about the substantive evil, is not open to consideration. It is sufficient that the statute itself be constitutional and that the use of the language comes within its prohibition. . . .

And finding, for the reasons stated, that the statute is not in itself unconstitutional, and that it has not been applied in the present case in derogation of any constitutional right, the judgment of the Court of Appeals is affirmed.

Mr. Justice Holmes, dissenting.

Mr. Justice Brandies and I are of opinion that this judgment should be reversed. The general principle of free speech, it seems to me, must be taken to be included in the Fourteenth Amendment, in view of the scope that has been given to the word 'liberty' as there used, although perhaps it may be accepted with a somewhat larger latitude of interpretation than is allowed to Congress by the sweeping language that governs or ought to govern the laws of the United States. If I am right, then I think that the criterion sanctioned by the full Court in *Schenck v. United States,* 249 U.S. 47, 52, applies. "The question in every case is whether the words used are used in such circumstances and are of such a nature as to create a clear and present danger that they will bring about the substantive evils that [the State] has a right to prevent." It is true that in my opinion this criterion was departed from in *Abrams v. United States,* 250 U.S. 616, but the convictions that I expressed in that case are too deep for it to be possible for me as yet to believe that it and *Schaefer v. United States,* 251 U.S. 466, have settled the law. If what I think the correct test is applied, it is manifest that there was no present danger of an attempt to overthrow the government by force on the part of the admittedly small minority who shared the defendant's views. It is said that this manifesto was more than a theory, that it was an incitement. Every idea is an incitement. It offers itself for belief and if believed it is acted on unless some other belief outweights it or some failure of energy stifles the movement at its birth. The only difference between the expression of an opinion and an incitement in the narrower sense is the speaker's enthusiasm for the result. Eloquence may set fire to reason. But whatever may be thought of the redundant discourse before us it had no chance of starting a present conflagration. If in the long run the beliefs expressed in proletarian dictatorship are destined to be accepted by the dominant forces of the community, the only meaning of free speech is that they should be given their chance and have their way.

If the publication of this document had been laid as an attempt to induce an uprising against government at once and not at some indefinite time in the future it would have presented a different question. The object would have been one with which the law might deal, subject to the doubt whether there was any danger that the publication could produce any result, or in other words, whether it was not futile and to remote from possible consequences. But the indictment alleges the publication and nothing more.

Myers v. United States
272 U.S. 52
1926

In *Myers v. United States* the Supreme Court upheld the right of the president to remove from office appointed officials. Frank Myers was a postmaster, appointed by President Woodrow Wilson in 1917, to a four-year term, who was removed from office in 1920, without the consent of the Senate. Myers sued in the Court of Claims to recover his salary, but lost his suit, and therefore appealed to the Supreme Court. Chief Justice William Howard Taft, speaking for the Court, denied the appeal and confirmed the removal; he supported this action on the belief that the early leaders of the nation wanted the president to efficiently execute the laws, and therefore could control his subordinates through removal. Legislative control of the executive—in this case the Senate—should be relatively weak in order not to violate the constitutional principle of separation of powers. In short, according to Taft, the removal power of the president could not be restricted by the Congress.

This case presents the question whether under the Constitution the President has the exclusive power of removing executive officers of the United States whom he has appointed by and with the advice and consent of the Senate.

Myers, appellant's intestate, was on July 21, 1917, appointed by the President, by and with the advice and consent of the Senate, to be a postmaster of the first class at Portland, Oregon, for a term of four years. On January 20, 1920, Myers' resignation was demanded. He refused the demand. On February 2, 1920, he was removed from office by order of the Postmaster General, acting by direction of the President....

By the...Act of Congress of July 12, 1876...under which Myers was appointed with the advice and consent of the Senate as a first-class postmaster, it is provided that

"Postmasters of the first, second and third classes shall be appointed and may be removed by the President by and with the advice and consent of the Senate and shall hold their offices for four years unless sooner removed or suspended according to law."

The Senate did not consent to the President's removal of Myers during his term. If this statute, in its requirement that his term should be four years unless sooner removed by the President by and with the consent of the Senate, is valid, the appellant, Myers' administratrix, is entitled to recover his unpaid salary for his full term, and the judgment of the Court of Claims must be reversed. The Government maintains that the requirement is invalid, for the reason that under Article II of the Constitution the President's power of removal of executive officers appointed by him with the advice and consent of the Senate is full and complete without consent of the Senate. If this view is sound, the removal of Myers by the President without the Senate's consent was legal and the judgment of the Court of Claims against the appellant was correct and must be affirmed, though for a different reason from that given by that court. We are therefore confronted by the constitutional question and can not avoid it.. . .

Our conclusion on the merits, sustained by the arguments before stated, is that Article II grants to the President the executive power of the Government, i.e., the general administrative control of those executing the laws, including the power of appointment and removal of executive officers—a conclusion confirmed by his obligation to take care that the laws be faithfully executed; that Article II excludes the exercise of legislative power by Congress to provide for appointments and removals, except only as granted therein to Congress in the matter of inferior offices; that Congress is only given power to provide for appointments and removals of inferior officers after it has vested, and on condition that it does vest, their appointment in other authority than the President with the Senate's consent; that the provisions of. . . Article II, which blend action by the legislative branch, or by part of it, in the work of the executive, are limitations to be strictly construed and not to be extended by implication; that the President's power of removal is further established as an incident to his specifically enumerated function of appointment by and with the advice of the Senate, but that such incident does not by implication extend to removals the Senate's power of checking appointments; and finally that to hold otherwise would make it impossible for the President, in case of political or other differences with the Senate or Congress, to take care that the laws be faithfully executed.

We come now to a period in the history of the Government when both Houses of Congress attempted to reverse this constitutional construction and to subject the power of removing executive officers appointed by the President and confirmed by the Senate to the control of the Senate—indeed, finally, to the assumed power in Congress to place the removal of such officers anywhere in the Government.

This reversal grew out of the serious political difference between the two Houses of Congress and Prsident Johnson.. . .

. . .[T]he chief legislation in support of the reconstruction policy of Congress was the Tenure of Office Act, of March 2, 1867,. . . providing that all officers appointed by and with the consent of the Senate should hold their offices until their successors should have in like manner been appointed and qualified, and that certain heads of departments, including the Secretary of War, should hold their offices during the term of the President by whom appointed and one month thereafter subject to removal by consent of the Senate. The Tenure of Office Act was vetoed, but it was passed over the veto. The House of Representatives preferred articles of impeachment against President Johnson for refusal to comply with, and for conspiracy to defeat, the legislation above referred to, but he was acquitted for lack of a two-thirds vote for conviction in the Senate. . . .

In spite of the foregoing Presidential declarations, it is contended that, since the passage of the Tenure of office Act, there has been general acquiesence by the Executive in the power of Congress to forbid the President alone to remove executive officers—an acquiescence which has changed any formerly accepted constitutional construction to the contrary. Instances are cited of the signed approval by President Grant and other Presidents of legislation in derogation of such construction. We think these are all to be explained, not by acquiescence therein, but by reason of the otherwise valuable effect of the legislation approved. Such is doubtless the explanation of the executive approval of the Act of 1876, which we are considering, for it was an appropriation act on which the section here in question was imposed as a rider. . . .

What, then, are the elements that enter into our decision of this case? We have first a construction of the Constitution made by a Congress which was to provide by legislation for the organization of the Government in accord with the Constitution which had just then been adopted, and in which there were, as representatives and senators, a considerable number of those who had been members of the Convention that framed the Constitution and presented it for ratification. It was the Congress that launched the Government. It was the Congress that rounded out the Constitution itself by the proposing of the first ten amendments which had in effect been promised to the people as a consideration for the ratification. It was the Congress in which Mr. Madison, one of the first in the framing of the Constitution, led also in the organization of the Government under it. It was a Congress whose constitutional decisions have always been regarded, as they should be regarded, as of the greatest weight in the interpretation of that fundamental instrument. . . .

We are now asked to set aside this construction, thus buttressed, and adopt an adverse view, because the Congress of the United States did so during a heated political difference of opinion between the then President and the majority leaders of Congress over the reconstruction measures adopted as a means of restoring to their proper status the States which attempted to withdraw from the Union at the time of the Civil War. The extremes to which the majority in both Houses carried legislative measures in that matter are now recognized by all who calmly review the history of that episode in our Government, leading to articles of impeachment against President Johnson, and his acquittal. Without animadverting on the character of the measures taken, we are certainly justified in saying that they should not be given the weight affecting proper constitutional construction to be accorded to that reached by the First Congress of the United States during a political calm and acquiesced in by the whole Government for three-quarters of a century, especially when the new construction contended for has never been acquiesced in by either the executive or the judicial departments. While this Court has studiously avoided deciding the issue until it was presented in such a way that it could not be avoided, in the references it has made to the history of the question, and in the presumptions it has indulged in favor of a statutory construction not inconsistent with the legislative decision of 1789, it has indicated a trend of view that we should not and can not ignore. When, on the merits, we find our conclusion strongly favoring the view which prevailed in the First Congress, we have no hesitation in holding that conclusion to be correct; and it therefore follows that the Tenute of Office Act of 1867, in so far as it attempted to prevent the President from removing executive officers who had been appointed by him by and with the advice and consent of the Senate, was invalid, and that subsequent legislation of the same effect was equally so.

For the reasons given, we must therefore hold that the provision of the law of 1876, by which the unrestricted power of removal of first class postmasters is denied to the President, is in violation of the Constitution, and invalid. This leads to an affirmance of the judgment of the Court of Claims.

Tyson & Brothers v. Banton
273 U.S. 418
1927

In this case the Supreme Court reviewed a New York statute which regulated resale theater ticket prices, a measure enacted to protect theater goers from being overcharged by brokers. Justice George Sutherland, speaking for the Court, argued that the resale of theater tickets did not constitute a matter affected with a public interest, and therefore held the statute unconstitutional as a violation of free contract. Sutherland accepted Chief Justice William Howard Taft's conceptionof public interest; in *Wolff Packing Co. v. Court of Industrial Relations* (1923) Taft essentially argued that the criterion was "the indispensable nature of the service and the exorbitant charges and arbitrary control to which the public might be subjected without regulation." For the Court majority the resale of theater tickets was obviously a service which did not meet this definition. Justice Oliver Wendell Holmes wrote a sharp dissent criticizing the majority for their narrow view of the concept of public interest. While Sutherland thought that only such businesses as utilities might be regulated, Holmes supported the position that any state legislature should regulate business whenever it believed the public welfare demanded it. Today, Holmes's view has triumphed and there is broad acceptance of the state's role in social legislation and business regulation.

Appellant is engaged in the business of reselling tickets of admission to theatres and other places of entertainment in the City of New York. . . .

[T]he price of or charge for admission to theatres, etc., is a matter affected with a public interest and subject to state supervision in order to safeguard the public against fraud, extortion, exorbitant rates and similar abuses. . . .

[T]he resale of any ticket or other evidence of the right of entry to any theatre, etc., [is forbidden] "at a price in excess of fifty cents in advance of the price printed on the face of such ticket or other evidence of the right of entry," such printing being required by that section. . . .

Strictly, the question for determination relates only to the maximum price for which an entrance ticket to a theatre, etc., may be resold. But the answer necessarily must be to a question of greater breadth. The statutory declaration. . . is that the price of or charge for admission to a theatre, place of amusement or entertainment or other place where public exhibitions, games, contests or performances are held, is a matter affected with a public interest. To affirm the validity. . . is to affirm this declaration completely, since appellant's business embraces the resale of entrance tickets to all forms of entertainment therein enumerated. And since the ticket broker is a mere appendage of the theatre, etc., and the *price of* or *charge for admission* is the essential element in the statutory declaration, it results that the real inquiry is whether every public exhibition, game, contest or performance, to which an admission charge is made, is clothed with a public interest, so as to authorize a law-making body to fix the maximum amount of the charge, which its patrons may be required to pay....

A business is not affected with a public interest merely because it is large or because the public are warranted in having a feeling of concern in respect of its maintenance. Nor is the interest meant such as arises from the mere fact that the public derives benefit, accommodation, ease or enjoyment from the existence or operation of the business; and while the word has not always been limited narrowly as strictly denoting "a right," that synonym more nearly than any other expresses the sense in which it is to be understood....

[T]he mere declaration by the legislature that a particular kind of property or business is affected with a public interest is not conclusive upon the question of the validity of the regulation. The matter is one which is always open to judicial inquiry. *Wolff Co. v. Industrial Court,* 262 U.S. 522, 536....

From the foregoing review it will be seen that each of the decisions of this court upholding governmental price regulation, aside from cases involving legislation to tide over temporary emergencies, has turned upon the existence of conditions, peculiar to the business under consideration, which bore such a substantial and definite relation to the public interest as to justify an indulgence of the legal fiction of a grant by the owner to the public of an interest in the use.

Lord Hale's statement that when private property is "affected with a public interest, it ceases to be *juris privati* only," is accepted by this court as the guiding principle in cases of this character....

A theatre or other place of entertainment does not meet this conception of Lord Hale's aphorism or fall within the reasons of the decisions of this court based upon it. A theatre is a private enterprise, which, in its relation to the public, differs obviously and widely, both in character and degree, from a grain elevator, standing at the gateway of commerce and exacting toll, amounting to a common charge, for every bushel of grain which passes on its way among the states; or stock yards, standing in like relation to the commerce in live stock; or an insurance company, engaged, as a sort of common agency, in collecting and holding a guaranty fund in which definite and substantial rights are enjoyed by a considerable portion of the public sustaining interdependent relations in respect to their interests in the fund. Sales of theatre tickets bear no relation to the commerce of the country; and they are not interdependent transactions, but stand, both in form and effect, separate and apart from each other, "terminating in their effect with the instances." And, certainly, a place of entertainment is in no legal sense a public utility; and, quite as certainly, its activities are not such that their enjoyment can be regarded under any conditions from the point of view of an emergency. . . .

We are of opinion that the statute assailed contravenes the Fourteenth Amendment and that the decree must be reversed.

Mr. Justice Holmes, dissenting.

We fear to grant power and are unwilling to recognize it when it exists. The States very generally have stripped jury trials of one of their most important characteristics by forbidding the judges to advise the jury upon the facts (*Graham v. United States,* 231 U.S. 474, 480), and when legislatures are held to be authorized to do anything considerably affecting public welfare it is covered by apologetic phrases like the police power, or the statement that the business concerned has been dedicated to a public use. The former expression is convenient, to be sure, to conciliate the mind to something that needs explanation: the fact that the constitutional requirement of compensation when property is taken cannot be pressed to its grammatical extreme; that property rights may be taken for public purposes without pay if you do not take too much; that some play must be allowed to the joints if the machine is to work. But police power often is used in a wide sense to cover and, as I said, to apologize for the general power of the legislature to make a part of the community uncomfortable by a change.

I do not believe in such apologies. I think the proper course is to recognize that a state legislature can do whatever it sees fit to do unless it is restrained by some express prohibition in the Constitution of the United States or of the State, and that Courts should be careful not to extend such prohibitions beyond their obvious meaning by reading into them conceptions of public policy that the particular Court may happen to entertain. Coming down to the case before us I think, as I intimated in *Adkins v. Children's Hospital,* 261 U.S. 525, 569, that the notion that a business is clothed with a public interest and has been devoted to the public use is little more than a fiction intended to beautify what is disagreeable to the sufferers. The truth seems to me to be that, subject to compensation when compensation is due, the legislature may forbid or restrict any business when it has a sufficient force of public opinion behind it. Lotteries were thought useful adjuncts of the State a century or so ago; now they are believed to be immoral and they have been stopped. Wine has been thought good for man from the time of the Apostles until recent years. But when public opinion changed it did not need the Eighteenth Amendment, notwithstanding the Fourteenth, to enable a State to say that the business should end. *Mugler v. Kansas,* 123 U.S. 623. What has happened to lotteries and wine might happen to theatres in some moral storm of the future, not because theatres were devoted to a public use, but because people had come to think that way.

But if we are to yield to fashionable conventions, it seems to me that theatres are as much devoted to public use as anything well can be. We have not that respect for art that is one of the glories of France. But to many people the superfluous is the necessary, and it seems to me that Government does not go beyond its sphere in attempting to make life livable for them. I am far from saying that I think this particular law a wise and rational provision. That is not my affair. But if the people of the State of New York speaking by their authorized voice say that they want it, I see nothing in the Constitution of the United States to prevent their having their will.

Nixon v. Herndon
273 U.S. 536
1927

In an effort to bar blacks from participating in Democratic party primaries—the decisive elections in the South—"white primaries" were legalized during the 1920s by state legislatures. The Supreme Court, in *Nixon v. Herndon,* found that such laws were unconstitutional; Justice Oliver Wendell Holmes, speaking for the Court, declared that they violated the equal protection clause of the Fourteenth Amendment since the statutes classified and discriminated among persons on the basis of color alone. Defeated on this front, the segregationists of most southern states proceeded to transform their Democratic party organization into private clubs, and thus excluded blacks from "private" primaries. During the 1940s, the Court also found this device unconstitutional.

This is an action against the Judges of Elections for refusing to permit the plaintiff to vote at a primary election in Texas. It lays the damages at five thousand dollars. The petition alleges that the plaintiff is a negro, a citizen of the United States and of Texas and a resident of El Paso, and in every way qualified to vote, as set forth in detail, except that the statute to be mentioned interferes with his right; that on July 26, 1924, a primary election was held at El Paso for the nomination of candidates for a senator and representatives in Congress and State and other offices, upon the Democratic ticket; that the plaintiff, being a member of the Democratic party, sought to vote but was denied the right by defendants; that the denial was based upon a Statute of Texas enacted in May, 1923,... "in no event shall a negro be eligible to participate in a Democratic party primary election held in the State of Texas," &c., and that this statute is contrary to the Fourteenth and Fifteenth Amendments to the Constitution of the United States. The defendants moved to dismiss upon the ground that the subject matter of the suit was political and not within the jurisdiction of the Court and that no violation of the Amendments was shown. The suit was dismissed and a writ of error was taken directly to this Court. Here no argument was made on behalf of the defendants but a brief was allowed to be filed by the Attorney General of the State.

The objection that the subject matter of the suit is political is little more than a play upon words. Of course the petition concerns political action but it alleges and seeks to recover for private damage. That private damage may be caused by such political aciton and may be recovered for in a suit at law hardly has been doubted.... If the defendants' conduct was a wrong to the plaintiff the same reason that allow a recovery for denying the plaintiff a vote at a final election allow it for denying a vote at the primary election that may determine the final result.

The important question is whether the statute can be sustained. But although we state it as a question the answer does not seem to us open to a doubt. We find it unnecessary to consider the Fifteenth Amendment, because it seems to us hard to imagine a more direct and obvious infringement of the Fourteenth. That Amendment, while it applies to all, was passed, as we know, with a special intent to protect the blacks from discrimination against them. *Slaughter House Cases,* 16 Wall. 36. *Strauder v. West Virginia,* 100 U.S. 303. That Amendment "not only gave citizenship and the privileges of citizenship to persons of color, but it denied to any State the power to withhold from them the equal protection of the laws.... What is this but declaring that the law in the States shall be the same for the black as for the white; that all persons, whether colored or white, shall stand equal before the laws of the States, and, in regard to the colored race, for whose protection the amendment was primarily designed, that no discrimination shall be made against them by law because of their color?"... The statute of Texas in the teeth of the prohibitions referred to assumes to forbid negroes to take part in a primary election the importance of which we have indicated, discriminating against them by the distinction of color alone. States may do a good deal of classifying that it is difficult to believe rational, but there are limits, and it is too clear for extended argument that color cannot be made the basis of a statutory classification affecting the right set up in this case.

Judgment reversed.

PART III

The Justices
of the
Supreme Court

■ ■ ■ ■ ■

1910-1930

Edward Douglas White

Edward Douglas White served on the Supreme Court for twenty-seven years, as an Associate Justice for sixteen years after his appointment by President Cleveland in 1894, and later as Chief Justice following Taft's decision in 1911, to elevate him from the ranks of the Court. Although White served on the Court for over a quarter of a century, he is not well-known and usually given credit for only one major contribution to jurisprudence: the "rule of reason." Fundamentally a conservative and an ardent champion of states' rights, White was indifferent to the development of strong national government.

Edward D. White was born on a Louisiana sugar plantation on November

3, 1845. He obtained a Catholic education and graduated from the Jesuit-run Georgetown College in 1857. In 1861, at the age of sixteen he joined the Confederate Army; he saw little action and went home two years later after the rebels were defeated at the siege of Port Hudson on the lower Mississippi. Now eighteen, young White decided to study law under a New Orleans lawyer named Edward Bermudez and at the law school of the University of Louisiana (Tulane). In 1868, he passed the bar and began his long career as a lawyer, politician, and jurist.

During the postwar years he remained loyal to the Confederate cause, but with the waning of Reconstruction he was able to enter politics and get elected to the state senate in 1874. In 1878, Governor Nicholls, an old friend of White's father, appointed the younger White, at the age of thirty-three, an Associate Justice of the Louisiana Supreme Court. Unfortunately, a change in the state constitution prohibited so young a man as White to remain on the court. Consequently, he returned to his law practice, prospered, and served as legal advisor to the newly chartered Tulane University. During the late 1880s, White again entered the political arena and in 1891, succeeded in gaining appointment as a United States senator from Louisiana. While in the Senate, he strongly fought against government interference with business, but supported high tariffs to protect Louisiana sugar and federal bounty payments to domestic sugar growers. Obviously, since he owned a sugar plantation, self-interest played a large role in determining positions White took on the Senate floor. White also deeply offended President Cleveland, who expected Democratic senators to support lower tariffs and to help eliminate preferred treatment of special interests such as sugar growers. Yet, despite their differences Cleveland nominated White to the Supreme Court on February 19, 1894. With the exception of the tariff issue, White generally supported the Cleveland administration, and the President thought it good politics to appoint a southerner.

Although White's record was rather inconsistent during his early years on the Court, he became increasingly conservative as he grew older. He adopted the liberal position in *Muller v. Oregon* (1908), when he voted to uphold an Oregon law limiting women to an eight-hour workday, and in *New York Central Railroad Co. v. White* (1917), when he supported a New York State workman's compensation act. By 1918, however, his thought was conclusively conservative as demonstrated by his positions in such cases as *Hammer v. Dagenhart* (1918) and *United States v. Doremus* (1919). In the first case he voted with the majority to void the Keating-Owen Child Labor Act (1916), which barred from interstate commerce all products manufactured by child labor, and in the second he wrote a minority opinion in a 5-4 decision that barely upheld the Harrison Narcotics Act (1914), which had been enacted in order to eliminate harmful drugs from the marketplace.

During White's term as Chief Justice (1911-21) he made a major contribution to American jurisprudence by applying his "rule of reason" to the Sherman Anti-Trust Act (1890). Basically, the "rule of reason" meant that not all trust combinations in restraint of trade were illegal, but only those which were unreasonable (arbitrary), or against the public interest. Earlier, the Court had in several cases denied White's argument for "reasonableness," but by 1911, in *Standard Oil Co. v. United States* a unanimous Court, with Chief Justice White writing the decision, agreed that the business practices of the oil monopoly constituted a "unreasonable" restraint of trade, rather than the "reasonable" restraint which the Court suggested would be permitted under the act. A short time later in *United States v. American Tobacco Co.* (1911) White repeated his argument, but this time found that the monopoly was "reasonable" and therefore did not call for dissolution as in *Standard Oil*. Thus in judicial proceedings concerning trusts two principles now became clear. One, it would be the Courts which decided what was "reasonable" under the Sherman Act and, two, it would be exceedingly difficult to eliminate big business from American society. Attorneys could easily demonstrate that large industries were far more efficient than small companies, and therefore enhanced the public interest. Under White, therefore, the American business system was safe from prosecution. For the time being the Sherman Act was effectively dead.

On May 13, 1921, White became seriously ill and on May 19, he died; William Howard Taft succeeded him in the Chief's chair. Although only a few legal scholars remember White today, he left an important legacy. His legal philosophy called for a pragmatic view of the law rather than blindly following precedents and fixed principles. This was intrinsically American in that our tradition sharply disdains adherence to rigid and inflexible ideological positions.

John Marshall Harlan

John M. Harlan, appointed by Rutherford B. Hayes in 1877, served on the Supreme Court for thirty-four years. He is perhaps best known for dissents which defined his legal philosophy: an uncompromising faith in Congress, not the judiciary, as the arbiter of political affairs and a strong belief in national authority. He consistently supported statutes which entrusted the federal government with the power to protect the national well-being. For example, when an income tax was struck down in *Pollock v. Farmers' Loan and Trust Co.* (1895), Harlan, in his dissent, declared that the majority decision "strikes at the very foundation of national authority, in that it denies to the general government a power which is or may become vital to the very existence and preservation of the Union in a national emergency." Other questions raised by Harlan dissents in such areas as civil liberties and civil rights have had a lasting impact on the American spirit. As a Justice of the Supreme Court he demanded not only adherence to the Thirteenth, Fourteenth, and Fifteenth Amendments, but elemental justice for all citizens. Dissenting in *Plessy v. Ferguson* (1896), Harlan argued that a state law which could segregate blacks on trains could segregate them anywhere else, and subsequent measures could do the same at will to other persons of whatever race, creed, or color. This argument would ultimately provide the reasoning for the legal overthrow of discrimination in the 1950s.

John M. Harlan was born on June 1, 1833, in Boyle County, Kentucky. He attended Centre College and Transylvania University where he studied law. His studies continued after graduation under his father and other lawyers. These early years also saw some public service as city attorney of Frankfurt, Kentucky, and as county judge. With the coming of Civil War he cast his lot with the Northern cause but stood firm on the slaveholder's right to his human property. After the war he reentered politics and by 1868, moved away from his Democratic origins to support the Republicans and their presidential candidate, General Ulysses S. Grant. His views on race and civil rights had also evolved and Harlan now accepted the Thirteenth Amendment. He was, however, unsuccessful in his bid for the governorship of Kentucky in 1871. In 1877, after Justice David Davis resigned from the Supreme Court, President Hayes wanted a responsible Southern Republican to fill the vacancy and Harlan fit the bill.

Harlan served only fourteen months on the White Court since he died on October 14, 1911. During his last days on the Court he prepared dissents for decisions which dealt with the great monopolies, *Standard Oil Co.* and *American Tobacco Co.* In these cases the majority of the Justices used the "rule of reason" to conclude that monopolies or trusts not "harmful or destructive" were not subject to Court condemnation under the Sherman Anti-Trust Act (1890). Harlan objected to their reasoning on two grounds. First, he took a narrow view of the Sherman Act; the statute had outlawed trusts and it was the duty of the Court to dissolve them. Second, Harlan strongly argued that the assumption of the "rule of reason" by the Justices contravened the role given to them by the Constitution. According to Harlan there were no good trusts, only bad ones which must be eliminated under the law. "I am compelled to say," he declared in his *Standard Oil* dissent, "that there is abroad in our land a most harmful tendency to bring about the amending of constitutions and legislative enactments by means alone of judicial construction."

Harlan wrote over three hundred dissents and many of these have been recognized as landmark judicial essays by legal scholars. He believed in a strong national government, which would be able to cope with the changing nature of modern industrialization. His dissents upholding human freedom and dignity have had a lasting effect on American law.

Joseph McKenna

Joseph McKenna was appointed to the Supreme Court by President William McKinley in 1898. Since he was a somewhat inexperienced lawyer, he was poorly prepared for the job. His early opinions are difficult to understand and filled with numerous references in an attempt to justify his decisions. Although in time McKenna gained confidence and polish, he never developed a consistent legal philosophy. He generally followed the lead of the conservative majority, especially in his later years on the Court.

Joseph McKenna was born on August 10, 1843, of Irish immigrant parents who came to America to escape famine. Although his father was only a baker, Joseph was sent to a Philadelphia Catholic school (St. Joseph's

College). In 1855, the family, in an effort to improve their economic status, moved to California and Joseph continued his education at local public schools. He also studied law on his own and in 1865, passed the California bar.

McKenna's first position, at the age of twenty-two, was as district attorney of Solano County. Most of his practical experience was gained, however, in the political arena rather than in the practice of law. He suffered several defeats in attempts to win a congressional seat before he was finally elected in 1884, and went off to Washington to join the Forty-ninth Congress. While in Congress, he befriended influential Republican politicians and through these contacts advanced his career. In 1892, President Benjamin Harrison appointed McKenna to the Ninth Circuit Court of Appeals. He now looked forward to an appointment to the Supreme Court and that oportunity came with the election to the presidency of his close political friend William McKinley. McKenna was elevated to the high court in 1898, after a short term as attorney general.

During his early years on the Court, McKenna strongly supported the use of the commerce clause to regulate and protect public health, social welfare, and morals. In *Hipolite Egg Co. v. United States* (1911), for example, he spoke for a unanimous Court in upholding the constitutionality of the Pure Food and Drug Act (1906). In *Hoke v. United States* (1913), which upheld the Mann (White Slave) Act (1910), he declared that the commerce power could be used to promote the general welfare, and, moreover, the purpose of regulation need only to be the welfare of the American people. Such positions not only reflected McKenna's views, but the majority of the Court which at this time sought to enlarge national power in order to deal with the effects of the industrial revolution.

As the Court moved to the right during the 1920s, so did McKenna, as was demonstrated by his position in several labor cases. In *Coppage v. Kansas* (1915) he joined the majority in voiding a Kansas state statute which outlawed yellow-dog contracts by which workers, upon or during employment, forswore membership in unions. McKenna argued that the law which applied to all private enterprises, rather than merely those which could be defined as serving the public interest, interfered too basically with individual contractual freedoms. And in *Adkins v. Children's Hospital* (1923) he aligned himself with his most conservative colleagues and voted to invalidate a minimum wage act for women in the District of Columbia.

In civil liberties cases McKenna supported the prevailing orthodoxy that the government could limit constitutional rights during wartime. He voted with the majority in *Schenck v. United States* (1919) in which the Espionage Act (1917) was upheld and in *Abrams v. United States* (1919) concurred with the majority opinion which validated Abrams's conviction for violating the Sedition Act (1918). In these and other cases McKenna accepted Holmes's "clear and present" danger doctrine, but went one step further to argue that

America's involvement in the war alone presented a "clear and present" danger under the acts. This narrow view of Holmes's doctrine demonstrated his conviction that the First Amendment was not absolute, but subject to severe restriction and limitation. A year later in *Pierce v. United States* (1920) McKenna discarded Holmes's position altogether and subscribed to Justice Mahlon Pitney's majority opinion which upheld the conviction under the Espionage Act of a socialist writer in spite of the fact that no evidence was produced to show any kind of relationship between the circulation of his pamphlet and the provisions of the act. Pitney substituted his "bad tendency" doctrine for Holmes's "clear and present danger" test and McKenna was convinced.

During his last years on the Court McKenna's views became increasingly rigid and dogmatic. He was more likely to support Justices George Sutherland, Willis Van Devanter, James C. McReynolds, and Pierce Butler than Oliver Wendell Holmes and Louis D. Brandies, and is therefore generally remembered as a staunch conservative who, in his early career, occasionally supported some of the basic goals of the Progressive movement. Joseph McKenna died on November 21, 1926, in Washington, D.C.

Oliver Wendell Holmes

If conservatives wish to preserve the *status quo,* liberals tend to emphasize the necessity for experiment, change, and reform. In numerous dissents, Oliver Wendell Holmes protested against a conservative Court majority which was disposed to view critically new forms of social legislation. His most memorable arguments can be found in those cases which dealt with civil liberties, child labor, labor relations, and price controls. While not totally wedded to the Progressive program, Holmes believed that the Supreme Court should not hinder social experimentation and certainly not write its brand of conservative laissez-faire economics into the Constitution.

Oliver Wendell Holmes was born in Boston, Massachusetts, on March 8,

1841. He attended a private Latin school and Harvard College, from which he was graduated in 1861. With the outbreak of the Civil War, Holmes volunteered for service in the Twentieth Massachusetts Regiment; he served for three years and was wounded three times. After the war he attended Harvard Law School, graduated in 1866, and was admitted to the bar the following year. Beyond the practice of law, he wrote several distinguished articles and books which enhanced his reputation in the legal community. Harvard Law School invited him to join its faculty and Holmes did teach for a short time. In 1882, he was appointed to the Massachusetts Supreme Judicial Court and served for almost twenty years until President Theodore Roosevelt appointed him to the United States Supreme Court in 1902.

Holmes is best known for his opinions and dissents concerning civil liberties, particularly freedom of speech. Fundamentally, Holmes held that the First Amendment guaranteed freedom of speech no matter how unpopular or shocking were the ideas disseminated by speakers and writers. Tolerance and immunity, however, were not unlimited. In *Schenck v. United States* (1919), which upheld the wartime Espionage Act (1917), he argued that absolute freedom of speech had never existed in peace or war. "Free speech," Holmes declared in his famous illustration, "would not protect a man in falsely shouting fire in a theatre, and causing a panic." He suggested that one must apply a "clear and present danger" test to all cases where freedom of speech was attacked. If the results were negative, government limitations would be valid.

In *Hammer v. Dagenhart* (1918) the Supreme Court found unconstitutional the Keating-Owen Child Labor Act (1916) which attempted to outlaw child labor by the use of the commerce clause of the Constitution. The statute prohibited the interstate shipment of any goods which had been manufactured with the assistance of any form of child labor. Justice Day, speaking for the majority, based his decision on the doctrine that "commerce succeeds to manufacture and is not part of it." This meant that the federal government had no constitutional power to regulate manufacturing and thus no control over child labor. Holmes, in his dissent, implied that the majority had not looked at constitutional precedent, but had been influenced by their own social philosophy. The Justices had thwarted social legislation which purged society of an evil for the sake of preserving a particular set of rigid concepts: laissez-faire economics.

Perhaps Holmes's most significant statement on labor relations was his dissent in *Truax v. Corrigan* (1921) where the Court majority struck down an Arizona statute which prohibited injunctions against picketing. Chief Justice Taft argued for the Court that picketing invalidly deprived men of their property rights without due process of law. Moreover, the law denied equal protection of the laws to all by granting to labor disputes immunity from the process of injunction. Justice Holmes countered by criticizing the concept that a business was a "property" entitled to special protection under the law.

"There is nothing," he declared, "that I more deprecate than the use of the Fourteenth Amendment beyond the absolute compulsion of its words to prevent the making of social experiments that an important part of the community desires.. . . " During the early years of the New Deal, legislation protecting labor unions from injunctions would be passed on the national level and upheld by the Court. Holmes's dissent had foreshadowed a more hospitable attitude on the part of congressmen and Justices in the area of industrial-labor relations.

On the issue of price controls Holmes also sharply differed from his conservative colleagues. Justice Sutherland, speaking for the majority in *Tyson & Brothers v. Banton* (1927), declared that control over prices was a valid legislative measure only when the business was one "affected with a public interest," like common carriers, banks and utilities. Holmes argued in response: "I think the proper course is to recognize that a state legislature can do whatever it sees fit to do unless it is restrained by some express prohibition in the Constitution of the United States." Moreover, he continued, "the notion that a business is clothed with a public interest and has been devoted to the public use is little more than a fiction intended to beautify what is disagreeable to the sufferers." In brief, Holmes thought it reasonable and proper for a legislature to restrict any business (in this case the law regulated the maximum prices at which brokers in New York State could sell theatre tickets) when it had sufficient force of public opinion behind it. The public control of business profits was for him a valid constitutional concern.

Holmes, along with Louis D. Brandies and Harlan F. Stone, represented the liberal view on a high bench which was dominated by conservatives bent on preserving the *status quo*. He is most remembered as a vigorous defender of civil liberties and an advocate of the "preservation of the free market in ideas."

On Janury 12, 1932, Holmes left the Court after several of his colleagues persuaded him that his age demanded resignation. He died in Washington, D.C. on March 6, 1935, at the age of nineth-three. He left most of the money in his estate to the United States of America. Congress approved the use of these funds for the preparation of a history of the Supreme Court which is still being written.

William Rufus Day

William R. Day was appointed to the Supreme Court by Theodore Roosevelt in February 1903. Although he took a conservative position on certain aspects of the commerce clause of the Constitutuion, he is best classified as a moderate liberal. He stood closer in legal philosophy to John H. Clarke, Charles Evans Hughes, and Louis Brandeis than to Willis Van Devanter, James C. Reynolds, and Mahlon Pitney.

Day was born on April 17, 1849, in Portage County, Ohio, thirty miles southwest of Cleveland. He attended local schools and in 1866, entered the University of Michigan. After graduation he spent a year reading law in a local judge's office in his hometown of Ravenna. In 1871, he returned to the

University of Michigan, and on completion of a year's study of law Day decided to settle in Canton, Ohio. He built a prosperous law firm, Lynch and Day, and made the most important contact of his life; Day became an intimate friend of William McKinley.

In 1886, Day was elected judge of the Court of Common Pleas, but only served six months. In 1889, he was nominated by President Benjamin Harrison to the United States District Court, but never filled the position. At this stage of his life Day was reluctant to give up his lucrative law practice. With the election of McKinley to the presidency, however, Day changed his mind about entering public service and accepted appointment as first assistant secretary of state. While working at the State Department, he busied himself primarily with the pressing problem of averting war with Spain over Cuba. Although Day opposed imperialism he, like all the other participants in the drama of 1898, was unable to control events and war did erupt. McKinley trusted him so greatly that he elevated Day to the secretaryship. It is a curious fact of history that the United States had an antiimperialist secretary of state in office at a time when the government was constructing an overseas empire.

After spending the fall of 1898 in Paris as head of the American delegation to the peace conference, Day expressed a desire to return to Canton, Ohio, and practice law. Yet in the end, he accepted an apointment to the United States Court of Appeals for the Sixth Circuit; as a member of that distinguished court he served with two future Supreme Court Justices, Horace Lurton and William Howard Taft. In 1903, Theodore Roosevelt, having been disappointed by Taft's reluctance to leave the Philippines where he was governor, chose Day to fill an opening on the Supreme Court caused by the resignation of George Shiras.

Day did not oppose the ideals of the Progressive Era, but because of his narrow view of the commerce clause of the Constitution, he supported the Court's opinion in *Hammer v. Dagenhart* (1918) which struck down the Keating-Owen Child Labor Act (1916). The statute, Day argued, was not a regulation of commerce, but an outright prohibition and as such as void. Moreover, he declared, the act "does not regulage transportation among the states, but aims to standardize the ages at which children may be employed in mining and manufacturing within the states." Justice Day stressed that earlier decisions had prohibited the transportation of goods in interstate commerce which were harmful; this prohibition had been necessary to save commerce itself from contamination, but the products of child labor were in themselves harmless as was their movement in commerce. Day was a decent man who must have been troubled by child labor. Yet he would not support legislation which prohibited it under his reading of the commerce clause. He was therefore unwilling to give the federal government the weapons necessary to wipe out this detestable institution. For Day, it was the responsibility of the states, rather than the federal government, to promote and protect public health, safety, and morals. In *Coppage v. Kansas* (1915), for example, he supprted, in a dissent, a Kansas statute which outlawed yellow-dog labor contracts, and in *Jones v. Portland* (1917) he held that local authorities had the right to establish a fuel yard to sell wood and coal.

On issues such as antitrust legislation stemming from the Sherman Act (1890), Day supported the liberal position. In 1920, the Court in *United States v. U.S. Steel* threw out charges against the great steel trust. Day, in a bitter dissent, attacked all monopolies, and argued against the notion that large industries were inevitable or desirable. Another illustration of Day's inclination to support liberal legislation is evident in *United States v. Doremus* (1919) in which the Court upheld the Harrison Anti-Narcotics Act (1914). The statute was designed to use the taxing power of the Constitution in order to control the traffic in drugs. "This act," Day charged, "may not be declared unconstitutional because its effect may be to accomplish another purpose as well as raising revenue." Day demanded that the federal government dissolve trusts and protect public health, but he would not sanction the use of federal authority to destroy child labor. Still, except for a stubborn determination to uphold an old-fashioned nineteenth-century idea about commerce, he basically supported the Court's attempt to adjust to new conditions caused by the industrialization of the nation.

Day retired from the Supreme Court in May 1923, and accepted an appointment to a commission to adjudicate claims between the United States and Germany left over from the First World War. On July 9, 1923, Justice William R. Day died at his summer home in Michigan.

Horace Harmon Lurton

Horace H. Lurton served on the Supreme Court for five years (1910-14) and contributed very little to constitutional jurisprudence. His decisions, especially those involving property, are marked by a strong desire to uphold the *status quo*. Lurton was reluctant to admit that early twentieth-century America was changing at a rapid rate, and that ideas and solutions of the past could not be applied to the present.

Lurton was born on February 26, 1844, in Newport, Kentucky. Several years later his parents moved the family to Tennessee where he spent most of his early life. He went to local schools and attended Douglas University (now extinct) in Chicago. The Civil War, however, interrupted his college education; Lurton volunteered and fought on the Southern side, was wounded and returned home with a medical discharge. His reenlistment meant more fighting as a member of a guerilla band under General John Hunt Morgan. Captured by Northern forces, Lurton was imprisoned but eventually was pardoned by President Lincoln.

With the end of the war Lurton decided to continue his education at the Cumberland University Law School. After graduation he immediately began to practice law, and in 1875, he was appointed presiding judge of the Sixth Chancery Division of Tennessee. His next major step was election to the Tennessee Supreme Court in 1886, where he remained until 1893, when he was appointed by President Cleveland to the Federal Court of Appeals. In 1910, President Taft appointed Lurton, who was sixty-five years old, to the United States Supreme Court.

Once on the Court Lurton put into practice his hard-and-fast conservative belief in fixed principles and precedents. In one of his most important decisions, *Henry v. A.B. Dick Co.* (1912), he defended the large manufacturer over the small retailer. The A.B. Dick Co. brought suit when one of its retailers refused to use A.B. Dick ink and stencils on its machines. Lurton argued that the company had created the market in the first place ·by the creation and marketing of a new invention. "Had he [the company] kept his invention to himself," he continued, "no ink could have been sold by others for use upon machines embodying that invention. By selling it subject to the restriction he [the company] took nothing from others and in no wise restricted their legitimate market." Justice Lurton, therefore, upheld the right of certain monopolies to set whatever restrictions they so desired on the distribution and retailing of products which they alone controlled. This view was one that subscribed to the old-fashioned idea of nineteenth-century laissez-faire and a deep belief in the sanctity of private property. Such decisions also had the effect of emasculating the Sherman Anti-Trust Act (1890).

Many of his contemporaries, celebrated jurists and lawyers, wrote lenghty and laudatory eulogies after Lurton's death on July 12, 1914. Outside the judicial chambers, a few like labor leader Samuel Gompers viewed him as a "narrow conservative" who worshiped property rights, but most commentators praised his ability and success as a lawyer and judge. Today, he is largely ignored by both constitutional and social historians.

Charles Evans Hughes

Charles Evans Hughes had two careers on the Supreme Court. He served as an Associate Justice from 1910 to 1916, and as Chief Justice from 1930 to 1941. During his first term of office, from which he resigned in order to run for the presidency, he generally steered a liberal course.

Hughes was born in Glens Falls, New York, on April 11, 1862. He studied at home and in local public grammar schools. At fourteen he was admitted to Madison College (now Colgate University), but later transferred to Brown University in Providence, Rhode Island. After graduation Hughes read law in the office of an attorney while earning money as a teacher of Greek, Latin, and mathematics. In 1882, he entered Columbia Law School and was graduated with highest honors in 1884. With such a record it was not difficult for him to procure a good position with a prominent law firm, but after a few years he turned away from the practice of law and in 1891, accepted a professorship at Cornell University. After two years he was back at his old job.

Hughes entered public life in 1905, when he became counsel to a New York State legislative committee investigating electric and gas rates. He discovered that the city of New York and consumers were being overcharged and recomended that a public service commission regulate rates and investigate complaints. In 1906, he was nominated by the Republican party for the New York State governorship; Hughes won by a margin of 57,897 votes and was the only Republican statewide candidate elected. Two years later he was reelected and served until he was appointed to the Supreme Court in 1910.

During his first term on the Court Hughes was involved in cases dealing with involuntary servitude, due process, equal protection, and the contract clauses of the Constitution. For example, in *Bailey v. Alabama* (1911) Hughes, speaking for the Court, voided a statute which had made it lawful for employers to compel employees to work off a debt. Such laws, he argued, "furnish the readiest means of compulsion. . .against the poor and ignorant, its most likely victims," and, he added, it is most important "to safeguard the freedom of labor upon which alone can enduring prosperity be based." And in *Miller v. Wilson* (1915) Justice Hughes, again speaking for the Court, upheld a California law which forbade the employment of women in certain businesses for more than eight hours a day. By holding for the state the Court had not restricted liberty of contract without due process of law or denied equal protection of the laws. The liberty of contract guaranteed by the Constitution, according to Hughes, mandated freedom from restraint and not immunity against measures to safeguard the public interest.

Some of the most important decisions of Justice Hughes were in the area of federal power and interstate commerce. Usually, he argued for a broad interpretation of the scope of federal interstate power. In *Baltimore & Ohio Railroad v. Interstate Commerce Commission* (1911) he held as constitutional the right of Congress to regulate hours of labor engaged in interstate commerce, and in the *Minnesota Rate Cases* (1913) he affirmed Congress's right to regulate both interstate and intrastate rail rates so that Congress would not be "thwarted by the co-mingling of interstate and intrastate operation." These and other cases enlarged the authority of the federal government, especially in transportation. Hughes fully understood America's need to possess a strong integrated railway system suitable for the new industrial age.

On June 7, 1916, Hughes was nominated for the presidency and therefore resigned from the Supreme Court. Thus, he ended his first term of service and a rather remarkably liberal phase of his career.

After defeat in the election he returned to the practice of law and spent most of his time advising corporations. In 1921, however, he was appointed Warren G. Harding's secretary of state; he served for four years and generally supported liberal foreign policy issues such as the entrance of the United States in the League of Nations and in the World Court, disarmament, and better relations with Latin America. (Hughes, however, refused to recognize the Soviet Union.) In March 1925, he resigned as secretary of state and once again entered private practice. From 1928 to 1930, he served as a judge on the Permanent Court of International Justice. On February 3, 1930, President Herbert Hoover nominated Hughes to succeed William Howard Taft to be Chief Justice of the Supreme Court.

During this second period of tenure on the Court Hughes wrote numerous decisions of great importance to American life. He supported civil liberties, civil rights, and the organizing activities of labor. On economic questions, however, he joined with other conservative Justices to strike down New Deal legislation enacted to overcome the damage wrought by the Great Depression.

On June 2, 1941, Hughes resigned from the Court because of "considerations of health and age." He died on August 17, 1948, at the age of eighty-six.

Willis Van Devanter

In December 1910, President William Howard Taft, after elevating Edward White to the Chief Justiceship, nominated Willis Van Devanter for the position of Associate Justice. During his twenty-six years on the Court, Van Devanter proved to be an unimaginative conservative principly interested in cases dealing with public lands, admiralty law, water rights, Indian affairs, and corporation law. While most of his work was important, these cases made for rather dull decisions, and his fellow Justices were happy to let him have them. Yet they seem to have respected him for is careful, meticulous, and learned opinions; William Howard Taft, Louis D. Brandeis, and Harlan F. Stone praised his craftsmanship, negotiation skills, and knowledge of judicial procedure.

Willis Van Devanter was born in Marion, Indiana, on April 17, 1859. He attended Marion public schools and Indiana Asbury University (De Pauw). In 1881, he graduated second in a class of sixty-five from the University of Cincinnati Law School. After several years of law practice in Indiana, Van Devanter moved on to the territory of Wyoming where he prospered in both the practice of law and Republican politics. He made a name for himself in public service by helping to revise and compile the territorial statutes of Wyoming, serving as city attorney of Cheyenne, and doing a creditable job as Chief Justice of the Territorial Supreme Court. On the national level his first position was with the Interior Department where he specialized in legal matters involving public lands and Indian affairs. In 1903, President Theodore Roosevelt appointed Van Devanter to the Eighth Circuit Court of Appeals. While on this court he busied himself with those matters he felt at home with: railroad cases, land claims, jurisdictional disputes, and questions of negligence. Indeed, much of this same work would consume his time on the United States Supreme Court.

Although Van Devanter is considered by most historians of the Supreme Court to have been a rigid conservative, he tended to take a liberal view on matters concerning the commerce clause of the Constitution. In *Kieran v. Portland* (1911) he upheld the Employers' Liability Act (1908) which applied to injured workers engaged in interstate commerce. And a year later in the *Second Employers' Liability Cases* he argued that Congress could do virtually anything "to save the act of interstate commerce from prevention or intervention or interruption, or to make that act more secure, more reliable, or more efficient."

On issues such as civil liberties, however, he demonstrated a strong inclination toward the *status quo,* and its comforting old formulas and principles. For example, in *Near v. Minnesota* (1931) he voted with the majority to uphold a state "press gag" law, and in *Nixon v. Condon* (1932) Van Devanter approved of a Texas white primary law invalidated by the Court. During the 1930s, he moved to the far right of the political spectrum voting against most New Deal measures which came before the Court such as the NRA, AAA, the gold clauses, and the Wagner Act.

In June 1937, Van Devanter resigned from the Court at the age of seventy-eight, retiring under a new law which gave him full pay. He moved to New York where he died on February 8, 1941. He was praised by lawyers and jurists for his thorough work on the Court, yet many people, during the harsh times of the Great Depression, had vilified him as a blind, stubborn reactionary who had lost contact with the real world.

Joseph Rucker Lamar

Joseph Rucker Lamar was a conservative southern lawyer who is viewed today as neither an original thinker nor as a person who understood the changing society of his day. Historians of the Supreme Court have largely ignored him and thus placed this Justice among the Court's forgotten men.

Lamar was born on October 14, 1857, on a plantation in Ruckersville, Georgia. He attended Richmond Academy in Augusta, Martin Institute, also in Georgia, and the Penn Lucy Academy in Baltimore. In 1877, he received his degree from Bethany College in West Virginia. After graduation he studied law at Washington and Lee University and in the office of a prominent Augusta attorney, Henry Clay Foster. Lamar joined the Foster firm in 1880, as a partner and spent the next thirty years practicing law, representing Richmond County in the lower house of Georgia's legislature, rewriting the state's law codes, and sitting on the Georgia Supreme Court. In 1910, he was appointed to the United States Supreme Court by President William Howard Taft.

Taft, a staunch conservative, viewed the Lamar appointment as a counterbalance, along with his other appointments (Horance H. Lurton, Charles Evans Hughes, Willis Van Devanter, and Mahlon Pitney), to the liberals (John Marshall Harlan, Oliver Wendell Holmes, Joseph McKenna, and William R. Day).

Lamar's work on the Court involved such diverse matters as the question of federal administrative powers, labor relations, and business regulation. In *United States v. Grimaud* (1911) speaking for the Court, he upheld Congress's right to authorize administrators to carry out the details and management of its policies. In fact, he declared that administrative rulings had the force of law and that violations might be punished as infractions of a criminal statute. Lamar's decision gave wide latitude to members of the executive branch in their administrative directives and helped to spawn numerous federal bureaus and agencies.

Labor viewed Lamar's decision in *Gompers v. Buck Stove and Range Co.* (1911) with much criticism and derision. Speaking for a unanimous Court, he upheld the legality of injunctions against secondary boycotts. Lamar's ruling supported business and undercut labor's ability to defend itself against unyielding employers. Referring particularly to labor's use of the boycott, he argued that the Court must extend its protective and restraining powers "to every device whereby property is irreparably damaged or commerce is illegally restrained."

A Kansas statute which regulated insurance company rates on the ground that the business of insurance was affected with a public interest was upheld by the Court in *German Alliance Insurance Co. v. Lewis* (1914). Lamar, in one of his few dissents, declared that the majority decision pointed "inevitable to the conclusion that the price of every article sold and the price of every service offered can be regulated by statute." This dissent marked Lamar as an economic conservative, more concerned with the welfare of business than with the public interest, and unable to comprehend the changing nature of American industrial society during the early twentieth century.

Although Lamar was highly praised for his work by his contemporaries, today we see him as a man who defended with great determination the property rights of the wealthy and powerful. His social and economic philosophy, conservative laissez-faire principles, was an outworn set of ideas which did not bring new insights to contemporary problems. In brief, as a member of the highest Court in the land, his achievements were limited and his influence minimal.

Lamar was unable to join his colleagues for the fall 1915 term because of a stroke he suffered in September. On January 2, 1916, at the age of fifty-eight, he died.

Mahlon Pitney

Mahlon Pitney was the last of five appointments to the Supreme Court made by President William Howard Taft. He was born near Morristown, New Jersey, on February 5, 1858, attended private schools, and graduated from Princeton University in 1879. Under his father's tutelage he studied law and was admitted to the New Jersey bar. In 1894, Pitney entered politics and was elected to the House of Representatives. He was reelected but resigned from the House on Janury 5, 1899, to accept election to the New Jersey senate. On February 5, 1901, Pitney was named to the New Jersey Supreme Court for a seven-year term by Governor Foster M. Voorhees where he remained until his appointment to the United States Supreme Court in 1912.

Pitney's Senate ratification was marked by bitter debate since progressive Republicans were displeased with his antiunion record while on the New Jersey Supreme Court. Their concerns were justified since, once on the Court, Pitney continued to oppose labor unions and their activities in his decisions. In *Coppage v. Kansas* (1915) Pitney, speaking for the majority, declared that "yellow-dog" contracts outlawed by a state statute were permissible; the law violated the Fourteenth Amendment's due process clause and had unlawfully deprived the employer of his freedom to make a contract. "Yellow-dog" contracts require workers to agree not to join any labor organization as a condition for securing or continuing their employment and Pitney's position was clear. He argued that while an individual has a legal right to join a union, he has no inherent right to do this and still remain in the pay of one who is unwilling to employ a union man.

Several years later in 1917, Pitney once again, took the side of business in an important labor case. Speaking for the Court in *Hitchman Coal and Coke Co. v. Mitchell* (1917), he stated that the company was free to make nonmembership in a union a condition of employment. Moreover, he declared that an injunction should be issued prohibiting union attempts to secure secret membership promises when these same workers had previously agreed to relinquish their employment in case they became union members. Other opinions in labor cases continued to express his bias against unions.

Pitney also exhibited an overwhelmingly narrow and conservative attitude in reference to civil liberties, an area in which he wrote several important decisions. For exampe, in *Pierce v. United States* (1920) Pitney ignored Holmes's "clear and present danger" test and adopted the rather vague "bad tendency" doctrine. A socialist pamphlet, it was argued, which attached conscription and the First World War *might* have a tendency to cause insubordination, disloyalty, and refusal of duty in the military forces of the United States.

Pitney suffered a stroke in August 1922, and resigned from the Court on December 31. Although he was a hardworking and conscientious jurist, he did not make any lasting contribution to American constitutional law.

James Clark McReynolds

James C. McReynolds, while Woodrow Wilson's attorney general, was thought to be a liberal because of his strong antitrust prosecutions, but after his appointment to the Supreme Court in 1914, he proved in reality to be a staunch conservative, who eventually developed into an extreme reactionary. In the opinion of his critics, he was a rude, puritanical, and intolerant individual bent on having his way without considering others.

McReynolds was born in Kentucky on February 3, 1862. His early life was spent on the family plantation where he was most influenced by his mother who brought him up according to strict fundamentalist teachings. At Vanderbilt University in Nashville he excelled at his studies and received his degree in 1882. After a year of graduate work he went on to the University of Virginia to study law. From 1884 to 1903, he practiced law in Nashville, mostly representing business corporations such as the Illinois Central Railroad. In 1903, he was appointed assistant attorney general, and in 1907, he was put in charge of prosecuting the tobacco trust; his work on that case established his reputation as a trustbuster. McReynold's support for Woodrow Wilson in 1912, led to his appointment to the position of attorney general in 1913. As attorney general he proved both controversial and inept; his bad temper did not help him in his dealings with congressmen and government officials. Because of the embarrassment he caused, Wilson shortened McReynold's career in the Cabinet by elevting him to the Supreme Court in 1914.

While on the Supreme Court McReynolds busied himself mostly with questions of admiralty and maritime jurisdiction, disputes of priority among creditors in bankruptcy proceedings, agreements with Indian tribes, and the validity of patents and copyrights. In dealing with these problems he was interested in the technical aspects of the law, statutory interpretation, and the procedures and jurisdiction of the federal courts. He also continued to favor, as in his days as attorney general, competition in the business world, and therefore supported the Sherman Anti-Trust Act (1890). In his opinion, the Federal Trade Commission Act had given the government too much power over business. In *Federal Trade Commission v. Gratz* (1920) he first argued that "unfair methods of competition" are not defined by the statute and then declared that the solution to this problem should come from the courts, not from the commission, which would "ultimately. . .determine as a matter of law, what they include." Since the courts generaly favored business, this decision severely undercut the commission's authority. McReynolds's position on the issue of monopolies showed both liberal and conservative facets. While he wanted competition in the marketplace, he also damaged the government's ability to accomplish this goal.

In areas such as the regulation of business there was no equivocation in his determination to protect freedom of contract and property rights: the centerpiece of conservative doctrine. In *Adams v. Tanner* (1917) the Court voided a Washington state statute which made it unlawful to receive fees from any person as payment for aid in securing employment. McReynolds stated that the law put an outright end to employment agencies and therefore the act was one of prohibition and not mere regulation. Such a prohibition of a lawful public business, he continued, lacked any social justification. The Washington state legislature had acted in order to protect consumers (job-hunters) from the abuses of employment agencies, but McReynolds opposed any government interferences in the conduct of "lawful" business. In another example, *Block v. Hirsh* (1919), McReynolds, in a bitter dissent, condemned a majority decision which approved of rent controls in Washington, D.C. He ranted that their opinion paved the way for socialism and for the complete destruction of private property rights.

The limitations of federal governmental authority, particularly the executive branch, was another important element of conservative policy which McReynolds supported with vigor. Dissenting in *Myers v. United States* (1926), he complained that the majority decision which upheld the President's right to dismiss a postmaster without congressional approval might make members of all administrative boards and commissions "subject to the President's pleasure or caprice." In McReynolds's view Congress should fix the conditions for removal. It is apparent that the society which the Justice desired was one where a weak national government, disposed to business, interfered very little with the lives of its citizens.

During the 1930s, Mr Reynolds became infamous for his opposition to social reform and for the bitterness and hatred he showed toward Franklin D. Roosevelt. He voted against more New Deal legislation than any other Justice on the Court. He retired in 1941, and lived for another five years in Washington, D.C., where he died on August 24, 1946. Along with Justices Willis Van Devanter, Pierce Butler, George Sutherland, Edward Terry Sanford, and Mahlon Pitney, McReynolds for over a generation supported conservative policies which favored privileges for business, a weak national government, and a strict constructionist view of the Constitution.

Louis Dembitz Brandeis

Louis D. Brandeis was successively a labor lawyer, a progressive reformer, and finally an Associate Justice of the United States Supreme Court. While on the high bench he sought to persuade his colleagues to accept his liberal views of the law; he was renowned for lengthy briefs, decisions, and dissents which were heavily weighted with facts and statistics as well as constitutional precedent. With great passion he argued that an analysis of the economic and social situation behind the case would demonstrate that the law was a "living organism," and that the Court had the capacity as well as the duty to "legislate" social change.

Brandeis was born in Louisville, Kentucky, on November 13, 1856. He attended Louisville public schools and at the age of sixteen entered the equivalent of high school in Dresden, Germany. Two years later he enrolled in Harvard Law School without having had the experience of a college education. Brandeis excelled in his studies and completed the course in two years. In 1878, he began to practice law, first in St. Louis, Missouri, and then in Boston, Massachusetts. Within a short time Brandeis became known as the People's Attorney since he worked, without fee, for a great variety of causes. He represented labor, sought cheaper utility rates and fought for railway and life insurance regulation. In each case he supported his arguments with sociological and economic data as well as the law; Brandeis's success rate demonstrated that it was very difficult for opponents to overcome his well-researched briefs.

On January 28, 1916, President Woodrow Wilson appointed Brandeis to the Supreme Court. His appointment stunned the business community, which looked upon Brandeis as a dangerous radical, since he had supported the labor movement and fought abuses in the world of transportation, banking, and insurance. After five months of Senate hearings, however, he was confirmed by a vote of 49 to 22.

Brandeis served on the Court for twenty-three years (1916-39). Throughout this period he consistently held the view that the majority of the Justices tended to settle constitutional questions by legal precedents which had been formulated several centuries ago under vastly different social conditions. As a result conservative Justices such as William Howard Taft did not understand modern society, particularly the new industrial age of the twentieth century. They were therefore incapable of writing decisions which formulated constitutional and legal precepts to meet new conditions. Brandeis sought to remedy this situaiton by educating the judiciary and the public through his decisions and dissents. The latter particularly have become mandatory reading for all those interested in constitutional law. In these documents filled with facts and statistics, he sought to gather every bit of information available to buttress his argument. Some jurists have called Brandeis a scientist of the law.

In areas such as labor relations and civil liberties one can observe Brandeis's deep differences with the majority of the Conservative Court. In *Truax v. Corrigan* (1921), for example, the Court declared unconstitutional an Arizona statute which banned state courts from granting injunctions against picketing. Chief Justice Taft argued that the law violated due process by protecting palpable wrongful injuries to property rights. Brandeis, in his dissent, argued that the injunction was an abuse which prevented equality in labor-management relations. He suggested that "the real motive in seeking the injunction was not originally to prevent property from being injured nor to protect the owner in its use, but to endow property with active, militant power which would make it dominant over men. In other words, that, under the guise of protecting property rights, the employer was seeking sovereign power."

In civil liberties cases, brought to the Court as a result of the violation of the Espionage and Sedition acts, Brandeis forcibly defended free speech in wartime. While several of his colleagues, employing circumstantial evidence, demanded the vigorous enforcement of the statutes, Brandeis sought strict application of Holmes's "clear and present danger" test. He believed that "the fundamental right of free men to strive for better conditions through new legislation and new institutions will not be preserved, if to secure it by argument to fellow citizens may be construed as criminal incitement to disobey the existing law." Justice Mahlon Pitney, speaking for the majority in *Pierce v. United States* (1920), rejected Holmes's "clear and present danger" test and Brandeis's arguments, and adopted the rather vague "bad tendency" doctrine which declared that the act was violated if literature or speech *might* have tendency to cause insubordination, disloyalty, and refusal of duty in the military forces of the United States. For Brandeis such an argument, which implied that statements which seemed "to those exercising judicial power to be unfair in its portrayal of existing evils, mistaken in its assumptions, unsound in reasoning, or intemperate in language" should be disallowed, was a severe and unlawful violation of the First Amendment. In Brandeis's estimation, *Pierce* was a challenge to the citizen's basic constitutional rights.

Brandeis was one of the most influential Justices of modern times. Along with Oliver Wendell Holmes and Harlan F. Stone he battled a conservative majority which adhered to the nineteenth-century philosophy of laissez-faire economics and the social *status quo*. He believed that changes in the law must be supported by well-researched evidence as well as constitutional precedent, that the Supreme Court should allow social experimentation, and that the law must be examined in terms of modern society. He served through the New Deal period, and so saw many of his views accepted by the public, by Congress, and by the Supreme Court. The "Peoples' Lawyer" retired from the bench in 1939, to devote what remained of his life to the Zionist cause; he died in Washington, D.C., on October 5, 1941.

John H. Clarke

John H. Clarke was elevated to the Supreme Court in 1916, by Woodrow Wilson. The President wished to appoint a progressive to replace Charles Evans Hughes, who had resigned in order to run for the presidency on the Republican ticket, and Clarke satisfied Wilson's wishes on most of the important issues that came before the Court. He supported the child labor law in his dissent of *Hammer v. Dagenhart* (1918); voiced approval of a federal tax on narcotics in *United States v. Doremus* (1919); and upheld labor's right to strike, picket, and conduct boycotts in *Duplex Printing Co. v. Deering* (1921) and in *Hitchman Coal and Coke Co. v. Mitchell* (1917). In the area of civil liberties, however, his record was far from liberal. For example, in *Abrams v. United States* (1919) Clarke, speaking for the majority, upheld the Sedition Act (1918), arguing that an antiwar pamphlet did "excite, at the supreme crisis of the war, disaffection, sedition, riots, and ...revolution." Oliver Wendell Holmes and Louis D. Brandeis found the case weak and criticized Clarke for taking seriously "the surreptitious publishing of a silly leaflet by an unknown man." Still, Clarke generally sided with Holmes and Brandeis on most issues and was looked upon by the progressive and liberal community as a counterweight to the conservative majority on the Court.

John Clark was born on September 18, 1857, in New Lisbon, Ohio. He went to New Lisbon High School and Western Reserve College where he graduated Phi Beta Kappa in 1877. The study of law under the supervision of his father came next, and in 1878, he passed the bar and began to practice law in New Lisbon. The law was, after a short time, mixed with journalism and politics when Clarke purchased a half interest in the Youngstown *Vindicator* and joined with other progressive Democrats in supporting both local and national liberal legislation. Yet he refused several nominations for public office and in 1897, joined a Cleveland law firm which represented major railroads in the Midwest. If at times there seemed to be contradictions at work in his life, Clarke, the corporation lawyer, still remained loyal to progressive principles. He continued to advocate reform and insisted that national power must be enlarged in order to cope with the changes wrought by the industrialization of American society. In 1914, President Wilson appointed Clarke to the Federal District Court of the Northern District of Ohio. His appointment raised questions among conservatives in the Senate, but he was confirmed. Two years later he was elevated to the United States Supreme Court.

Although Clarke only served six years on the Court, he made his mark, not only in defending progressive legislation, but in the area of antitrust law. In a series of antitrust cases—*United States v. Reading Railroad Co.* (1920), *United States v. United States Steel Corp.* (1920), and *United States v. Lehigh Valley Railroad* (1920)—he argued that large companies had purchased other firms, monopolized whole industries, and therefore eliminated competition. His arguments were persuasive enough to convince his associates to agree to disolve both the Reading and Lehigh combinations. During the 1930s, these cases would be used by the Court as a precedent for major antitrust decisions.

On September 1, 1922, Clarke resigned from the Court, explaining that his resignation was based on his desire to work for American entrance in the League of Nations as well as family duties. Liberals, who saw Clarke as a progressive force on an overly conservative Court, felt betrayed. Perhaps the real reasons for his departure were the tedious work and the discomfort caused by the clash of personalities of nine strong-minded men. In retirement, Clarke made numerous speeches, and wrote a book, *America and World Peace,* urging American participation in the world organization. During the 1930s, he warmly supported the New Deal and Roosevelt's attempt to enlarge the Supreme Court. He died on March 22, 1945.

William Howard Taft

William Howard Taft ranks among the most successful politicians and public servants in American history. From 1881 to 1930, his positions included the following: prosecuting attorney of Ohio, Superior Court judge in Cincinnti, solicitor general of the United States, Federal Circuit Court judge, governor general of the Philipines, Cabinet member, president of the United States, and Chief Justice of the Supreme Court. His appointment by President Harding to the Chief's chair on June 30, 1921, at the age of sixty-four, provided Taft with a new career at an age when most men retire.

Taft's legal philosophy was congruent with that of America's leading industrialists and financiers. He firmly defended the *status quo,* which meant that he was a defender of laissez-faire, economic privilege, and private property. He looked upon the Court "as a bulwark to enforce the guarantee that no man shall be deprived of his property without due process of law." Yet, while he was a staunch conservative, he was not an outright reactionary. The politician in him was often moved to face the realities of a new industrial era and to deal with complex social problems in a manner of genuine humanitarianism.

Taft was born in Cincinnati, Ohio, on September 15, 1857. He attended a public high school, graduated from Yale in 1878, studied at Cincinnati Law School, and was admitted to the Ohio bar in 1880. His long and successful career now commenced. Although his true love was the law, Taft, a man of great ambition, deeply involved himself in Washington politics. This led to government service in the Philippines and a Cabinet position as secretary of war under Theodore Roosevelt. The greatest prize, the presidency, was literally handed to him by Roosevelt in 1908. Curiously, Taft would have preferred appointment to the Supreme Court which he regarded as more desirble than election to the presidency. He had developed a distaste for politics and longed to once again enjoy the restrained atmosphere of the courts rather than the hectic and excited ambiance of national government.

In March 1913, Taft, out of office, was offered a professorship of Constitutional Law by Yale University; he accepted the position but pined for an appointment to the Supreme Court. With the election of Warren G. Harding, a Republican, and the death of Chief Justice Edward D. White, his chances increased enormously. On June 30, Harding appointed Taft Chief Justice and the nomination was confirmed with only four dissenting votes— progressive Senators William E. Borah, Hiram Johnson, Robert M. LaFollette, and Populist demagogue Tom Watson. After more than thirty years of dreaming, Taft's greatest goal was finally achieved.

Taft came to the Court intent on reforming the national judicial system which had become sluggish due to clogged dockets. The pressure he applied through speeches and articles in legal periodicals helped to produce the Judicial Act (1922) which modernized the system by allowing judges to meet and smooth out the rough spots which had prevented an efficient judiciary. A Judges' Law (1925) giving the Supreme Court greater control over its docket, was the next step in his reform program. Unfortunately, the third piece of his plan, a rules-of-procedure revision, failed to pass Congress. Still, Taft accomplished enough to achieve recognition as a great legal reformer.

Taft was the most "political" of Chief Justices in American history. As a former president, he never hesitated to freely give advice to Presidents Harding, Coolidge, and Hoover. Influencing appointments to lower federal courts consumed an inordinate amount of his time and, when vacancies occurred, he sent numerous recommendations to the attorney general and the president. Taft wished to see the entire court system filled with men whose political philosophy mirrored his own. He viewed the courts as a bulwark against "radicals" as well as progressives in the other branches of government. It is interesting that his recommendations disregarded party affiliation; one's political viewpoint was all that mattered.

Taft's conservatism on the Court was immediately demonstrated in his first major opinion, *Truax v. Corrigan* (1921), where he argued that an Arizona statute forbidding state courts from issuing injunctions against picketing was unconstitutional; the law violated due process by protecting palpably wrongful injuries to property rights. Accordingly, since conducting a business is a property right, he declared that a law which deprived the owners of an enterprise access to their premises could not be held valid. Taft's opinion showed a rather severe distaste for laws beneficial to social experimentation in general, and labor in particular. In another major decision, *Bailey v. Drexel Furniture* (1922), Taft, speaking for the Court, voided the second Child Labor Law which attempted to eliminate the evil of child labor through the taxing power of Congress. Liberals correctly charged that taxation as a regulatory device had long been recognized as constitutional, but for Taft the welfare of children was less important than the prnciples of laissez-faire economics and the health of the *status quo*. Yet in *Adkins v. Children's Hospital* (1923) he dissented when the Court majority found a District of Columbia minimum wage labor law for women and children unconstitutional. He argued that low-paid employees, "in their necessitous circumstances are prone to accept pretty much anything that is offered. They are peculiarly subject to the overreaching of the harsh and greedy employer."

Occasionally, Taft was able to examine a question unhampered by conservative dogma and produce a humane judgment. Unfortunately, in most cases he opposed with all his heart and his considerable legal weight the "progressive" position. Had he more often concurred in decisions with Oliver Wendell Holmes, Louis D. Brandeis, and Harlan F. Stone, the Court might have produced a record more sympathetic to the dramatic changes that were transforming America into a great industrial society. Perhaps, for example, a more liberal Court might have made the rights of labor a reality during the 1920s, and thus prevented the great violence of the 1930s, which erupted when industrial unions attempted to organize workers. In any event, Taft never had to face the great trial of the depression when his confident assumptions about the wisdom of American business enterprise would have been surely tested. Because of illness he resigned from the Court on February 3, 1930, and a little over a month later, on March 8, 1930, the Chief Justice died.

George Sutherland

George Sutherland was a conservative who strongly believed in laissez-faire economics and the sanctity of private property. Among the members of the conservative bloc on the Supreme Court during the 1920s and 1930s, he was the ablest jurist and best thinker. Some have called him the group's intellectual spokesman.

Born in England on March 25, 1862, Sutherland was brought to America by his parents in 1864. The family settled in the territory of Utah where young George studied at local schools in between various jobs such as clothing store clerk and Wells Fargo agent. He then attended Brigham Young Academy (later Brigham Young University); studied briefly at the University of

Michigan Law School under McIntyre Cooley, a specialist in constitutional law; and worked in various law offices. After thirteen years of law practice Sutherland, in 1896, won election as a Republican to the Utah legislature. In 1900, he moved up to the United States Congress where he served one term in the House of Representatives, and in 1905, he won election to the Senate. While in Congress he supported reform legislation—the Food and Drug Act (1906), the Postal Savings Act, and the Hepburn Act. At this stage of his political career he had not yet developed a hard-and-fast conservative position on the issues of the day, but a few years later, during the first Wilson administration, he would condemn the Federal Reserve Act (1913), the Federal Trade Commission, and the Clayton Anti-Trust Act (1914).

At the end of his first term in the Senate Sutherland was unable to gain renomination and spent the next few years practicing law in Washington, D.C. When the Republicans, under Warren G. Harding, recaptured the White House in 1920, he was apointed to various government committees and represented the Unitd States in arbitration proceedings before The Hague Tribunal. In 1922, Justice John H. Clarke resigned from the Supreme Court and Harding appointed Sutherland to the high bench.

Almost immediately Sutherland played an active role on the Court. In *Adkins v. Children's Hospital* (1923), which dealt with a minimum wage law in Washington, D.C., he spoke for the Court majority and made a lengthy atack upon all minimum wage legislation as economically and socially unsound. Specifically, such legislation, according to Sutherland, ignored the rights of employers, leaving them the privilege of abandoning their businesses as an alternative for going on at a loss. Emphasizing that the issue narrowed down to that of freedom of contrct, he stated that "to sustain the individual freedom of action contemplated by the Constitution, is not to strike down the common good but to exalt it; for surely the good of society as a whole cannot be better served than by the preservation against arbitrary restraints of the liberties of its constituent members."

After this decision was written Sutherland found that he had become a leader of the conservative Justices, who often looked to him as their spokesman, especially when dealing with the troublesome issue of business regulation. In *Tyson Brothers v. Banton* (1927), for example, Sutherland voided a New York statute which prohibited brokers of theater tickets from reselling seats for more than fifty cents over the box office price. The legislature, in passing this law, proclaimed that it was in the public interest to regulate such transactions in order to prevent price gouging. Sutherland argued that the law violated freedom of contract, would lead to the fixing of prices, and was especially perilous since "such subversions are not only illegitimate but are fraught with the danger that having begun on the ground of necessity, they will continue on the score of expediency, and finally, as a mere matter of course." The following year in *Ribnik v. McBride,* a case in which the Court struck down a state law which set fees charged by employment agencies, he reiterated his position on freedom of contract and business regulation by charging that the fixing of prices was beyond the power of legislatures. And again, in *Williams v. Standard Oil Co.* (1929) Sutherland voided a statute which fixed gasoline prices, declaring that a legislature could not set prices unless a business was explicitly vested with a public interest such as special monopolies like utilities.

During the 1930s, Justice Sutherland consistently voted to hold unconstitutional most of the New Deal legislation of the Roosevelt administration that came before the Court. While not exactly a reactionary, he was a staunch conservative who refused to acknowledge the harsh economic conditions of the period. He died on July 18, 1942, at the age of seventy-six.

Pierce Butler

Pierce Butler, a railroad attorney, was an extreme reactionary, blind to the great changes that were occurring in modern American industrial society during the early twentieth century, and firmly against social reform. His confirmation to the Supreme Court was strenuously opposed by progressive Senators George Norris (Nebraska), Robert La Follette (Wisconsin), and Senator-elect Henrik Shipstead (Minnesota). Opponents were objected to Butler because he was a leading advocate of the largest railroads and due to his role in the dismissal of two college professors at the University of Minnesota. One professor was involved with railroad valuations and the other advocated municipal ownership of street railays which conflicted with

Butler's work and views as a representative of railroads. Butler's nomination easily overcame the disapproval of his critics, and he was confirmed on January 2, 1923; the vote was 61 to 8.

Butler was born on March 17, 1866, on a farm in Minnesota. His parents were immigrants from Ireland who came to the United States after the potato famine of the 1840s. After studying at local county schools, Butler entered Carleton College and graduated in 1887. A year later, after reading law at a law firm in St. Paul, he was admitted to the Minnesota bar. His career then followed a path which included law practice, principly railroad litigation; and public service. He was state's attorney for Ramsey County, which included the city of St. Paul; a federal attorney under Attorney General George Wickersham; and finally a United States Supreme Court Justice.

Butler's decisions and dissents consistently demonstrate an all-out effort to support freedom from governmental restraint for business and a disdain for civil liberties and civil rights. For example, in *Jay Burns Baking Co. v. Bryan* (1924) the Court struck down a Nebraska statute fixing standard weights for bread. The intent of the law was to minimize fraud and thus protect the consumer. Butler, for the Court, stated that practical conditions would make it difficult to comply with the statute, and that it imposed an "intolerable burden" upon bakers. And in a dissent to *Euclid v. Ambler* (1926) which upheld the constitutionality of zoning laws, he argued for the freedom of expanding business rather than for protection of homeowners.

In cases dealing with civil liberties Butler sought to limit freedom of expression for the press, minor political opinion, and labor. In *Near v. Minnesota* (1931) he supported a Minnesota "press gag" law which had been passed by legislators seeking to silence a paper, the *Saturday Press,* which was anti-Semitic, but also effectively investigated crime involving officials in Minneapolis. Unconcerned with First Amendment questions, Butler argued that the *Press* threatened the peace and order of the state and therefore deserved no constitutional protection. Rejecting the decision of the majority, he supported the conviction of a woman found guilty of displaying a red flag in public (*Stromberg v. California,* 1931). And in *Hague v. Committee of Industrial Organizations* (1939) he found nothing wrong with a municipal ordinance which essentially prohibited labor meetings in public parks. In civil rights cases Butler showed the same lack of sympathy for elemental justice. He opposed granting a new trial for accused blacks who were denied due process *(Scottsboro Case)* in *Powell v. Alabama* (1932), and in *Nixon v. Condon* (1932) he did not join his colleagues in rejecting an all-white Texas primary law.

During the 1930s, Butler wrote numerous dissents opposing New Deal legislation. With great vigor he condemned government intervention in American life, even when its purpose was to salvage society from the destruction of the Great Depression. When Butler died on November 16, 1939, President Franklin D. Roosevelt replaced him with a Michigan liberal,

Attorney General Frank Murphy. Butler's contribution to constitutional law was minimal, and his career is neglected by legal scholars and is unknown to the public.

Edward Terry Sanford

Edward Terry Sanford was an undistinguished conservative Justice on both the Federal District Court and the Supreme Court. He generally followed the lead of Chief Justice William Howard Taft, and their voting records were remarkably similar. His work has generated little interest in the historical and legal scholarly communities, and no one has been stimulated to write anything of signficance about his career.

Sanford was born in Knoxville, Tennessee, on July 23, 1865. He attended local private schools and several colleges and universities. Graduating *magna cum laude* from Harvard Law School, he went on to pass the Tennessee bar in 1888. Next, he practiced law in Knoxville until he moved to Washington,

D.C., in 1906, to work as a special assistant to the attorney general. After serving in this office, he became attorney general in 1907, Federal District Judge in 1908, and finally Supreme Court Justice in 1923.

On the Supreme Court Sanford's most important decisions were in the area of civil liberties; his record clearly shows a lack of sympathy for First Amendment rights. In *Gitlow v. New York* (1925), for example, he expressed the Court's position that the word *liberty* in the due process clause of the Fourteenth Amendment included freedom of speech and of the press, and that the First Amendment bound the states as well as the federal government. Nevertheless, he found the statute in question (a criminal anarchy law which made it illegal to promote, by written or spoken word, the overthrow of organized government by force) constitutional because Gitlow advocated the violent overthrow of government through the publication of a pamphlet, *The Left Wing Manifesto*. The Court therefore upheld Gitlow's conviction—and argued that there was no infringement on the freedom of speech—even though there was no proof of any danger to society. To Sanford "free speech did not confer an absolute right to speak or publish, without responsiblity, whatever one may choose." He warned that even though no evidence had been presented by the government of any revolutionary activity caused by the publication of the pamphlet, the state had a right to stamp out any sparks that "may kindle a fire that, smoldering for a time, may burst into a sweeping and destructive conflagration." Justice Sanford replaced Holmes's "clear and present danger" test with the rather vague "bad tendency" doctrine of *Pierce v. United States* (1920).

In another significant case, *Whitney v. California* (1927), in which the Court upheld a state criminal syndicalism law imposing heavy fines and imprisonment for joining an organization that favored violence in a political cause or labor dispute, Sanford again instituted the doctrine of "bad tendency." He viewed with alarm "united and joint action" which "involves . . . greater danger to the public peace and security than the isolated utterance and act of individuals." Thus Sanford demanded that all subversive activities which threatened the American form of goverment, no matter how remote, must be opposed. Justice Sanford was essentially saying that even though the protection of civil liberty was an obligation that applied to the states as well as the federal goverment, the states could, in fact, diminish such rights with little justification. Louis D. Brandeis, in a concurring opinion to *Whitney,* in which he showed greater tolerance, argued that the statute should be qualified by requiring that a serious, immediate menace must be proved. "Only an emergency can justify repression," and "such must be the rule if authority is to be reconciled with freedom."

On March 8, 1930, Sanford died at the age of sixty-four. His mentor, Chief William Howard Taft, died on the same day.

Harlan Fiske Stone

When Harlan Fiske Stone was appointed to the Supreme Court by President Calvin Coolidge in 1925, it was assumed that he would join the conservatives—Pierce Butler, Willis Van Devanter, James McReynolds, and George Sutherland. During his tenure as professor and dean of Columbia Law School, he wrote articles and gave lectures which demonstrated a commitment to the basic principles of laissez-faire economics. Yet, after a short time, Stone joined Oliver Wendell Holmes and Louis D. Brandeis in numerous dissents which favored social reform and understood the changing nature of American industrial society. He also sharply criticized his conservative colleagues for interposing their own social and economic philosophy under the guise of interpreting the Constitution.

Stone was born in Chesterfield, New Hampshire, on October 11, 1872. He attended public schools, graduated Phi Beta Kappa from Amherst College and studied law at Columbia University; the New York State bar admitted him in 1899. With his legal training behind him, Stone chose to practice law with a Wall Street firm. Liberals, such as Senator George W. Norris (Neb.), would later charge that since he had been an attorney for men of great weath, he was unfit for public office. In 1903, Stone joined the staff of the Columbia University Law School; from 1915 to 1923, he was the institution's dean. During the First World War he served on the board of inquiry charged with the duty of examining men who claimed exemption from military service. Stone forcibly stated his position, with reference to the objectors, when he declared that "liberty of conscience has a moral and social value which makes it worthy of preservation at the hands of the State." President Coolidge called Stone to Washington in 1924, to assume the duties of the office of the attorney general. Coolidge was obviously looking for someone of impeccable reputation to put in order the Justice Department after the corrupt and disruptive Harding period. One year later President Coolidge appointed Harlan F. Stone to the Supreme Court.

With the exception of *Bedford Stone Co. v. Journeymen Stonecutters* (1927), Stone wrote liberal decisions and dissents. In that particular case he concurred in a decision written by Justice Sutherland which defined as unfair competition a union's efforts to prevent members from finishing products of nonunion labor. "I should have doubted," Stone argued, "whether the Sherman Act prohibited a labor union from peacably refusing to work upon material produced by non-union labor or by a rival union, even though interstate commerce was affected.... But this view was rejected in *Duplex Printing v. Deering* (1921) and a decree was authorized restraining in precise terms any agreement not to work or refusal to work, such as involved here." Perhaps, Stone felt obliged to take a conservative position in a labor matter because of Chief Justice William Howard Taft's insistence that he support the majority. In any event, after *Bedford* Stone consistently supported the liberal position; and if influenced at all, it was by Holmes and Brandeis.

Stone joined Holmes and Brandeis, for example, in opposing the conservative majority in *Ribnick v. McBride* (1928); a critical case in which a state law regulating employment agencies was invalidated. Sutherland, for the Court, contended that a business was regulable only when it was "devoted to public use and its use thereby, in effect, granted by the public." Stone, in his dissent, countered, "Price regulation is within the state's power whenever any combination of circumstances seriously curtails the regulative force of competition so that buyers or sellers are placed at such a disadvantage in the bargaining struggle that a legislature might reasonably anticipate serious consequences to the community as a whole." Sutherland would possibly limit state regulation to utilities, while Stone wanted the doctrine of public interest abandoned in favor of a recognition of the general right of any state legislature to regulate private business wherever it thought the public welfare demanded it.

In yet another example, *St. Louis, O'Fallon Railway Co. v. United States* (1929), where the majority substantially limited the Interstate Commerce Commission's ability to determine the basis for railway rate fixing, Stone, Brandeis, and Holmes declared that the practical effect of the decision was to defeat the intent of Congress which was to provide the public with adequate rail service. The Interstate Commerce Commission's authority to regulate the great railroads, and thereby insure competition, was held as a cardinal civic activity among liberals.

During the 1930s, Stone supported Franklin D. Roosevelt's New Deal program; the President reciprocated by elevating him to the Chief's chair in 1941. When Stone died in Washington, D.C., on April 22, 1946, there was an outpouring of praise for his work on the Court, not only by jurists and lawyers, but by the public.

Justice	State	Appointed by	Replacced	Term	Life Span
John Jay	NY	Washington	—	1789-1795	1745-1829
John Rutledge	SC	Washington	—	1789-1791	1739-1800
William Cushing	MA	Washington	—	1789-1810	1732-1810
James Wilson	PA	Washington	—	1789-1798	1742-1798
John Blair	VA	Washington	—	1789-1796	1732-1800
James Iredell	NC	Washington	—	1790-1799	1751-1799
Thomas Johnson	MD	Washington	Rutledge	1791-1793	1732-1819
William Paterson	NJ	Washington	Johnson	1793-1806	1745-1806
John Rutledge	SC	Washington	Jay	1795-	1739-1800
Samuel Chase	MD	Washington	Blair	1796-1811	1741-1811
Oliver Ellsworth	CT	Washington	Rutledge	1796-1800	1745-1807
Bushrod Washington	VA	John Adams	Wilson	1798-1829	1762-1829
Alfred Moore	NC	John Adams	Iredell	1799-1804	1755-1810
John Marshall	VA	John Adams	Ellsworth	1801-1835	1755-1835
William Johnson	SC	Jefferson	Moore	1804-1834	1771-1834
H. Brockholst Livingston	NY	Jefferson	Paterson	1806-1823	1757-1823
Thomas Todd	KY	Jefferson	—	1807-1826	1765-1826
Gabriel Duvall	MD	Madison	Chase	1811-1835	1752-1844
Joseph Story	MA	Madison	Cushing	1811-1845	1779-1845
Smith Thompson	NY	Monroe	Livingstone	1823-1843	1768-1843
Robert Trimble	KY	John Quincy Adams	Todd	1826-1828	1777-1828
John McLean	OH	Jackson	Trimble	1829-1861	1785-1861
Henry Baldwin	PA	Jackson	Washington	1830-1844	1780-1844
James M. Wayne	GA	Jackson	Johnson	1835-1867	1790-1867
Roger B. Taney	MD	Jackson	Marshall	1836-1864	1777-1864
Philip P. Barbour	VA	Jackson	Duvall	1836-1841	1783-1841
John Catron	TN	Van Buren	—	1837-1865	1786-1865
John McKinley	AL	Van Buren	—	1837-1852	1780-1852
Peter V. Daniel	VA	Van Buren	Barbour	1841-1860	1784-1860
Samuel Nelson	NY	Tyler	Thompson	1845-1872	1792-1873
Levi Woodbury	NH	Polk	Story	1845-1851	1784-1851
Robert C. Grier	PA	Polk	Baldwin	1846-1870	1794-1870
Benjamin R. Curtis	MA	Fillmore	Woodbury	1851-1857	1809-1874
John A. Campbell	AL	Pierce	McKinley	1853-1861	1811-1889
Nathan Clifford	ME	Buchanan	Curtis	1858-1881	1803-1881
Noah H. Swayne	OH	Lincoln	McLean	1862-1881	1804-1884
Samuel F. Miller	IA	Lincoln	Daniel	1862-1890	1816-1890
David Davis	IL	Lincoln	Campbell	1862-1877	1815-1886
Stephen J. Field	CA	Lincoln	—	1863-1897	1816-1899
Salmon P. Chase	OH	Lincoln	Taney	1864-1873	1808-1873
William Strong	PA	Grant	Grier	1870-1880	1808-1895
Joseph P. Bradley	NJ.	Grant	—	1870-1892	1813-1892
Wald Hunt	NY	Grant	Nelson	1872-1882	1810-1886
Morrison R. Waite	OH	Grant	Chase	1874-1888	1816-1888
John Marshall Harlan	KY	Hayes	Davis	1877-1911	1833-1911
William B. Woods	GA	Hayes	Strong	1880-1887	1824-1887
Stanley Matthews	OH	Garfield	Swayne	1881-1889	1824-1889
Horace Gray	MA	Arthur	Clifford	1881-1902	1828-1902
Samuel Blatchford	NY	Arthur	Hunt	1882-1893	1820-1893
Lucius Q.C. Lamar	MS	Cleveland	Woods	1888-1893	1825-1893
Melville W. Fuller	IL	Cleveland	Waite	1888-1910	1833-1910
David J. Brewer	KS	Benjamin Harrison	Matthews	1889-1910	1837-1910
Henry B. Brown	MI	Benjamin Harrison	Miller	1890-1906	1836-1913
George Shiras	PA	Benjamin Harrison	Bradley	1892-1903	1832-1924
Howell E. Jackson	TN	Benjamin Harrison	Lamar	1893-1895	1832-1895
Edward D. White	LA	Cleveland	Blatchford	1894-1910	1845-1921

(Chief Justices in Italics)

Justice	State	Appointed by	Replaced	Term	Life Span
Rufus W. Peckham	NY	Cleveland	Jackson	1895-1909	1838-1909
Joseph McKenna	CA	McKinley	Field	1898-1925	1843-1926
Oliver Wendell Holmes	MA	Theodore Roosevelt	Gray	1901-1932	1841-1935
William R. Day	OH	Theodore Roosevelt	Shiras	1903-1922	1849-1923
William H. Moody	MA	Theodore Roosevelt	Brown	1906-1910	1853-1917
Horace H. Lunon	TN	Taft	Peckham	1909-1914	1844 1914
Charles E. Hughes	NY	Taft	Brewer	1910-1916	1862-1948
Edward D. White	LA	Taft	Fuller	1910-1921	1845-1921
William Van Devanter	WY	Taft	White	1910-1937	1859-1941
Joseph R. Lamar	GA	Taft	Moody	1910-1916	1857-1916
Mahlon Pitney	NJ	Taft	Harlan	1912-1922	1858-1924
James C. McReynolds	TN	Wilson	Lunon	1914-1941	1862-1946
Louis D. Brandeis	MA	Wilson	Lamar	1916-1939	1856-1941
John H. Clarke	OH	Wilson	Hughes	1916-1922	1857-1945
William H. Taft	CT	Harding	White	1921-1930	1857-1930
George Sutherland	UT	Harding	Clarke	1922-1938	1862-1942
Pierce Butler	MN	Harding	Day	1922-1939	1866-1939
Edward T. Sanford	TN	Harding	Pitney	1923-1930	1865-1930
Harlan F. Stone	NY	Coolidge	McKenna	1925-1941	1872-1946
Charles E. Hughes	NY	Hoover	Taft	1930-1941	1862-1948
Owen J. Roberts	PA	Hoover	Sanford	1930-1945	1875-1955
Benjamin N. Cardozo	NY	Hoover	Holmes	1932-1938	1870-1938
Hugo L. Black	AL	Franklin D. Roosevelt	Van Devanter	1937-1971	1886-1971
Stanley F. Reed	KY	Franklin D. Roosevelt	Sutherland	1938-1957	1884-1980
Felix Frankfurter	MA	Franklin D. Roosevelt	Cardozo	1939-1962	1882-1965
William O. Douglas	CT	Franklin D. Roosevelt	Brandeis	1939-1975	1898-1980
Frank Murphy	MI	Franklin D. Roosevelt	Butler	1940-1949	1890-1949
James F. Byrnes	SC	Franklin D. Roosevelt	McReynolds	1941-1942	1879-1972
Harlan F. Stone	NY	Franklin D. Roosevelt	Hughes	1941-1946	1872-1946
Robert H. Jackson	NY	Franklin D. Roosevelt	Stone	1941-1954	1892-1954
Wiley B. Rutledge	IA	Franklin D. Roosevelt	Byrnes	1943-1949	1894-1949
Harold H. Burton	OH	Truman	Roberts	1945-1958	1888-1964
Fred M. Vinson	KY	Truman	Stone	1946-1953	1890-1953
Tom C. Clark	TX	Truman	Murphy	1949-1967	1899-1977
Sherman Minton	IN	Truman	Rutledge	1949-1956	1890-1965
Earl Warren	CA	Eisenhower	Vinson	1953-1969	1891-1978
John Marshall Harlan	NY	Eisenhower	Jackson	1955-1971	1899-1971
William J. Brennan, Jr.	NJ	Eisenhower	Minton	1956-1990	1906-
Charles E. Whittaker	MO	Eisenhower	Reed	1957-1962	1901-1973
Potter Stewart	OH	Eisenhower	Bunon	1958-1981	1915-1985
Byron R. White	CO	Kennedy	Whittaker	1962-1993	1917-
Arthur J. Goldberg	IL	Kennedy	Frankfurter	1962-1965	1908-1990
Abe Fortas	TN	Lyndon B. Johnson	Goldberg	1965-1969	1910-1980
Thurgood Marshall	MD	Lyndon B. Johnson	Clark	1967-1991	1908-1993
Warren E. Burger	MN	Nixon	Warren	1969-	1907-
Harry A. Blackmun	MN	Nixon	Fortas	1970-1994	1908-
Lewis F. Powell, Jr.	VA	Nixon	Black	1972-1981	1907-
William R. Rehnquist	AZ	Nixon	Harlan	1972-	1924-
John Paul Stevens	IL	Ford	Douglas	1975-	1920-
Sandra Day O'Connor	AZ	Reagan	Stewart	1981-	1930-
William R. Rehnquist	AZ	Reagan	Burger	1986-	1924-
Antonin Scalia	NJ	Reagan	Rehnquist	1986-	1936-
Anthony Kennedy	CA	Reagan	Powell	1988-	1936-
David Souter	NH	Bush	Brennan	1990-	1939-
Clarence Thomas	GA	Bush	Marshall	1991-	1948-
Ruth Bader Ginzberg	NY	Clinton	White	1993-	1933-
Stephen Breyer	MA	Clinton	Blackman	1994-	1938-

Bibliography

Berman, Edward. *Labor and the Sherman Act.* New York: Harper Brothers, 1930.

Bickel, Alexander M. "Mr. Taft Rehabilitates the Court." *Yale Law Journal* 79 (1969).

————, ed. *The Unpublished Opinions of Mr. Justice Brandeis.* Cambridge, Mass.: Harvard University Press, 1957.

Bitterman, Henry John. *State and Federal Grants-in-Aid.* New York: Mentzer, Bush & Co., 1938.

Brown, Francis Joseph. *The Social and Economic Philosophy of Pierce Butler.* Washington, D.C.: The Catholic University of America Press, 1945.

Brown, Ray A. "Police Power—Legislation for Health and Personal Safety." *Harvard Law Review* 42 (May 1929). A study of the balance between police power and state social legislation.

Buenker, John D. "The Urban Political Machine and the Seventeenth Amendment." *Journal of American History* LVI (September 1969).

————. "Urban Liberalism and the Federal Income Tax Amendment." *Pennsylvania History* XXXVI (April 1969).

Cardozo, Benjamin N. *The Nature of the Judicial Process.* New Haven: Yale University Press, 1921. A collection of lectures Cardozo gave at the Yale Law School.

Cassidy, Lewis C. "An Evaluation of Chief Justice White." *Mississippi Law Journal* 10 (February 1938).

Chafee, Zechariah, Jr. *Freedom of Speech.* New York: Harcourt, Brace, & Howe, 1920. Chafee discusses wartime civil liberties cases.

Coben, Stanley A. *A. Mitchell Palmer: Politician.* New York: Columbia University Press, 1963. This book is especially incisive on the Red Scare of the early 1920s.

Corwin, Edward S. *Commerce Power Versus State Rights.* Princeton: Princeton University Press, 1936.

————. "Tenure of Office and the Removal Power under the Constitution." *Columbia Law Review* 27 (April 1927). The Myers case is analyzed by a distinguished legal scholar.

Danelski, David J. *A Supreme Court Justice is Appointed.* New York: Random House, 1964. A study of the appointment and confirmation of

Pierce Butler in 1922.

Dishman, Robert B. "Mr. Justice White and the Rule of Reason." *Review of Politics* 13 (1951). Dishman's article is a very useful study of an important Supreme Court doctrine.

Faulkner, Harold U. *The Quest for Social Justice, 1898-1914.* New York: Macmillan, 1931. Faulkner discusses the Pure Food and Livestock acts.

Flexner, Eleanor. *A Century of Struggle: The Woman's Rights Movement in the United States.* Cambridge, Mass.: Harvard University Press, 1959. An excellent and objective history of the feminist movement.

Frankfurter, Felix. "Hours of Labor and Realism in Constitutional Law." *Harvard Law Review* 29 (February 1916). A survey of maximum-hours cases by a future Supreme Court Justice.

———. *Mr. Justice Holmes and the Supreme Court.* Cambridge, Mass.: Harvard University Press, 1961. An excellent short study of Holmes's legal and constitutional philosophy.

Fuller, Raymond G. *Child Labor and the Constitution.* New York: Thomas Y. Crowell Co., 1923. Fuller's book is out-of-date but still useful.

Grantham, Dewey W., Jr. "The White Primary and the Supreme Court." *South Atlantic Quarterly* 48 (1949).

Hamilton, Walton H. "Affection with a Public Interest." *Yale Law Journal* 39 (1930). An important article on a critical Supreme Court doctrine.

Hendel, Samuel. *Charles Evans Hughes and the Supreme Court.* New York: King's Crown Press, 1951. The author looks at Hughes as Associate Justice and Chief Justice.

Hicks, John D. *Republican Ascendancy, 1921-1933.* New York: Harper & Row, 1960. A readable general account of the period.

Highsaw, Robert Baker. *Edward Douglas White: Defender of the Conservative Faith.* Baton Rouge: Louisiana State University Press, 1981.

Hoogenboom, Ari and Olive. *A History of the ICC: From Panacea to Palliative.* New York: W.W. Norton & Co., Inc., 1976. A general history of the Interstate Commerce Commission.

Howe, Mark DeWolfe. *Justice Oliver Wendell Holmes.* 2 vols. Cambridge, Mass.: Harvard University Press, 1957, 1962.

Howell, Ronald F. "Conservative Influence on Constitutional Development, 1923-1937: The Judicial Theory of Justices Van Devantor, McReynolds, Sutherland, and Butler." Ph.D. dissertation, The Johns Hopkins University, 1952.

Klinkhamer, Marie Carolyn. *Edward Douglas White: Chief Justice of the United States.* Washington, D.C.: The Catholic University of America Press, 1943. Klinkhamer gives us a useful overview, but this is basically an uncritical work.

Konefsky, Samuel J. *The Legacy of Holmes and Brandeis.* New York: Macmillan, 1956.

Kutler, Stanley. "Chief Justice Taft, National Regulation, and the Commerce Clause." *Journal of American History* 51 (1965).

Lamar, Clarinda P. *The Life of Joseph Rucker Lamar, 1857-1916.* New York: G.P. Putnam's Sons, 1926. A biography written by Lamar's wife.

Latham, Frank B. *Great Dissenter: Supreme Court Justice John Marshall Harlan, 1833-1911.* New York: Cowles Book Co., 1970.

Leavitt, Donald Carl. "Attitudes and Ideology on the White Supreme Court." Ph.D. dissertation, Michigan State University, 1970.

Lemons, Stanley. *The Woman Citizen: Social Feminism in the 1920s.* Urbana, Ill.: University of Illinois Press, 1973. Among several issues Lemons discusses the effort by women to obtain a constitutional amendment guaranteeing equality of the sexes.

Lerner, Max, ed. *The Mind and Faith of Justice Holmes: His Speeches, Essays, Letters, and Judicial Opinions.* New York: Modern Library, 1943. Lerner's brief commentaries are excellent.

Link, Arthur. *Woodrow Wilson and the Progressive Era.* New York: Harper & Row, 1954. A competent general study by the biographer of Wilson.

McDevitt, Matthew. *Joseph McKenna, Associate Justice of the United States.* Washington, D.C.: The Catholic University of America Press, 1946. While this book is useful, it is an uncritical biography.

McHargue, Daniel S. "President Taft's Appointments to the Supreme Court." *Journal of Politics* 12 (1950).

McLean, Joseph E. *William Rufus Day: Supreme Court Justice from Ohio.* Baltimore: The Johns Hopkins University Press, 1946. This account of Day's life is useful for its treatment of his judicial career.

Mason, Alpheus T. *Brandeis: A Free Man's Life.* New York:: The Viking Press, 1946. A scholarly biography which argues that Brandeis was essentially conservative.

———. *Harlan Fiske Stone: Pillar of the Law.* New York: The Viking Press, 1956.

———. "The Conservative World of Mr. Justice Sutherland." *American Political Science Review* 32 (1938).

———. *The Supreme Court from Taft to Burger.* Baton Rouge: Louisiana State University Press, 1979. Contains a good chapter on the Supreme Court during the Progressive Era.

———. *William Howard Taft: Chief Justice.* New York: Simon & Schuster, 1965.

Mendelson, Wallace. "Clear and Present Danger: From Schenck to Dennis." *Columbia Law Review* 52 (March 1952).

Merz, Charles. *The Dry Decade.* Garden City: Doubleday, Doran, 1931. Merz deals with the Eighteenth Amendment and Prohibition.

Mock, James R. *Censorship, 1917.* Princeton: Princeton Unviersity Press, 1941. Mock provides a good general view of the wartime curb of civil liberties.

Murphy, Paul. *The Constitution in Crisis Times.* New York: Harper & Row,

1972. A good overview of constitutional development during the 1920s.

————. *World War I and the Origin of Civil Liberties in the United States.* New York: W.W. Norton & Co., 1979.

Nobitt, Harding Coolidge. "The Supreme Court and the Progressive Era." Ph.D. dissertation, University of Chicago, 1955. Nobitt analyzes the Justices' voting records.

O'Brien, Kenneth B., Jr. "Education, Americanization and the Supreme Court in the 1920s." *American Quarterly* 13 (1961).

Paschal, Joel Francis. *Mr. Justice Sutherland: A Man Against the State.* Princeton: Princeton University Press, 1951. Paschal has written a sympathetic but critical biography of a conservative Justice.

Paxson, Frederic L. *America at War, 1917-1918.* Boston: Houghton Mifflin Co., 1939. There is much detail on wartime constitutional problems in this book.

Peterson, Horace C., and Fite, Gilbert C. *Opponents of War, 1917-1918.* Madison, Wis.: University of Wisconsin Press, 1957. Well-written account of wartime repression.

Powell, T.R. "The Judiciality of Minimum Wage Legislation." *Harvard Law Review* 37 (March 1924). Powell looks at the *Adkins Case.*

Preston, William. *Aliens and Dissenters: Federal Supression of Radicals, 1900-1933.* Cambridge, Mass.: Harvard University Press, 1963. Preston does a good job on the IWW.

Pringle, Henry F. *Life and Times of William Howard Taft.* 2 vols. New York: Farrar & Rinehard , 1939.

Pusey, Merlo J. *Charles Evans Hughes.* 2 vols. New York: Macmillan, 1951.

Ragan, Fred D. "Justice Oliver Wendell Homes, Jr., Zechariah Chafee, Jr., and the Clear and Present Danger Test for Speech: The First Year, 1919." *Journal of American History* 58 (June 1971).

Roelofs, Vernon William. "William R. Day: A Study in Constitutional History." Ph.D. dissertation, University of Michigan, 1942.

Scheiber, Harry N. *The Wilson Administration and Civil Liberties, 1917-1921.* Ithaca: Cornell University Press, 1960.

Stone, Harlan Fiske. "Fifty Years' Work of the Supreme Court." *American Bar Association Journal* 14 (1928).

Taft, William Howard. *The Anti-Trust Act and the Supreme Court.* New York: Harper Brothers, 1914. Taft gives the reader his views on the Sherman Act.

————. "The Jurisdiction of the Supreme Court under the Act of February 13, 1925." *Yale Law Journal* 1 (1925). Taft on court reform.

Todd, Alden L. *Justice on Trial: The Case of Louis D. Brandeis.* New York: McGraw-Hill Book Co., 1964. A history of the Senate battle over the confirmation of Brandeis to the Supreme Court in 1916.

Urofsky, Melvin I. *A Mind of One Piece: Brandeis and American Reform.* New York: Charles Scribner's Sons, 1971.

Warner, Hoyt Landon, *The Life of Mr. Justice Clarke: A Testament to the Power of Liberal Dissent in America.* Cleveland: Western Reserve University Press, 1959. A lucid summary of Clarke's career.

Warren, Charles. *Congress, the Constitution, and the Supreme Court.* Boston: Little, Brown and Co., 1925.

Warren, Earl. "Chief Justice William Howard Taft." *Yale Law Journal* 67 (1958).

Weinstein, James. *The Corporate Ideal in the Liberal State, 1900-1918.* Boston: Beacon Press, 1968. A New Left view of the history of Progressive reform.

White, Edward D. "The Supreme Court of the United States." *American Bar Association Journal* 7 (1921).

Wood, Stephen B. *Constitutional Politics in the Progressive Era: Child Labor and the Law.* Chicago: University of Chicago Press, 1968. Wood's book is the best study on this subject.